Algorithms for Emergency Medicine

Algorithms for Emergency Medicine

Edited by

Mark Harrison

Consultant in Emergency Medicine,
Northumbria Specialist Emergency Care Hospital,
UK

and

Ala Mohammed

Consultant in Emergency Medicine,
Sunderland Royal Hospital,
UK

OXFORD
UNIVERSITY PRESS

OXFORD
UNIVERSITY PRESS

Great Clarendon Street, Oxford, OX2 6DP,
United Kingdom

Oxford University Press is a department of the University of Oxford.
It furthers the University's objective of excellence in research, scholarship,
and education by publishing worldwide. Oxford is a registered trade mark of
Oxford University Press in the UK and in certain other countries

© Oxford University Press 2023

The moral rights of the authors have been asserted

First Edition published in 2023

Published in the United States of America by Oxford University Press
198 Madison Avenue, New York, NY 10016, United States of America

British Library Cataloguing in Publication Data
Data available

Library of Congress Control Number is on file at the Library of Congress

ISBN 978–0–19–882913–3

DOI: 10.1093/med/9780198829133.001.0001

Printed and bound by
CPI Group (UK) Ltd, Croydon, CR0 4YY

Oxford University Press makes no representation, express or implied, that the
drug dosages in this book are correct. Readers must therefore always check
the product information and clinical procedures with the most up-to-date
published product information and data sheets provided by the manufacturers
and the most recent codes of conduct and safety regulations. The authors and
the publishers do not accept responsibility or legal liability for any errors in the
text or for the misuse or misapplication of material in this work. Except where
otherwise stated, drug dosages and recommendations are for the non-pregnant
adult who is not breast-feeding

Links to third party websites are provided by Oxford in good faith and
for information only. Oxford disclaims any responsibility for the materials
contained in any third party website referenced in this work.

PREFACE

Delivering Emergency Medicine involves constant challenges to the emergency clinician, reflected by the wide breadth of conditions that are encountered, the necessity for the frequent need to deal with multiple severely unwell patients, the time constraints of acute illnesses, and the urgency needed in diagnosis and treatment.

Algorithms for Emergency Medicine is designed to be a 'straight to the point' reference to help face these challenges and allow the busy emergency clinician to respond and deliver appropriate care in a timely fashion.

The book is divided into ten sections (e.g. Practical procedures, Airway and breathing, Cardiovascular) and each section is comprised of a number of topics. Each topic is divided into an information section, which provides essential knowledge, tips, and salient points on the topic, and an algorithm, which is aimed to guide the clinician in a step-by-step manner in managing these conditions. These are based on the Royal College of Emergency Medicine curriculum for those who would like to train or obtain experience in delivering Emergency Medicine which contains up-to-date evidence and knowledge.

This book would have not been possible without the dedication and commitment by the authors and the willingness to share their experience in delivering emergency care.

We hope that this book will be useful for Emergency Nurse Practitioners, new doctors starting their placement in the Emergency Department, and trainee doctors working towards specializing in Emergency Medicine.

Ala Mohammed
Mark Harrison

CONTENTS

DETAILED CONTENTS

CONTRIBUTORS

Charlotte Bates
Consultant in Emergency Medicine
Northumbria Specialist Emergency Care Hospital
UK

Dave Bramley
Chief Medical Officer
Great North Air Ambulance Service
UK

Laurence Chuter
Consultant in Emergency Medicine
Musgrove Park Hospital
UK

Damian Garwell
Consultant in Emergency Medicine
Northumbria Specialist Emergency Care Hospital
UK

Mark Harrison
Consultant in Emergency Medicine
Northumbria Specialist Emergency Care Hospital
UK

Ala Mohammed
Consultant in Emergency Medicine
Sunderland Royal Hospital
UK

Alister T. Oliver
Consultant in Emergency Medicine
Northumbria Specialist Emergency Care Hospital
UK

ABBREVIATIONS

6-CIT	six-item Cognitive Impairment Test
AAA	abdominal aortic aneurysm
AAGBI	Association of Anaesthetists of Great Britain and Ireland
ABCDE	airway, breathing, circulation, disability, exposure
ABG	arterial blood gas
ABPI	ankle-brachial pressure index
AC	alternating current
ACE	angiotensin-converting enzyme
ACJ	acromioclavicular joint
ACL	anterior cruciate ligament
ACS	acute coronary syndrome
AE	air entry
AED	automated external defibrillator
AF	atrial fibrillation
AKI	acute kidney injury
AKIN	Acute Kidney Injury Network
ALL	acute lymphoblastic leukaemia
ALS	advanced life support
ALT	alanine transaminase
AP	antero-posterior
APLS	advanced paediatric life support
APTT	activated partial thromboplastin time
ARDS	acute respiratory distress syndrome
ASIA	American Spinal Injury Association
AST	aspartate transaminase
ATLS	advanced trauma life support
ATN	acute tubular necrosis
AUR	acute urinary retention
AVM	arteriovenous malformation
AVPU	alert, to voice, to pain, unconscious
AXR	abdominal X-ray
BASHH	British Association for Sexual Health and HIV
BBV	blood-borne virus
BE	base excess
BiPAP	bilevel positive airway pressure
BLS	basic life support
BM	Boehringer Mannheim (fingerprick glucose)
BNF	British National Formulary
BP	blood pressure
BPH	benign prostatic hyperplasia
BSA	body surface area
BTS	British Thoracic Society
BVM	bag-valve-mask
C spine	cervical spine
C&S	culture and sensitivity
CAM	Confusion Assessment Method
CCF	congestive cardiac failure
CCU	coronary care unit
CIWA-Ar	clinical institute withdrawal assessment for alcohol (revised)
CK	creatinine kinase
CNS	central nervous system
COPD	chronic obstructive pulmonary disease
CPAP	continuous positive airway pressure
Cr	creatinine
CRP	C-reactive protein
CRT	capillary refill time
CSF	cerebrospinal fluid
CSU	catheter specimen urine
CT	computed tomography

CTPA	computed tomography pulmonary angiography
CURB	confusion, urea, respiratory rate, blood pressure
CXR	chest X-ray
D&V	diarrhoea and vomiting
DBP	diastolic blood pressure
DIC	disseminated intravascular coagulation
DIPJ	distal interphalangeal joint
DKA	diabetic ketoacidosis
DM	diabetes mellitus
DMARD	disease-modifying antirheumatic drug
DNACPR	do not attempt cardiopulmonary resuscitation
DTs	delirium tremens
DVT	deep vein thrombosis
EBV	Epstein–Barr virus
ECG	electrocardiogram
ECHO	echocardiogram
ED	Emergency Department
eFAST	extended focused assessment with sonography
EGSYS	Evaluation of Guidelines in Syncope Study
EHS	exertional heat stroke
ENT	ear, nose, and throat
ESR	erythrocyte sedimentation rate
ET	endotracheal tube
ETCO$_2$	end-tidal carbon dioxide
FAST	face, arm, speech, time
FAST	focused assessment with sonography
FB	foreign body
FBC	full blood count
FDP	flexor digitorum profundus
FDS	flexor digitorum superficialis
FEV	forced expiratory volume
FFP	fresh frozen plasma
FH	family history
Fr	French
FU	follow-up
FVC	forced vital capacity
G&S	group and save
GABHS	group A beta-haemolytic streptococcus
GCA	giant cell arteritis
GCS	Glasgow Coma Scale
GGT	γ-glutamyltransferase
GI	gastrointestinal
GRACE	global registry of acute coronary events
GTN	glyceryl trinitrate
GUM	genito-urinary medicine
h/o	history of
Hb	haemoglobin
HB	hepatitis B
HBIg	hepatitis B immunoglobulin
HCG	human chorionic gonadotropin
HCO$_3$	bicarbonate
HCV	hepatitis C virus
HDU	high dependency unit
HHS	hyperosmolar hyperglycaemic state
HIV	human immunodeficiency virus
HR	heart rate
HTX	haemothorax
ICD	intercostal chest drain
ICP	intracranial pressure
IDA	iron deficiency anaemia
Ig	immunoglobulin
IHD	ischaemic heart disease
IM	intramuscular
INR	internalized normalized ratio
IO	intraosseous
ITU	intensive therapy unit

IV	intravenous
IVF	in vitro fertilization
IVU	intravenous urogram
JVP	jugular venous pressure
K	potassium
KUB	kidney, ureter, and bladder
LA	local anaesthesia
LBBB	left bundle branch block
LCL	lateral collateral ligament
LFT	liver function test
LGIB	lower gastrointestinal bleeding
LMA	laryngeal mask airway
LMWH	low molecular weight heparin
LOC	loss of consciousness
LP	lumbar puncture
LRTI	lower respiratory tract infection
LSD	lysergic acid diethylamide
LVF	left ventricular failure
MAP	mean arterial pressure
MC&S	microscopy, culture, and sensitivity
MCA	Mental Capacity Act
MCHb	mean corpuscular haemoglobin
MCL	medial collateral ligament
MCPJ	metacarpophalangeal joint
MCV	mean corpuscular volume
MDMA	3,4-methyl-enedioxy-methamphetamine
MHA	Mental Health Act
MI	myocardial infarction
MILS	manual in-line stabilization
MOI	mechanism of injury
MRI	magnetic resonance imaging
MSU	mid-stream urine
MTS	Mental Test Score
NAI	non-accidental injury
NBM	nil by mouth

NEB	nebulizer
NEHS	non-exertional heat stroke
NG	nasogastric
NHL	non-Hodgkin lymphoma
NIBP	non-invasive blood pressure
NIBP	non-invasive blood pressure
NICE	National Institute for Health and Care Excellence
NIV	non-invasive ventilation
NP	nasopharyngeal
NPIS	National Poisons Information Service
NPV	negative predictive value
NSAIDs	non-steroidal anti-inflammatory drugs
NSTEMI	non-ST elevation myocardial infarction
NT-pro BNP	N-terminal pro B-type natriuretic peptide
O&G	obstetrics and gynaecology
O/P	outpatient
OD	overdose
OP	oropharyngeal
ORT	oral rehydration therapy
OT	occupational therapy
PaCO$_2$	partial pressure of carbon dioxide
PaO$_2$	partial pressure of oxygen
PBF	peripheral blood film
PCI	percutaneous coronary intervention
PCL	posterior cruciate ligament
PE	pulmonary embolus
PEA	pulseless electrical activity
PEEP	positive end-expiratory pressure
PEFR	peak expiratory flow rate
PEP	post-exposure prophylaxis
PICU	paediatric intensive care unit
PID	pelvic inflammatory disease
PIPJ	proximal interphalangeal joint
PMH	past medical history

PN	percussion note	SOB	shortness of breath
PO	per os (by mouth)	SOFA	Sequential Organ Failure Assessment
PPE	personal protective equipment	SOL	space occupying lesion
PPI	proton pump inhibitor	SP	suprapubic
PR	per rectum	SpO$_2$	peripheral oxygen saturations
PT	prothrombin time	SSRI	selective serotonin reuptake inhibitor
PTX	pneumothorax	STAT	statim (immediately)
PU	passed urine	STEMI	ST-elevation myocardial infarction
PV	per vagina	SVC	superior vena cava
PVD	peripheral vascular disease	SVT	supraventricular tachycardia
qSOFA	Quick Sequential Organ Failure Assessment	TB	tuberculosis
		TIA	transient ischaemic attack
RBC	red blood cell	TIMI	thrombolysis in myocardial infarction
RIDDOR	Reporting of Injuries, Diseases and Dangerous Occurrences Regulations	TMJ	temporomandibular joint
		TSH	thyroid stimulating hormone
RIFLE	Risk, Injury, Failure, Loss of kidney function, and End-stage kidney disease	U&E	urea and electrolytes
		UGIB	upper gastrointestinal bleeding
		UO	urine output
ROSIER	recognition of stroke in the emergency room	URTI	upper respiratory tract infection
		US	ultrasound
RR	relative risk	USS	ultrasound scan
RR	respiratory rate	UTI	urinary tract infection
RSI	rapid sequence induction	V/Q	ventilation/perfusion
RWS	Revised Wells score	VBG	venous blood gas
SAD	supraglottic airway device	VF	ventricular fibrillation
SAH	subarachnoid haemorrhage	VT	ventricular tachycardia
SaO$_2$	oxygen saturations	WBC	white blood cell
SBP	systolic blood pressure	WFNS	World Federation of Neurological Surgeons
SIGN	Scottish Intercollegiate Guidance Network		
		WHO	World Health Organization
SIRS	systemic inflammatory response syndrome		

SECTION 1

Practical procedures

1. Basic life support

Personal safety

- Check for your personal safety and that patient surroundings are safe
- Wear gloves and other protective equipment, e.g. apron, eye protection

Call for help

Check for signs of life: Loudly ask 'Are you OK?' and gently shake shoulders.

If response:

- Call for urgent medical help—use hospital protocol to contact resus/medical team
- Assess using airway, breathing, circulation, disability, exposure (ABCDE) approach
- Give O_2 as guided by pulse oximetry
- Attach monitoring equipment and take vital signs
- Obtain intravenous (IV) access and take bloods as appropriate (e.g. full blood count (FBC), urea and electrolytes (U&E), C-reactive protein (CRP), glucose, liver function test (LFT), coagulation test, group and save (G&S), lactate)—consider venous/arterial blood gas (ABG)

If no response:

- Lie patient on back
- Open airway: Head tilt, chin lift if **no** trauma/Jaw thrust is suspicion of trauma
- Look, listen, and feel for breathing and assess carotid pulse at same time (<10 s)

If pulse present/other signs of life: ABCDE approach, O_2, monitoring, IV access, await medical team

If no pulse/no sign of life:

- Ask colleague to call the resuscitation team and to collect the resuscitation trolley
- **Start CPR**
  - Place heel of one hand in the middle of the lower half of sternum and place the other hand on top
  - Depth of compressions should be 5–6 cm at rate of 100–120 compressions per minute
  - Allow complete recoil of chest between compressions
  - Give 30 compressions followed by 2 ventilations (minimize any interruptions in CPR)
- **Ventilation**
  - Use whatever equipment is available, e.g. bag mask, pocket mask, or supraglottic airway device (SAD) (e.g. laryngeal mask airway (LMA)) and self-inflating bag. Consider mouth to mouth ventilation if nothing else available. Minimize air leak by forming good seal if using bag mask
  - Use inspiratory time of 1 s and ensure visible chest rise
  - Give supplementary O_2 when possible
- **Defibrillation**
  - When available, apply pads to chest (one beneath right clavicle and one in left mid-axillary line)
  - Assess rhythm: if indicated (i.e. ventricular fibrillation (VF)/pulseless ventricular tachycardia (VT)) charge machine, stand clear, remove O_2, and deliver shock, minimizing gaps in CPR. (*Note*: If using automated external defibrillator (AED), follow audio-visual prompts)
  - **When resuscitation team arrives, progress to advanced life support (ALS)**

If respiratory arrest (i.e. has a pulse but not breathing):

- Ventilate lungs, checking for pulse and response every 10 breaths
- **If any doubt about presence of pulse, start CPR**

Further reading

Soar J, Deakin CD, Nolan JP, Perkins GD, Yeung J, Couper K, . . . Hampshire S. Adult advanced life support guidelines. Retrieved from https://www.resus.org.uk/library/2021-resuscitation-guidelines/adult-advanced-life-support-guidelines, 2021.

Algorithm for basic life support

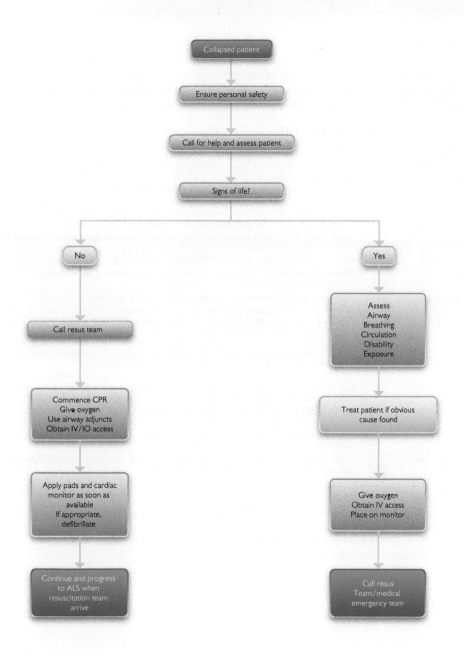

Collapsed patient

↓

Ensure personal safety

↓

Call for help and assess patient

↓

Signs of life?

No

↓

Call resus team

↓

Commence CPR
Give oxygen
Use airway adjuncts
Obtain IV/IO access

↓

Apply pads and cardiac
monitor as soon as
available
If appropriate,
defibrillate

↓

Continue and progress
to ALS when
resuscitation team
arrive

Yes

↓

Assess
Airway
Breathing
Circulation
Disability
Exposure

↓

Treat patient if obvious
cause found

↓

Give oxygen
Obtain IV access
Place on monitor

↓

Call resus
Team/medical
emergency team

2. Airway protection

Introduction

The gold standard in airway protection is the passage of a cuffed tube into the trachea. However, even in cases where this is clearly indicated, and the appropriate staff and equipment are available, it cannot happen instantly. It is essential that all practitioners who are expected to deal with emergency presentations are capable of emergency airway assessment and management. Table 1.1 lists methods of optimizing an airway.

Table 1.1 Methods of optimizing an airway

Method	Information
Patient position	Unconscious patients with no suspicion of spinal injury should be placed in the recovery position with close monitoring.
	Ideally the trolley should be capable of being tipped head-down in case of vomiting.
	In some cases of facial trauma or foreign body obstruction, for example, patients may present sitting forwards, sometimes even holding their own tongue/mandible to maintain their airway. Invariably they do this better than you can: let them, and request additional help.
	Supine patients who it is not appropriate to place in the recovery position should be managed on a trolley which can be tipped head-down, and if spinal injury is not suspected, then the 'sniffing the morning air' position should be achieved; alternatively a jaw thrust can be used.
Suction	Suction should be performed using a Yankauer-type suction catheter under direct vision. Consider using a tongue depressor to facilitate this.
Airway adjuncts	Oropharyngeal (OP) airway should be used in the absence of a gag reflex.
	Nasopharyngeal (NP) airway is very useful where trismus is present or there is a risk of precipitating vomiting with an OP airway. This should preferentially be avoided in cases of serious head injury; however, if the patient is hypoxic and other methods of airway maintenance have failed, then the risk of worsening secondary brain injury because of hypoxia is likely to outweigh the small risk of inadvertently introducing the NP airway through a base of skull fracture. After placement, position may be confirmed by intraoral palpation or inspection.
	SADs are useful in cardiac arrest cases and failed intubation scenarios during RSI as they can be inserted rapidly and offer some degree of (but not complete) airway protection. However, they may precipitate vomiting or laryngospasm and as such are not recommended in the non-anaesthetized patient where other methods are effective.
Rapid sequence induction of anaesthesia	The gold standard in airway protection in the passage of a cuffed tube into the trachea. This requires appropriate staff, monitoring, and equipment, and it is essential that an airway is maintained during the preparation time involved.
Surgical airway	In the apnoeic peri-arrest or actual cardiac arrest patient with an airway that is unmanageable by any other means, this must be performed immediately.

Further reading

Lloyd G. 'Basic airway management', RCEM Learning, 2020; https://www.rcemlearning.co.uk/references/basic-airway-management/ (accessed March 22).

Brady MP, Becker JU. 'Best Practices: Emergency Airway Management', Medscape, 2016; https://reference.medscape.com/features/slideshow/airway-management#page=1 (accessed March 22).

Algorithm for airway protection

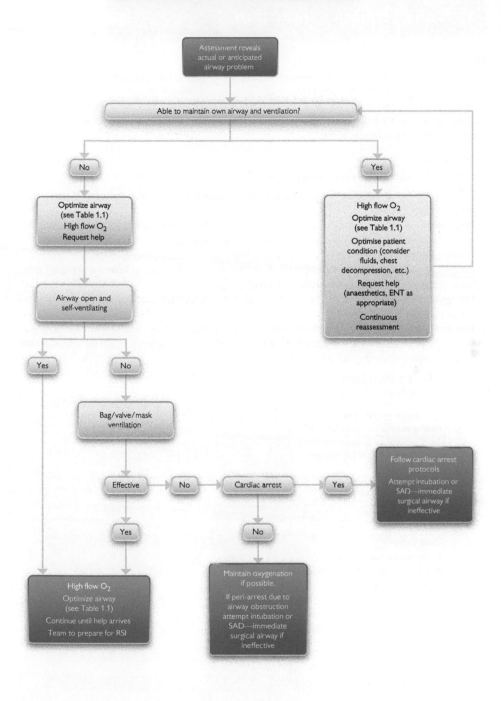

3. Rapid sequence induction

Introduction

In all cases of RSI, the benefits and risks must be evaluated. This must include consideration of who (patient **and** clinician), when, and where to perform this.

However, in time-critical airway or ventilation problems, transferring a patient to another part of the hospital is not possible. As such, the Emergency Department should be able to facilitate a safe and effective RSI of anaesthesia and manage predictable complications.

Checklist

In order to do this, a checklist should **always** be used (Table 1.2) and the '6 Ps' approach followed:

- **Pre-oxygenation**—should be delivered using tight-fitting mask and circuit with reservoir bag (e.g. bag-valve-mask (BVM) or Mapleson C)
- **Preparation**—all the items listed in the checklist, along with optimizing the patient's current condition. This may include using fluids, sedation, chest decompression, pelvic splintage, etc.
- **Premedication**—if required, e.g. fentanyl in isolated head injuries
- **Paralysis and sedation**—appropriate agents include thiopentone (3–5 mg/kg) or ketamine (2 mg/kg) with suxamethonium (1.5 mg/kg) or rocuronium (1.2 mg/kg)
- **Passage of the tube**—routine use of a bougie is recommended, but this should be passed carefully to avoid airway trauma
- **Post-intubation care**—appropriate monitoring (minimum of SPO_2, end-tidal carbon dioxide ($ETCO_2$), non-invasive blood pressure (NIBP), 3-lead electrocardiogram (ECG)), ongoing sedation, and paralysis. Consider head-up position in raised intracranial pressure

Table 1.2 RSI checklist

	Checked
Pre-oxygenation taking place	
Baseline observations (ECG, SpO_2, BP)	
2× IV access One connected to fluid and runs easily	
Suction working	
Airway adjuncts (OP/NP)	
Endotracheal tube (ET) size chosen, cuff tested	
Syringe 10 mL for cuff	
Tape or tie	
Elastic bougie	
Laryngoscopes: two working	
Alternative laryngoscope blades available	
Heat and moisture exchange filter	
Catheter mount	
SAD and emergency cricothyroidotomy kit available	
Induction agent and paralysis agent prepared Maintenance of paralysis and sedation agents prepared Drug giver briefed	
Ventilator and BVM connected to O_2	
Monitoring, including ECG, NIBP, SpO_2, $ETCO_2$	
Stethoscope	
Premedication if required	
Inline immobilizer briefed	
Cricoid pressure person briefed	

Further reading

Difficult Airway Society, 2022; https://www.das.uk.com.

Algorithm for rapid sequence induction

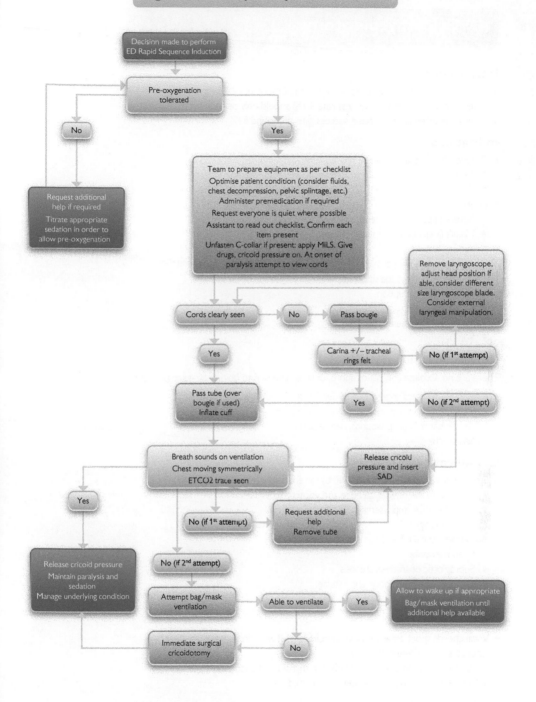

Decision made to perform ED Rapid Sequence Induction

Pre-oxygenation tolerated

No

Yes

Request additional help if required

Titrate appropriate sedation in order to allow pre-oxygenation

Team to prepare equipment as per checklist
Optimise patient condition (consider fluids, chest decompression, pelvic splintage, etc.)
Administer premedication if required
Request everyone is quiet where possible
Assistant to read out checklist. Confirm each item present
Unfasten C-collar if present: apply MILS. Give drugs, cricoid pressure on. At onset of paralysis attempt to view cords

Remove laryngoscope, adjust head position If able, consider different size laryngoscope blade. Consider external laryngeal manipulation.

Cords clearly seen

No

Pass bougie

Yes

Carina +/− tracheal rings felt

No (if 1st attempt)

Pass tube (over bougie if used)
Inflate cuff

Yes

No (if 2nd attempt)

Breath sounds on ventilation
Chest moving symmetrically
ETCO2 trace seen

Release cricoid pressure and insert SAD

Yes

No (if 1st attempt)

Request additional help
Remove tube

Release cricoid pressure
Maintain paralysis and sedation
Manage underlying condition

No (if 2nd attempt)

Attempt bag/mask ventilation

Able to ventilate

Yes

Allow to wake up if appropriate
Bag/mask ventilation until additional help available

Immediate surgical cricoidotomy

No

4. Cricothyroidotomy

Introduction

- Accounts for ~1% of all secured airways in the Emergency Department
- Needle cricothyroidotomy (success rate 40%) should only be used for 30–45 minutes
- Surgical cricothyroidotomy has a success rate of around 84%

Indications

- To save life—a situation where you 'can't intubate and can't ventilate'
  - Other airway techniques should have been attempted first
  - Consider use of bougie if difficult placement
- Likely aetiology:
  - Severe upper airway haemorrhage
  - Maxillofacial injuries or abnormal facial anatomy
  - Airway trauma
    - Inhalational or thermal
    - Foreign body in the upper airway
    - Laryngeal disruption
  - Airway oedema
  - Mass (tumour, haematoma, abscess)
  - Supraglottitis

Contraindications

There are no absolute contraindications, only relative due to being a life-saving measure:

- Age under 10 years undesirable; under 5 years should be avoided
- Pre-existing laryngeal pathology (epiglottitis, cancer)
- Anatomic barriers (stab wounds, haematoma)
- Coagulopathy

Complications

- Substantial complication rate (10–40%) for emergency cricothyroidotomy
  - Damage to the thyroid cartilage and vocal chords
  - Subcutaneous emphysema
  - Haemorrhage
  - Extra-tracheal tube placement (false-passage)
  - Pneumothorax
  - Supraglottic or tracheal stenosis
  - Oesophageal perforation and fistulae
  - Infection

Anatomy

- Vocal chords short distance above thyroid notch (avoid this area)
- Cricoid is a complete cartilaginous ring
- Cricothyroid membrane located between thyroid and cricoid cartilages
- 30% of population have veins lateral to the midline

Further reading

Cook TM, Woodall N, Frerk C. Fourth National Audit Project. Major complications of airway management in the UK: results of the Fourth National Audit Project of the Royal College of Anaesthetists and the Difficult Airway Society. Part 1: anaesthesia. *Br J Anaesth* 2011;106:617–631.

Hubble MW, Wilfong DA, Brown LH, Hertelendy A, Benner RW. A meta-analysis of prehospital airway control techniques part II: alternative airway devices and cricothyrotomy success rates. *Prehosp Emerg Care* 2010;14(4):515–530.

Spiegel JE, Shah V. Surgical management of the failed airway: a guide to percutaneous cricothyrotomy. *Anesthesiology News* 2012;38(8):57–61.

Algorithm for cricothyroidotomy

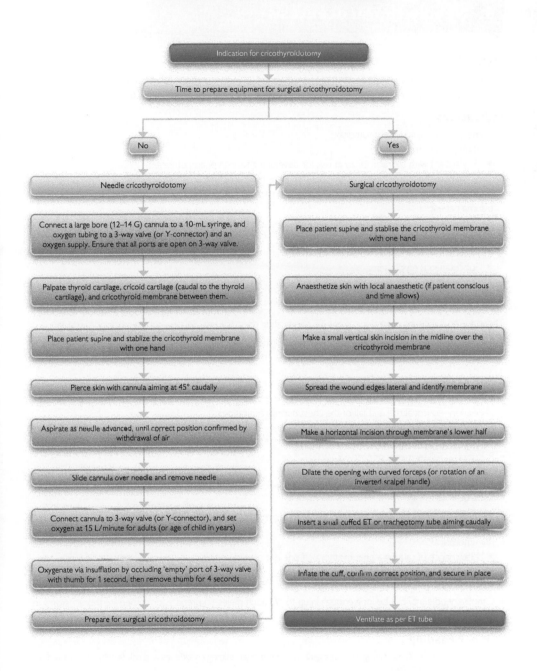

Indication for cricothyroidotomy

Time to prepare equipment for surgical cricothyroidotomy

No

Yes

Needle cricothyroidotomy

Connect a large bore (12–14 G) cannula to a 10-mL syringe, and oxygen tubing to a 3-way valve (or Y-connector) and an oxygen supply. Ensure that all ports are open on 3-way valve.

Palpate thyroid cartilage, cricoid cartilage (caudal to the thyroid cartilage), and cricothyroid membrane between them.

Place patient supine and stablize the cricothyroid membrane with one hand

Pierce skin with cannula aiming at 45° caudally

Aspirate as needle advanced, until correct position confirmed by withdrawal of air

Slide cannula over needle and remove needle

Connect cannula to 3-way valve (or Y-connector), and set oxygen at 15 L/minute for adults (or age of child in years)

Oxygenate via insufflation by occluding 'empty' port of 3-way valve with thumb for 1 second, then remove thumb for 4 seconds

Prepare for surgical cricothroidotomy

Surgical cricothyroidotomy

Place patient supine and stablise the cricothyroid membrane with one hand

Anaesthetize skin with local anaesthetic (if patient conscious and time allows)

Make a small vertical skin incision in the midline over the cricothyroid membrane

Spread the wound edges lateral and identify membrane

Make a horizontal incision through membrane's lower half

Dilate the opening with curved forceps (or rotation of an inverted scalpel handle)

Insert a small cuffed ET or tracheotomy tube aiming caudally

Inflate the cuff, confirm correct position, and secure in place

Ventilate as per ET tube

5. Needle thoracocentesis

Definition

- A procedure where a needle and catheter are inserted through the chest wall into the pleural space
  - The catheter provides a pathway for the release of accumulated pressure within the pleural space

Indications

- Primary spontaneous pneumothorax
- Tension pneumothorax
  - Any patient with thoracic injury at risk for developing tension pneumothorax
    - Increased risk with penetrating wound or signs of rib fracture
- A needle decompression should also be considered if any of the following indications are present in the trauma patient:
  - Patients with decreased or absent breath sounds, and examination consistent with pneumothorax, or tension pneumothorax
  - Patients with shortness of breath and/or respiratory distress
  - Subcutaneous emphysema
  - Tracheal deviation

Contraindications

There are no significant contraindications if a penetrating chest trauma. Relative contraindications include:

- Secondary spontaneous pneumothorax (underlying lung disease)
- Traumatic pneumothorax without tension

Clinical decision making

- Based on mechanism of injury (MOI) and a noted increase in difficulty breathing
- Inspection—unequal rise and fall of the chest during respirations
- Auscultation—decreased breath sounds
- Percussion—hyper-resonant to percussion
- Palpation—flail segments or crepitus

Complications

- Local cellulitis
- Local haematoma (2%)
- Pleural infection, empyema
- Pneumothorax
  - 11% chance of causing a pneumothorax if one not present initially
- Haemothorax (0.8%)
- Subcutaneous emphysema
- Cannula needle may not be long enough in up to 1/3 adult males, so prepare for immediate thoracostomy in peri-arrest situation

Further reading

Celik B, Sahin E, Nadir A, Kaptanoglu M. Iatrogenic pneumothorax: etiology, incidence and risk factors. *Thorac Cardiovasc Surg* 2009;57(5):286–290.

Algorithm for needle thoracocentesis

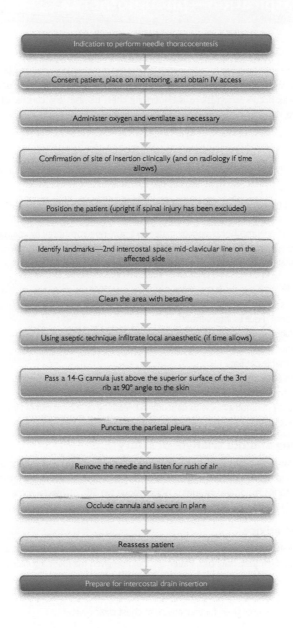

Indication to perform needle thoracocentesis

↓

Consent patient, place on monitoring, and obtain IV access

↓

Administer oxygen and ventilate as necessary

↓

Confirmation of site of insertion clinically (and on radiology if time allows)

↓

Position the patient (upright if spinal injury has been excluded)

↓

Identify landmarks—2nd intercostal space mid-clavicular line on the affected side

↓

Clean the area with betadine

↓

Using aseptic technique infiltrate local anaesthetic (if time allows)

↓

Pass a 14-G cannula just above the superior surface of the 3rd rib at 90° angle to the skin

↓

Puncture the parietal pleura

↓

Remove the needle and listen for rush of air

↓

Occlude cannula and secure in place

↓

Reassess patient

↓

Prepare for intercostal drain insertion

6. Pleural aspiration—pneumothorax

Introduction

A pneumothorax can be spontaneous or traumatic. Spontaneous pneumothorax can be subdivided into primary and secondary pneumothorax. Primary pneumothorax occurs in the absence of underlying lung disease. Secondary pneumothorax occurs when there is underlying chest disease (e.g. chronic obstructive pulmonary disease (COPD), asthma, malignancy, tuberculosis (TB)) or evidence of underlying lung disease on examination or chest X-ray (CXR).

Indications

British Thoracic Society (BTS) guidelines suggest that a pneumothorax should be aspirated in the following circumstances:

- Primary spontaneous pneumothorax with difficulty in breathing and/or a rim of pneumothorax on CXR >2 cm (measured at the level of the hilum). A >2-cm pneumothorax is by definition a large pneumothorax and a 2-cm radiographic pneumothorax approximates to a 50% pneumothorax by volume
- Secondary spontaneous pneumothorax with no difficulty in breathing and a 1- to 2-cm rim of pneumothorax on CXR

Contraindications

- Tension pneumothorax should undergo immediate needle decompression
- Traumatic pneumothorax requires intervention
- Bilateral pneumothoraces
- Previous pneumothorax within last 2 weeks
- Haemodynamically unstable patient
- Anticoagulated patient (await internalized normalized ratio (INR) prior to attempted aspiration)
- Spontaneous pneumothoraces suitable for conservative management
- Secondary spontaneous pneumothorax with difficulty in breathing or >2-cm rim of air on CXR should be treated with Seldinger chest drain

Patient positioning and the triangle of safety

Whilst performing aspiration of a pneumothorax, the patient should be positioned sitting upright, with the hand of the affected side behind the head. The triangle of safety for aspiration of the pneumothorax lies between the lateral edges of the pectoralis major and latissimus dorsi, above the 5th intercostal space and below the base of the axilla.

Patient discharge advice

Patients who are suitable for discharge should be referred for follow-up in the chest clinic, and information should be sent to their GP to confirm their diagnosis. Patients should be given the following information:

- Return to the ED immediately if they experience breathlessness or chest pain
- They should avoid diving for life
- They should avoid air travel until given further advice at chest clinic review

Further reading

Maskell N. British Thoracic Society Pleural Disease Guidelines— 2010 update. *Thorax* 2010;65:667–669.

Ramrakha P, Moore K, Sam, A. Oxford Handbook of Acute Medicine. Oxford, UK: Oxford University Press. Retrieved 2 May, 2022, from https://oxfordmedicine.com/view/10.1093/med/9780198797425.001.0001/med-9780198797425, 2019–11.

Wyatt J, Taylor R, de Wit K, Hotton E. Oxford Handbook of Emergency Medicine. Oxford, UK: Oxford University Press. Retrieved 2 May, 2022, from https://oxfordmedicine.com/view/10.1093/med/9780198784197.001.0001/med-9780198784197, 2020–08.

Algorithm for pleural aspiration—pneumothorax

Pneumothorax suitable for attempted aspiration

Yes → **No** → Discontinue pathway and consider alternative management

Confirm side of pneumothorax clinically and on CXR
Gain consent from patient

- Prepare equipment
- Aseptic technique
- Position patient

- Clean skin with appropriate wash (e.g. chlorhexidine) and allow to dry

Identify 2nd intercostal space and infiltrate 1% lignocaine just above 3rd rib in the mid-clavicular line

Attach syringe to a pleural aspirate needle or a large IV cannula and insert into 2nd intercostal space, aspirating to confirm entry into pleural space

Ask patient to hold their breath and remove needle, whilst advancing cannula–secure cannula with tape if desired
Attach 3-way tap and 50-mL syringe to cannula

Aspirate 50 mL of air and expel through the other lumen of the three-way tap
Repeat aspiration until resistance to suction is felt, patient coughs excessively, or 2.5 L of air has been aspirated

Withdraw cannula and cover site with occlusive dressing

Arrange post-procedure CXR

Aspiration adequate?
(Breathing improved, rim of pneumothorax <2 cm)

Yes → Observe for 2 hours. If remains asymptomatic plan for discharge and refer for chest clinic follow-up.
Provide Discharge Advice

No → Do not repeat aspiration unless technical difficulties
Plan for insertion of Seldinger chest drain
Plan for admission

7. Intercostal drain—seldinger

Indications

- Pneumothorax
- Malignant pleural effusion

Predrainage

- Correct coagulopathy or platelet defect if possible
- Explain procedure to patient and record informed consent
- Place patient on monitoring for pulse oximetry, ECG, and blood pressure (BP)
- Premedication (benzodiazepine or opioid) to reduce patient distress unless contraindicated
- Position patient slightly recumbent, with ipsilateral hand behind patient's head to expose axillary area and 'triangle of safety' (Figure 1.1)
  - Lateral edge of latissimus dorsi (posteriorly)
  - Lateral border of pectoralis major (anteriorly)
  - Line superior to horizontal level of the nipple or 5th IC space (inferiorly)
  - Base of the axilla (superiorly)
- Alternatively: patient sat upright leaning forwards over adjacent table with a pillow
- Confirm site of drain insertion by reviewing clinical signs and chest radiograph
- Prophylactic antibiotics not routinely indicated

Drainage

- Common position for insertion is in the mid-axillary line through the 'safe triangle'
  - For apical pneumothoraces, 2nd intercostal space in mid-clavicular line
- Aseptic technique with skin cleansing using iodine or chlorhexidine
- Local anaesthetic (LA) prior to insertion of drain (up to 3 mg/kg of lidocaine)
- Insertion of a small-bore (8–14 French (Fr)) drain with aid of a guidewire by Seldinger technique does not require blunt dissection
- Position of tube tip should be apically for pneumothorax or basally for pleural effusion
  - However, any tube position can be effective, and a functioning drain should not be repositioned because of its radiographic position
- Secure drain with stay suture to prevent it falling out—such as 1-0 silk
- Connect chest tube to a single flow drainage system (e.g. underwater seal bottle)
  - Position confirmed with swinging and bubbling

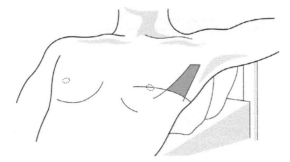

Figure 1.1 Safe triangle for intercostal drain insertion.
Reproduced with permission from Murray et al. Oxford Handbook of Clinical Medicine 7e, 2007, Oxford University Press.

Further reading

Laws D, Neville E, Duffy J. BTS guidelines for the insertion of a chest drain. *Thorax* 2003;58(Suppl II):ii52–ii59.

Algorithm for intercostal drain—seldinger

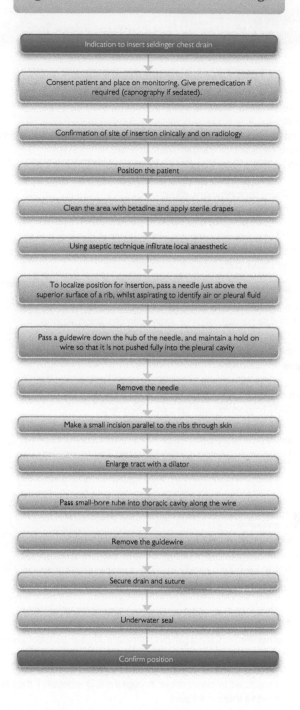

Indication to insert seldinger chest drain

Consent patient and place on monitoring. Give premedication if required (capnography if sedated).

Confirmation of site of insertion clinically and on radiology

Position the patient

Clean the area with betadine and apply sterile drapes

Using aseptic technique infiltrate local anaesthetic

To localize position for insertion, pass a needle just above the superior surface of a rib, whilst aspirating to identify air or pleural fluid

Pass a guidewire down the hub of the needle, and maintain a hold on wire so that it is not pushed fully into the pleural cavity

Remove the needle

Make a small incision parallel to the ribs through skin

Enlarge tract with a dilator

Pass small-bore tube into thoracic cavity along the wire

Remove the guidewire

Secure drain and suture

Underwater seal

Confirm position

8. Intercostal drain—open

Indications
- Traumatic haemothorax
- Traumatic pneumothorax
- Open pneumothorax
- Selected patients with suspected severe lung injury (e.g. multiple rib fractures or pulmonary contusions) who need positive-pressure ventilation or transport via road or air
- Traumatic cardiac arrest (either insert bilateral intercostal drains (ICDs) or perform bilateral finger thorocostomies)
- Empyema and complicated parapneumonic effusion
- Postsurgical (e.g. thoracotomy, oesophagectomy, cardiac surgery)

Contraindications
- Patient unstable: no contraindications
- Patient stable: consider coagulopathy/multiple pleural adhesions

Equipment
- Personal protective equipment (sterile gloves and gown, consider face shield)
- Skin antiseptic solution (use hospital policy, e.g. iodine/chlorhexidine in alcohol)
- Sterile drapes and swabs
- A selection of syringes and needles
- LA (e.g. 1% lignocaine +/– adrenaline)
- Scalpel and blade
- Instrument for blunt dissection (e.g. curved clamp)
- A chest tube (size 28–32 Fr in adults) with the trocar discarded
- Connecting tubing
- Underwater seal drain
- Suture (e.g. 0 or 1-0 silk)
- Dressing and tape

Complications
- Damage to intercostal nerve, artery, or vein
- Infection, e.g. thoracic empyema
- Creation of false track
- Persistent pneumothorax
- Subcutaneous emphysema
- Organ damage, e.g. liver, spleen, lung, heart, diaphragm
- Chronic pain

Other considerations
- Antibiotics should be considered in trauma patients having an ICD inserted, especially with penetrating trauma
- Patients should be referred to a thoracic surgeon if the ICD yields >1.5 L of blood immediately OR if there is persistent blood loss via the ICD (e.g. >200 mL/hour for 2 hours)
- A ruptured bronchus is suggested by persistent air through the ICD, especially if the lung fails to expand; this needs urgent discussion with a thoracic surgeon
- Consider Seldinger drain in non-traumatic pneumothorax
- Consider conservative management for small isolated traumatic pneumothoraces with no haemothorax

Further reading
Maskell N. British Thoracic Society Pleural Disease Guidelines—2010 update. *Thorax* 2010;65:667–669.
American College of Surgeons. ATLS: advanced trauma life support for doctors: student course manual. Chicago, IL: American College of Surgeons, 2008.

Algorithm for intercostal drain—open

Identify need for open ICD

Preparation:
- **Obtain consent:** ideally written, but in emergency setting verbal is adequate. If patient is unable to give consent, perform procedure if deemed in the best interests of the patient
- **Ensure assistant is present**
- **Monitoring:** ensure patient is attached to full monitoring and has 100% oxygen (unless any contraindications to high flow oxygen)
- **Consider parenteral analgesia** e.g. IV morphine

Procedure
1. Position patient appropriately—classically supine or at 45° (depending on other injuries) with arm fully abducted or held behind patient's head.
2. Determine insertion site: commonly 5th intercostal space, just anterior to the mid-axillary line on the affected side
3. Don full personal protective equipment
4. Prepare equipment on procedure trolley
5. Maintain asepsis
6. Clean skin with appropriate antiseptic solution
7. Surgically drape the chest
8. Insert local anaesthetic to skin and down to rib periosteum
9. Make 2- to 3-cm transverse incision on upper border of the rib and bluntly dissect down through tissues
10. Puncture the parietal pleura and insert a gloved finger into the pleural cavity to release adhesions and to ensure that you are in the pleural space
11. Insert the chest tube into the pleural cavity with the aid of a clamp, and look for fogging of air or passage of blood in the drain tube
12. Connect the end of the tube with the underwater seal
13. Suture tube in place and apply a dressing
14. Ensure tube is secure

Post procedure
Re-evaluate patient
Obtain CXR

9. Arterial blood gas sampling

Indications

Arterial blood gas (ABG) sampling is useful:

- In patients with respiratory disease who are at risk of inadequate ventilation and tissue oxygenation.
- In critically ill patients
- In those with metabolic disease (e.g. diabetic ketoacidosis)
- In poisoning and drug overdose.

Contraindications

Contraindications are relative and patient risk should be weighed against the importance of sampling.

- Areas of infected skin/cellulitis overlying the sample site (due to the risk of inoculation with bacteria)
- Patients with coagulopathy or who are anticoagulated.
- Consideration should also be given to the presence of collateral circulation (see section 'Selection of a suitable artery') due to the risk of thrombus formation.

Complications

- The commonest complication is local haematoma at the site of sampling.
- Other complications include intra-arterial thrombus and infection at the sampling site.

Selection of a suitable artery

ABG sampling can be performed using the radial, brachial, or femoral arteries. If the radial artery is to be used, a modified Allen test should ideally be performed to assess and confirm good collateral circulation. To do this, ask the patient to make a fist and apply occlusive pressure to both radial and ulnar arteries with your thumbs. Ask the patient to clench their fist until the palmar skin is blanched. Release the pressure over the ulnar artery only and watch to ensure the palm becomes pink. Repeat the process again, this time releasing pressure on the radial artery only to ensure the palm becomes pink. If pressure release over either artery fails to allow blood flow to the palm and colour to return within 15 seconds, consider a different site for ABG sampling.

To access the radial artery the patient should be positioned supine, with the forearm supinated and the wrist dorsiflexed to approx. 40° if possible.

To access the brachial artery the patient is positioned supine, with the shoulder in slight abduction, the elbow extended, and the forearm fully supinated.

To access the femoral artery the patient is positioned supine, with the legs in the anatomical position.

Use of local anaesthetic

LA does not tend to be used routinely as the insertion of LA is itself painful. If LA is to be utilized 0.5–1.0 mL of 1% lignocaine can be injected subcutaneously using an orange needle over the intended site of arterial puncture. Care should be taken to aspirate prior to instilling the anaesthetic agent to ensure that the artery has not been punctured and so avoid intra-arterial administration of the LA.

ABG normal values

pH	7.35–7.45
PaO_2	10.0–13.0 kPa on room air
$PaCO_2$	4.7–6.0 kPa
HCO_3	22–26 mmol/L
BE	−2 to +2
SaO_2	>95%

(As a rule of thumb, PaO_2 should usually be around 10 kPa less than inspired partial pressure. Practically, this means PaO_2 should be numerically around 10 less than the inspired O_2 concentration (%).)

Further reading

Danckers M. Arterial Blood Gas Sampling. https://emedicine.medscape.com/article/1902703-overview, 2020.
Wyatt JP, Illingworth RN, Graham CA, Hogg K, Robertson C, Clancy M. Oxford Handbook of Emergency Medicine, 4th edn. Oxford: Oxford University Press, 2012.

Algorithm for arterial blood gas sampling

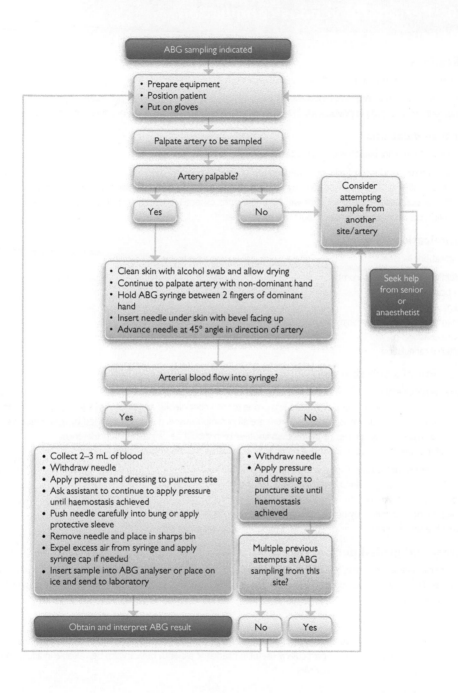

ABG sampling indicated

- Prepare equipment
- Position patient
- Put on gloves

Palpate artery to be sampled

Artery palpable?

Yes | No

Consider attempting sample from another site/artery

- Clean skin with alcohol swab and allow drying
- Continue to palpate artery with non-dominant hand
- Hold ABG syringe between 2 fingers of dominant hand
- Insert needle under skin with bevel facing up
- Advance needle at 45° angle in direction of artery

Seek help from senior or anaesthetist

Arterial blood flow into syringe?

Yes | No

- Collect 2–3 mL of blood
- Withdraw needle
- Apply pressure and dressing to puncture site
- Ask assistant to continue to apply pressure until haemostasis achieved
- Push needle carefully into bung or apply protective sleeve
- Remove needle and place in sharps bin
- Expel excess air from syringe and apply syringe cap if needed
- Insert sample into ABG analyser or place on ice and send to laboratory

- Withdraw needle
- Apply pressure and dressing to puncture site until haemostasis achieved

Multiple previous attempts at ABG sampling from this site?

Obtain and interpret ABG result

No | Yes

10. Peripheral venous cannulation

Indications

Peripheral venous cannulas are used for:

- The administration of IV fluids, blood and blood products, drugs, and parenteral nutrition.
- They are also inserted prophylactically in unstable patients and before certain procedures are commenced.

Contraindications

Peripheral venous cannulation is contraindicated:

- Where there is evidence of infection over the site of insertion.
- Relative contraindications include avoiding forearm veins in patients with renal failure (who may require arteriovenous fistulae) and small veins with low flow rates, especially when irritant drugs are to be used
- Established arteriovenous fistulas should not be cannulated.

Complications

Complications include:

- Infection, phlebitis and thrombophlebitis
- Emboli
- Pain
- Haematoma or haemorrhage
- Extravasation
- Arterial cannulation.

Selection of a suitable vein

In general, peripheral veins in the upper limb are used in preference to those in the lower limb, as they cause less interference with a patient's mobility and are less prone to thrombophlebitis and thrombosis. In the upper limb the dorsal hand veins, cephalic veins, and basilic veins are all commonly used. If a limb is affected by lymphoedema, is infected, or has sustained injuries or burns, then another limb should be cannulated in preference.

If a suitable vein is difficult to identify, a number of techniques may be useful. These include:

- Try a different limb to see if veins are more readily visible
- Ask the patient to open and close their fist when the tourniquet is in situ
- Gently tap or stroke the site
- Enlist the help of gravity, by holding the limb down
- Place the limb in warm water or apply heat pack/warm towel to the site

Ultrasound-guided peripheral cannulation

If peripheral veins are not readily visible and the above techniques do not help, US-guided cannulation is a useful technique. The linear/vascular probe can be used to visualize veins and a cannula can then be inserted using the standard technique.

Topical anaesthetic

In non-emergent situations, topical anaesthetic creams and gels may be applied to the skin to decrease the pain associated with cannulation. This is particularly useful in paediatric patients, but can also be valuable in adults who are very anxious or have a fear of needles.

Further reading

Campbell J. Intravenous cannulation: potential complications. *Prof Nurse* 1997;12(8 Suppl):S10–S13.
Clutton-Brock TH. Vascular access. How to set up a drip and keep it going. *Br J Hosp Med* 1984;32:162, 164, 166–167.
Shlamovitz GZ. Intravenous Cannulation. https://emedicine.medscape.com/article/1998177-overview, 2021.
Waitt C, Waitt P, Piromohamed M. Intravenous therapy. *Postgrad Med J* 2004;80:1–6.

Algorithm for peripheral venous cannulation

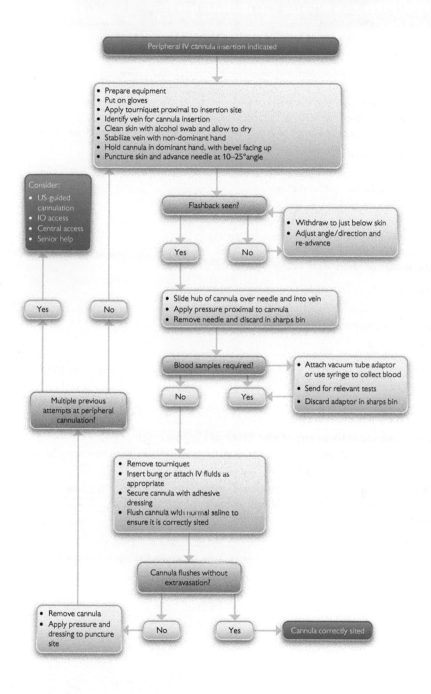

Peripheral IV cannula insertion indicated

- Prepare equipment
- Put on gloves
- Apply tourniquet proximal to insertion site
- Identify vein for cannula insertion
- Clean skin with alcohol swab and allow to dry
- Stabilize vein with non-dominant hand
- Hold cannula in dominant hand, with bevel facing up
- Puncture skin and advance needle at 10–25°angle

Consider:
- US-guided cannulation
- IO access
- Central access
- Senior help

Flashback seen?

- Withdraw to just below skin
- Adjust angle/direction and re-advance

Yes   No

Yes   No

- Slide hub of cannula over needle and into vein
- Apply pressure proximal to cannula
- Remove needle and discard in sharps bin

Blood samples required?

- Attach vacuum tube adaptor or use syringe to collect blood
- Send for relevant tests
- Discard adaptor in sharps bin

No   Yes

Multiple previous attempts at peripheral cannulation?

- Remove tourniquet
- Insert bung or attach IV fluids as appropriate
- Secure cannula with adhesive dressing
- Flush cannula with normal saline to ensure it is correctly sited

Cannula flushes without extravasation?

- Remove cannula
- Apply pressure and dressing to puncture site

No   Yes   Cannula correctly sited

11. Central venous cannulation

Indications

- If the patient requires medications that need central access to allow administration such as inotropes or amiodarone
- If a patient has very poor peripheral venous access and needs a more definitive line
- As part of fluid balance monitoring in the critically ill patient
- If a patient requires a rapid infusion of fluid or blood, such as in haemorrhagic shock secondary to trauma

Contraindications

There are no absolute contraindications for central line insertion, but a risk versus benefit approach should be considered in the following circumstances:

- If the patient has a coagulopathy that hasn't been addressed
- Infection in the tissues around the insertion site
- If there is local thrombosis causing venous obstruction
- Raised intracranial pressure. A femoral line should be considered in this situation
- Local damage such as a burn or a contaminated wound

Consent

Consent for this procedure should cover the following risks:

- Bleeding—local or from arterial puncture
- Infection
- Failure of procedure
- Pneumothorax and damage to other local structures
- Pain
- Thrombus formation
- Uncooperative patient

Ultrasound identification of the internal jugular vein

The following features will help differentiate between the carotid artery and the internal jugular vein:

- It usually lies lateral to the carotid artery within the carotid sheath
- The internal jugular vein should be compressible, whereas the carotid artery will not be
- Valsalva manoeuvre will increase the diameter of the vein
- Doppler flow will show blood flowing away from the probe

Further reading

Hatfield A, Bodenham A. Ultrasound for central venous access. *Continuing Education in Anaesthesia, Critical Care & Pain* 2005;5(6):187–190.

Algorithm for central venous cannulation

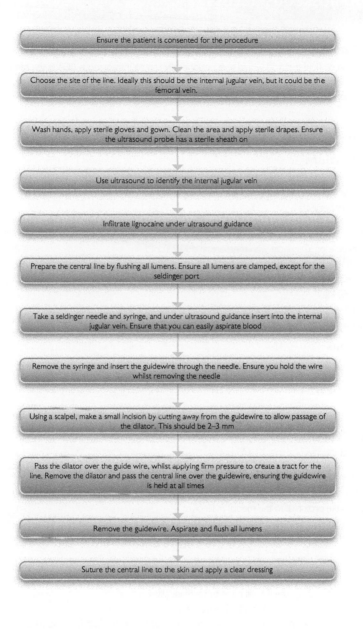

Ensure the patient is consented for the procedure

Choose the site of the line. Ideally this should be the internal jugular vein, but it could be the femoral vein.

Wash hands, apply sterile gloves and gown. Clean the area and apply sterile drapes. Ensure the ultrasound probe has a sterile sheath on

Use ultrasound to identify the internal jugular vein

Infiltrate lignocaine under ultrasound guidance

Prepare the central line by flushing all lumens. Ensure all lumens are clamped, except for the seldinger port

Take a seldinger needle and syringe, and under ultrasound guidance insert into the internal jugular vein. Ensure that you can easily aspirate blood

Remove the syringe and insert the guidewire through the needle. Ensure you hold the wire whilst removing the needle

Using a scalpel, make a small incision by cutting away from the guidewire to allow passage of the dilator. This should be 2–3 mm

Pass the dilator over the guide wire, whilst applying firm pressure to create a tract for the line. Remove the dilator and pass the central line over the guidewire, ensuring the guidewire is held at all times

Remove the guidewire. Aspirate and flush all lumens

Suture the central line to the skin and apply a clear dressing

12. Intraosseous access

Important points

- Any medication or fluid that you would give peripherally can go intraosseous (IO) at the same dose
- Any age patient can have an IO needle inserted
- Each medication given needs to be flushed with 5 mL of normal saline

Indications

- Any situation where IV access is proving difficult/impossible, e.g. burns, circulatory collapse, cardiac arrest

Contraindications

- Vascular damage or fracture proximal to the intended site of insertion
- Infection in the skin overlying the intended site of insertion
- Osteogenesis imperfecta

Equipment

- Manual IO needle or IO needle with mechanical driver (drill)
- Select the correct IO needle:
  - 15 mm: 3–39 kg
  - 25 mm: >40 kg
  - 45 mm: proximal humeral site, or excessive subcutaneous tissue
- Three-way tap with primed extension set with 0.9% saline

Complications

- Epiphyseal injury
- Bleeding
- Skin necrosis
- Infection
- Through and through bone penetration
- Subcutaneous infiltration
- Iatrogenic fracture

Possible sites for insertion

- Proximal tibia: approx. 2.5 cm distal to the tibial tuberosity on the antero-medial aspect of the tibia
- Distal tibia: 2.5 cm proximal to the medial malleolus
- Distal femur: 2.5 cm proximal to the lateral femoral condyle on the antero-lateral surface
- Proximal humerus: at the greater trochanter on the antero-lateral aspect

Notes

- Bone marrow can be tested for BM, cultures, or group and save
- Any fluid inserted through the IO will need to be manually syringed
- Continually assess to ensure patency of IO placement
- Remove IO needle as soon as two IV accesses have been obtained and within 24 hours of insertion

Further reading

American College of Surgeons. ATLS: advanced trauma life support for doctors: student course manual. Chicago, IL: American College of Surgeons, 2008.

Advanced LifeAdvanced Life Support Group. Advanced Paediatric Life Support: A Practical Approach to Emergencies (APLS), 6th edn. Wiley-Blackwell, 2016.

Algorithm for intraosseous access

Preparation
- Explain the procedure to patient/relative and obtain consent if appropriate.
- Identify the insertion site
- Sterilize the skin
- Support the limb on a blanket

Manual IO insertion

1. Insert local anaesthetic (e.g. 1% lignocaine) subcutaneously if needed
2. Firmly grasp the handle and use a twisting motion to insert the needle at a 90°angle to the bone. Stop when you feel the give of breaching the medullary cavity
3. Remove stylet and confirm placement by aspiration of bone marrow (*Note*: failure to aspirate bone marrow does not necessarily signify incorrect IO placement)

Mechanical IO insertion (with drill)

1. Local anaesthetic to the skin is not needed
2. Select correct IO needle size and place needle into drill
3. Insert the needle at 90° to the skin up to the 5-mm black line on the shaft of the needle
4. Remove the drill and the stylet of the IO needle, leaving the needle itself in the medullary cavity
5. Confirm placement by aspiration of bone marrow
6. *Note*: failure to aspirate bone marrow does not necessarily signify incorrect IO placement

Attach the 3-way tap and extension set, and flush the IO with 0.9% saline

Look for soft tissue swelling around the IO site—this may suggest incorrect IO positioning

Secure IO needle to leg with tape or consider a plaster of Paris back slab to ensure leg immobilization

13. Urinary catheterization

Important safety notes

- Adult urinary catheters are manufactured in two lengths: female length (20–26 cm) and standard length (40–45 cm). The use of standard-length catheters in females poses no safety issues. However, if a female-length catheter is accidentally used for a male, the 'balloon' inflated with sterile water to retain the catheter will be within the urethra, rather than the bladder, and can then cause severe trauma
- Most widely used types of catheter contain latex. If the patient is allergic to latex, an all-silicone catheter must be used

Technique for insertion

1. Obtain an assistant/chaperon
2. Choose an appropriate size catheter (e.g. 12–14 Fr) and appropriate length (see above) and prepare your equipment
3. Position the patient in supine with legs slightly apart
4. Wash and dry your hands, then put on sterile gloves
5. Clean thoroughly around the urethral meatus (retract the foreskin if applicable) using an antiseptic solution like chlorhexidine
6. Insert LA gel and hold the meatus close; wait for 5 minutes for it to work
7. a) Hold the penis vertically with one hand and gently advance the catheter with the other hand, until all is inserted
   b) Part the labia with one hand and gently advance the catheter with the other hand, until all is inserted
8. Wait until urine starts flowing through the catheter
9. Inflate the balloon using 10 mL of sterile water, ensuring that it does not cause any pain, and attach a catheter bag
10. Gently pull on the catheter until resistance is felt
11. Reposition the foreskin if applicable

Useful tips

- Instruct the patient to try to void when you feel resistance passing the catheter. This will sometimes open the sphincter, allowing the catheter to pass
- Use forceps to aid advancing and applying gentle pressure to the catheter as it advances; this will provide better grip to the catheter and stops slipping

Further reading

NPSA alert (NPSA/2009/RRR02): Female urinary catheters causing trauma to adult males. *Nurs Times* 30 April 2010.

Algorithm for urinary catheterization

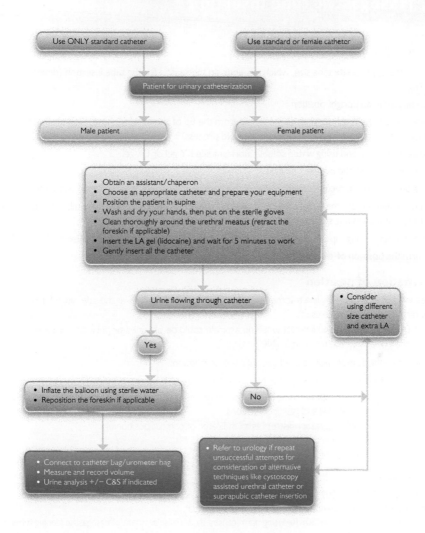

Use ONLY standard catheter

Use standard or female catheter

Patient for urinary catheterization

Male patient

Female patient

- Obtain an assistant/chaperon
- Choose an appropriate catheter and prepare your equipment
- Position the patient in supine
- Wash and dry your hands, then put on the sterile gloves
- Clean thoroughly around the urethral meatus (retract the foreskin if applicable)
- Insert the LA gel (lidocaine) and wait for 5 minutes to work
- Gently insert all the catheter

Urine flowing through catheter

Yes

- Consider using different size catheter and extra LA

- Inflate the balloon using sterile water
- Reposition the foreskin if applicable

No

- Connect to catheter bag/urometer bag
- Measure and record volume
- Urine analysis +/- C&S if indicated

- Refer to urology if repeat unsuccessful attempts for consideration of alternative techniques like cystoscopy assisted urethral catheter or suprapubic catheter insertion

14. Nasogastric tube insertion

Technique for insertion

1. Choose the appropriate tube size, which depends on the reason for the tube insertion (drainage or feeding)
2. Place patient in an upright position
3. Measure the tube length (it must be measured from the tip of the patient's nose, loop around their ear, and then down to roughly 5 cm below the xiphoid process)
4. Lubricate the tube end using water-soluble lubricant like KY gel or LA gel
5. Insert it into one of the patient's nostrils
6. The tube should be directed straight towards the back of the patient, parallel to the nasal floor
7. When the tube enters the oropharynx and glides down the posterior pharyngeal wall, the patient may gag; ask the patient to mimic swallowing or give some water to sip through a straw
8. Secure the tube using tape
9. Confirm the position of the tube before using it

Confirmation of position

- pH testing is used as the first-line test method, with pH between 1 and 5.5 as the safe range for right position (pH indicator paper must be used)
- X-ray is used only as a second-line test when no aspirate could be obtained or pH indicator paper has failed to confirm the position of the nasogastric (NG) tube

The following methods **must not** be used to confirm tube position:

- Auscultation of air insufflated through the NG tube ('whoosh' test)
- Testing acidity/alkalinity of aspirate using blue litmus paper—blue litmus paper is not sensitive enough to distinguish between bronchial and gastric secretions
- Interpreting absence of respiratory distress as an indicator of correct positioning
- Monitoring bubbling at the end of the NG tube
- Observing the appearance of NG tube aspirate

Further reading

NPSA alert (NPSA/2011/PSA002): Reducing the harm caused by misplaced nasogastric feeding tubes in adults, children and infants. http://www.gbukenteral.com/pdf/npsa-alert-2011.pdf.

NPSA alert (Reference number 0180): Reducing harm caused by the misplacement of nasogastric feeding tubes. https://www.england.nhs.uk/publication/patient-safety-alert-nasogastric-tube-misplacement-continuing-risk-of-death-and-severe-harm/

Algorithm for nasogastric tube insertion

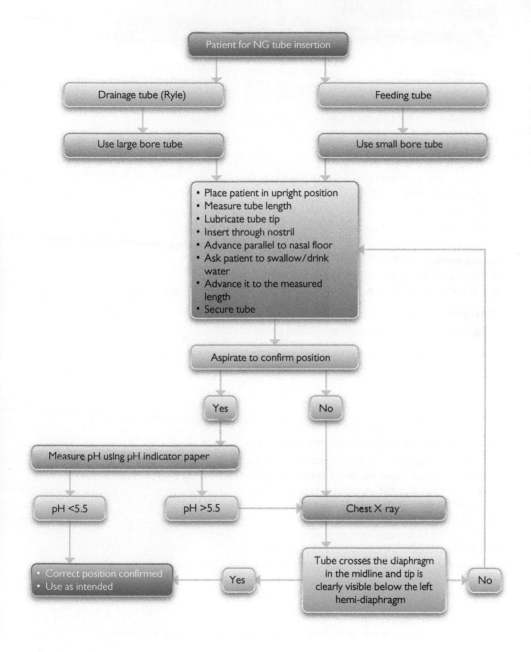

Patient for NG tube insertion

Drainage tube (Ryle) → Use large bore tube

Feeding tube → Use small bore tube

- Place patient in upright position
- Measure tube length
- Lubricate tube tip
- Insert through nostril
- Advance parallel to nasal floor
- Ask patient to swallow/drink water
- Advance it to the measured length
- Secure tube

Aspirate to confirm position

Yes / No

Measure pH using pH indicator paper

pH <5.5 / pH >5.5

Chest X ray

- Correct position confirmed
- Use as intended

Yes

Tube crosses the diaphragm in the midline and tip is clearly visible below the left hemi-diaphragm

No

15. Arterial cannulation and arterial pressure monitoring

Indications

- The need for continuous BP monitoring, such as the critically ill or unstable patient
- If recurrent arterial samples are required
- If normal BP monitoring is not possible due to an injury such as burns

Contraindications

Absolute contraindications include:

- Any vascular impairment to the limb intended for use
- Raynaud syndrome
- Full thickness burns

Relative contraindications include:

- Partial thickness burns
- Local infection
- Previous vascular surgery in the affected area
- Inadequate collateral flow, such as ulnar artery insufficiency in the Allen test

Complications

- Radial artery occlusion secondary to indwelling catheter
- Bleeding
- Local infection
- Limb ischaemia
- Thrombosis
- Air embolism
- Median nerve damage

Preparing arterial pressure monitoring

- Spike a 500-mL bag of normal saline with the transducer set
- Place saline in a pressure bag and inflate pressure bag up to 300 mmHg
- Attach transducer holder and saline to IV pole
- Connect transducer to transducer holder, ensuring transducer cable is pointing down
- Prime tubing and remove all air bubbles
- Connect transducer cable to monitor port
- Connect distal part of tubing to patient's arterial line
- Expose port on transducer to atmosphere (port closed to the patient) and press zero on monitor
- Close port to atmosphere and open port to the patient
- Arterial tracing should now be present on the monitor

Further reading

Core EM video on monitoring set up. https://coreem.net/procedures/how-to-set-up-an-arterial-line/.

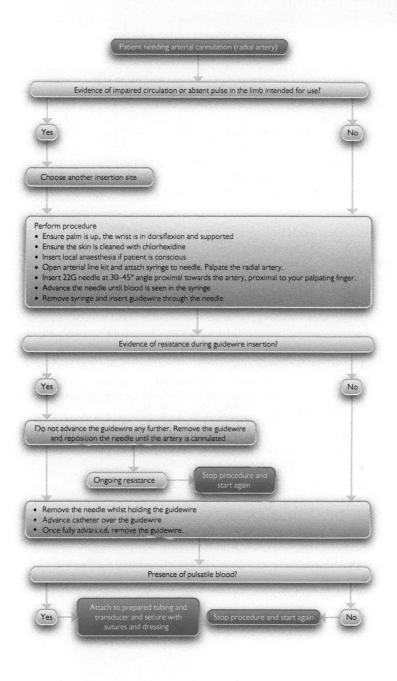

Patient needing arterial cannulation (radial artery)

Evidence of impaired circulation or absent pulse in the limb intended for use?

Yes

No

Choose another insertion site

Perform procedure
- Ensure palm is up, the wrist is in dorsiflexion and supported
- Ensure the skin is cleaned with chlorhexidine
- Insert local anaesthesia if patient is conscious
- Open arterial line kit and attach syringe to needle. Palpate the radial artery.
- Insert 22G needle at 30–45° angle proximal towards the artery, proximal to your palpating finger.
- Advance the needle until blood is seen in the syringe
- Remove syringe and insert guidewire through the needle

Evidence of resistance during guidewire insertion?

Yes

No

Do not advance the guidewire any further. Remove the guidewire and reposition the needle until the artery is cannulated

Ongoing resistance

Stop procedure and start again

- Remove the needle whilst holding the guidewire
- Advance catheter over the guidewire
- Once fully advanced, remove the guidewire.

Presence of pulsatile blood?

Yes

Attach to prepared tubing and transducer and secure with sutures and dressing

Stop procedure and start again

No

16. Lumbar puncture

Consent

It is important as with any procedure to ensure fully informed consent is obtained prior to performing the procedure. If you are doing the procedure, you should be able to consent the patient.

- Outline the reason the procedure is being done. This might be as a diagnostic test in a suspected central nervous system infection
- Explain the procedure and the steps involved to the patient
- Explain the risks associated with the procedure
- Common risks include back pain at the site of insertion, post spinal headache, shooting pain down the legs during the procedure, and bleeding if on anticoagulants
- Less common risks include bleeding at the insertion site, lower limb neurology, and infection at insertion site

Complications

- Post spinal headache can begin anywhere between 24 and 48 hours after the lumbar puncture has been done. It is usually relieved by lying down. Simple analgesia can be given, and it is usually self-limiting. If severe, an anaesthetic review should be sought for consideration of an epidural blood patch
- Infection can occur in any of the anatomical sites involved with the lumbar puncture. These include cellulitis, epidural and spinal abscesses, and potentially discitis. Correct sterile technique will reduce the risk of this occurring
- A bloody spinal tap may occur secondary to trauma to local tissues when performing the lumbar puncture. It will usually result in a false positive for red blood cells in the cerebrospinal fluid (CSF) cell count
- Bleeding in the epidural and subdural space can occur but is rare. It is important to check whether the patient is on anticoagulants or is known to have a coagulopathy. If the platelet count is below 50 the procedure should be delayed and advice should be sought from the haematologist
- When withdrawing the spinal needle, it is important to ensure that the stylet is replaced in the needle to prevent damage to spinal structures

Further reading

West Suffolk Hospital. Lumbar puncture and consent patient leaflet. https://www.wsh.nhs.uk/cms-documents/patient-leaflets/neurology/5561-1lumberpunctureandconsent.pdf, 2018.

Algorithm for lumbar puncture

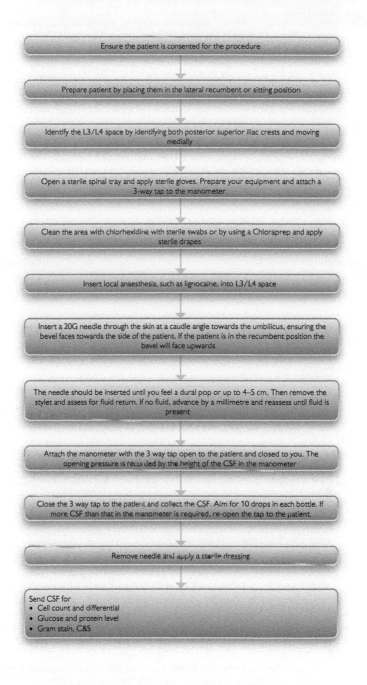

Ensure the patient is consented for the procedure

↓

Prepare patient by placing them in the lateral recumbent or sitting position

↓

Identify the L3/L4 space by identifying both posterior superior iliac crests and moving medially

↓

Open a sterile spinal tray and apply sterile gloves. Prepare your equipment and attach a 3-way tap to the manometer

↓

Clean the area with chlorhexidine with sterile swabs or by using a Chloraprep and apply sterile drapes

↓

Insert local anaesthesia, such as lignocaine, into L3/L4 space

↓

Insert a 20G needle through the skin at a caudle angle towards the umbilicus, ensuring the bevel faces towards the side of the patient. If the patient is in the recumbent position the bevel will face upwards

↓

The needle should be inserted until you feel a dural pop or up to 4–5 cm. Then remove the stylet and assess for fluid return. If no fluid, advance by a millimetre and reassess until fluid is present

↓

Attach the manometer with the 3 way tap open to the patient and closed to you. The opening pressure is recorded by the height of the CSF in the manometer

↓

Close the 3 way tap to the patient and collect the CSF. Aim for 10 drops in each bottle. If more CSF than that in the manometer is required, re-open the tap to the patient.

↓

Remove needle and apply a sterile dressing

↓

Send CSF for
- Cell count and differential
- Glucose and protein level
- Gram stain, C&S

17. Abdominal paracentesis/ascetic tap

Introduction

Paracentesis is a method of obtaining a sample of abdominal free fluid either as a diagnostic or as a therapeutic intervention.

Indications

- In the Emergency Department the most common reason to perform paracentesis is for the diagnosis or exclusion of spontaneous bacterial peritonitis.
- Other indications include:
  - Therapeutic drainage of massive chronic ascites
  - To relieve either abdominal pain or respiratory splinting
  - To aid diagnosis in new-onset ascites.

Contraindications

- Acute abdomen requiring surgery

The following are relative contraindications and require a senior clinician to assess the perceived risks of carrying out compared to delaying the procedure:

- Thrombocytopenia (platelet count <20 × 10³/μL) or INR >2.0
- Pregnancy
- Distended urinary bladder
- Abdominal wall cellulitis
- Distended bowel
- Intra-abdominal adhesions

Procedure

Pericardiocentesis packs should be used where available: IV cannulas, a three-way tap, a 50-mL syringe, and a giving set may be fashioned together as an alternative, but this should only be used by someone already familiar with this technique.

   With the patient either supine with head of bed raised by 30° or in lateral decubitus position, the left or right lower quadrants are the preferred puncture sites (lower side if in lateral position). Dullness to percussion or confirmation of fluid using US is necessary prior to puncture. To avoid the inferior epigastric artery, aim for 2–4 cm cephalad and medial to the anterior superior iliac spine.

Complications

- Complications include puncture of bowel or mesentery.
- Rarely there may be spontaneous bleeding from mesenteric varices following large volume drainage.
- Abdominal wall haematomas are uncomfortable but rarely significant.
- Post-paracentesis hypotension may be managed with fluid replacement: commonly, albumin is used in these cases; however, other plasma expanders may be used as an alternative.
- A persistent leak should be initially managed with direct pressure, and if continuing, consider horizontal mattress suture around the site or alternatively apply a urostomy bag to collect and measure fluid loss.

Further reading

Moore KP, Aithal GP. Guidelines on the management of ascites in cirrhosis. *Gut* 2006;55(Suppl VI):vi1–vi12.
Shlamovitz GZ. Paracentesis. https://emedicine.medscape.com/article/80944-overview, 2020.
Wong CL, Holroyd-Leduc J, Thorpe KE, Straus SE. Does this patient have bacterial peritonitis or portal hypertension? How do I perform a paracentesis and analyze the results? *JAMA* 2008;299(10):1166–1178.

Algorithm for abdominal paracentesis/ascetic tap

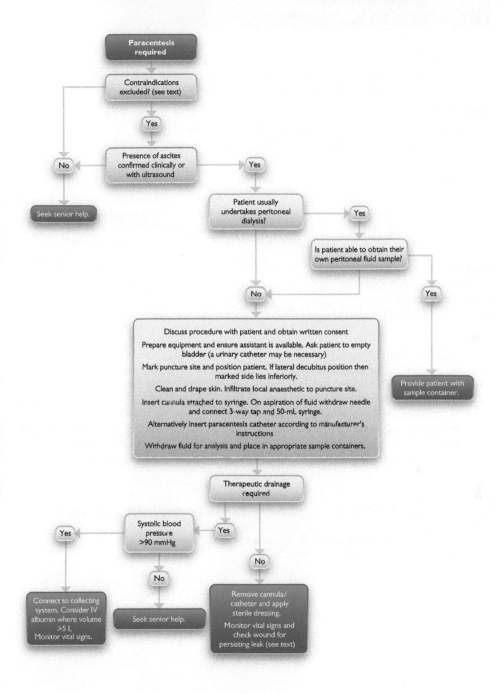

Paracentesis required

Contraindications excluded? (see text)

Yes

Presence of ascites confirmed clinically or with ultrasound

No → Seek senior help.

Yes

Patient usually undertakes peritoneal dialysis?

Yes → Is patient able to obtain their own peritoneal fluid sample?

No

Yes → Provide patient with sample container.

Discuss procedure with patient and obtain written consent

Prepare equipment and ensure assistant is available. Ask patient to empty bladder (a urinary catheter may be necessary)

Mark puncture site and position patient. If lateral decubitus position then marked side lies inferiorly.

Clean and drape skin. Infiltrate local anaesthetic to puncture site.

Insert cannula attached to syringe. On aspiration of fluid withdraw needle and connect 3-way tap and 50-mL syringe.

Alternatively insert paracentesis catheter according to manufacturer's instructions

Withdraw fluid for analysis and place in appropriate sample containers.

Therapeutic drainage required

Yes → Systolic blood pressure >90 mmHg

Yes → Connect to collecting system. Consider IV albumin where volume >5 L Monitor vital signs.

No → Seek senior help.

No → Remove cannula/catheter and apply sterile dressing. Monitor vital signs and check wound for persisting leak (see text)

18. DC cardioversion

Introduction

Electrical cardioversion is an effective method of restoring sinus rhythm in a variety of cardiac arrhythmias. It is the responsibility of the practitioner delivering the shock to ensure the safety of the team.

Indications

- Cardiac arrest due to ventricular fibrillation or ventricular tachycardia
- Haemodynamically compromised patient with either a broad or a narrow complex tachycardia
- Stable patient with persistent dysrhythmia (e.g. atrial fibrillation)

Contraindications

- The only contraindications involve risks to safety of the operator or patient and include water across the chest (e.g. in cases of drowning) and removal or avoidance of glyceryl trinitrate (GTN) medication patch if this lies between the two pads

Complications

- Failure to restore sinus rhythm
- Post-procedure chest discomfort
- Thromboembolic stroke
- Induction of a different arrhythmia

Notes

All European defibrillators are marked with the numbers 1–3: 1 selects energy, 2 charges, and 3 delivers the shock.

It should be noted that if a synchronized shock is to be delivered, the practitioner must hold the shock button down until the shock has been delivered: this may not be instantaneous.

The energy delivered depends on the machine used; practitioners must be familiar with the equipment they will be using. Values quoted in the algorithm are for a Philips Heartstart biphasic defibrillator.

If sedation is required, a separate clinician is required to deliver this (not the same person who is doing the cardioversion.) This requires an assessment of sedation risk and may need urgent anaesthetic assistance.

Following cardioversion, an immediate pulse check should take place, along with recording BP. An ECG should then be performed.

Further reading

Resuscitation Council UK. Adult Advanced Life Support. Retrieved from https://www.resus.org.uk/library/2021-resuscitation-guidelines, 2021.

Resuscitation Council UK. Peri-arrest arrhythmias. Retrieved from https://www.resus.org.uk/library/2021-resuscitation-guidelines/adult-advanced-life-support-guidelines, 2021.

Algorithm for DC cardioversion

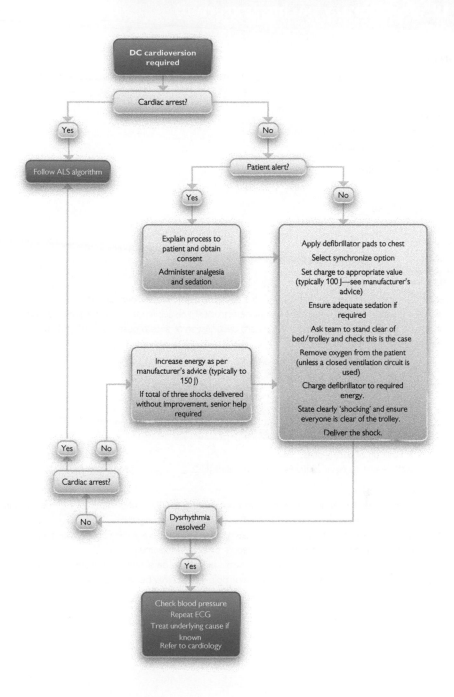

DC cardioversion required

Cardiac arrest?

Yes → Follow ALS algorithm

No → Patient alert?

Yes → Explain process to patient and obtain consent

Administer analgesia and sedation

No → Apply defibrillator pads to chest

Select synchronize option

Set charge to appropriate value (typically 100 J—see manufacturer's advice)

Ensure adequate sedation if required

Ask team to stand clear of bed/trolley and check this is the case

Remove oxygen from the patient (unless a closed ventilation circuit is used)

Charge defibrillator to required energy.

State clearly 'shocking' and ensure everyone is clear of the trolley.

Deliver the shock.

Increase energy as per manufacturer's advice (typically to 150 J)

If total of three shocks delivered without improvement, senior help required

Cardiac arrest?

Yes / No

Dysrhythmia resolved?

No

Yes → Check blood pressure
Repeat ECG
Treat underlying cause if known
Refer to cardiology

19. Temporary pacing (external)

Introduction

External pacing is a potentially life-saving emergency intervention to restore or increase heart rate in order to preserve cardiac output.

Indications

- Bradycardia resulting in cardiovascular compromise
- Syncope due to bradycardia

Contraindications

There are no absolute contraindications.

Complications

- Failure to respond
- Chest discomfort at site of pads
- Inability to tolerate procedure (sedation is frequently required)

Procedure

It is essential that practitioners are familiar with the equipment used in their own department.

Note: most pacing machines require the monitor electrodes to be applied as well as the pacing/defibrillator pads.

Pacing pads may be applied in either the standard defibrillation or antero-posterior (AP) positions (Figure 1.2).

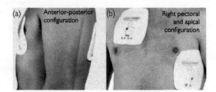

Figure 1.2 Position of pacing pads.

Reproduced with the kind permission of the Resuscitation Council (UK).

Sedation of the unwell bradycardic patient is hazardous and should only be undertaken by experienced clinicians. Monitoring in such cases should include SPO_2, NIBP, ECG, and nasal capnography.

Fist pacing (to the centre of the chest with increasing force until capture is seen on the monitor) is sometimes necessary whilst obtaining help and equipment needed for external electric pacing.

Early cardiology referral is essential: complete heart block may be a finding in acute myocardial infarction. Transvenous pacing is nearly always required, and inotropic support may be needed in some cases.

In cases of failure to capture, consider changing to alternative pad position.

Further reading

Gammage M. Temporary cardiac pacing. *Heart* 2000;83:715–720.

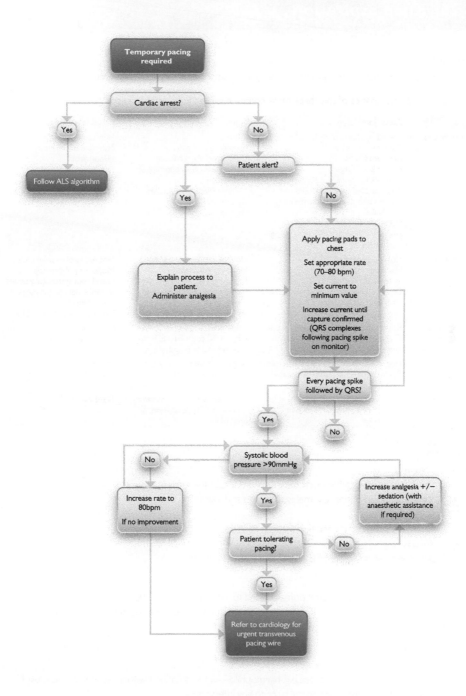

Algorithm for temporary pacing (external)

Temporary pacing required

Cardiac arrest?

Yes → Follow ALS algorithm

No → Patient alert?

Yes → Explain process to patient. Administer analgesia

No → Apply pacing pads to chest

Set appropriate rate (70–80 bpm)

Set current to minimum value

Increase current until capture confirmed (QRS complexes following pacing spike on monitor)

Every pacing spike followed by QRS?

Yes → Systolic blood pressure >90mmHg

No

No → Increase rate to 80bpm

If no improvement

Systolic blood pressure >90mmHg

Yes → Patient tolerating pacing?

No → Increase analgesia +/− sedation (with anaesthetic assistance if required)

Patient tolerating pacing?

Yes → Refer to cardiology for urgent transvenous pacing wire

20. Knee aspiration

Introduction

Table 1.3 shows the characteristics of the three most common causes for a swollen knee.

Table 1.3 Characteristics of the three most common causes for a swollen knee

	Septic joint	Gout	Pseudogout
Risk factors	Preceding history of arthritis Recent knee injury Knee prosthesis Recent knee surgery Immunodeficiency (e.g. human immunodeficiency virus (HIV), chemotherapy, diabetes mellitus) Alcoholics Sickle cell disease Sexually transmitted disease, especially gonorrhoea	Trauma Diuretics and aspirin Diet, especially rich foods Increased alcohol consumption Renal failure Myeloproliferative disorders Cytotoxic drugs Previous history of gout	Haemochromotosis Hyperparathyroidism Hypothyroid Diabetes mellitus Wilson's disease Previous history of pseudogout
Presentation	Hot red swollen painful knee Usually monoarthritis Systemically unwell Gross reduction in range of movement Inability to weight bear	Hot red swollen painful knee Mono- or polyarthritis Usually not systemically unwell Variable reduction in range of movement Variable ability to weight bear	Hot red swollen painful knee Mono- or polyarthritis Usually not systemically unwell Variable reduction in range of movement Variable ability to weight bear
Blood tests	Raised white blood cell (WBC) count, CRP, and erythrocyte sedimentation rate (ESR) is characteristic	Urate may be raised or normal CRP, WBC count, and ESR may be normal or raised	CRP, WBC count, and ESR may be normal or raised
Microscopy	High WBC count, usually polymorphs Positive Gram stain (may be negative if patient on antibiotics)	Negative birefringent crystals (monosodium urate)	Positive birefringent crystals (calcium pyrophosphate)
Treatment	Analgesia, antibiotics Refer to orthopaedics for a joint washout	Non-steroidal anti-inflammatory drugs (NSAIDs), colchicine, or prednisolone	NSAIDs

Causes

- Acute injuries
  - Blood in the knee, e.g. anterior cruciate ligament (ACL) tears, fractures
  - Synovial fluid accumulation, e.g. meniscal injuries and ligamentous sprains
- Chronic conditions
  - E.g. arthritis or any other condition that can flare up
- Spontaneous
  - Rapid knee swelling, e.g. septic arthritis, gout, and pseudogout

Indications

- The procedure of knee aspiration is primarily used to identify septic arthritis
- It can be used to symptomatically drain a haemarthrosis or a swollen joint secondary to arthritis,
- It can also confirm gout and pseudogout.

Contraindications

- Infection over site of planned aspiration
- Patient with known bleeding disorder, e.g. haemophilia—in these patients with a swollen joint, all **must** be discussed with the haematologist on call prior to any intervention
- **All** cases with a prosthetic knee do **not** aspirate in the ED—refer to orthopaedics for aspiration in theatre

Further reading

Ramrakha P, Moore K, Sam A. Oxford Handbook of Acute Medicine. Oxford, UK: Oxford University Press, 2019–11. Retrieved 2 May, 2022, from https://oxfordmedicine.com/view/10.1093/med/9780198797425.001.0001/med-9780198797425.

Algorithm for knee aspiration

Decision to perform knee aspiration

Preparation
- Explain procedure
- Obtain consent
- Use full aseptic precautions

Procedure tips
- Lie patient as flat as comfort allows.
- Relaxation of the quadriceps muscle facilitates insertion
- Aim to keep the knee in extension
- Squeezing the superior and medial aspect of the knee joint may aid the aspiration

Local anaesthetic
- Surgically prepare skin with skin antiseptic and drapes
- Infiltrate local anaesthetic (e.g. 1% lignocaine) just posterior and lateral to the mid point of the patella
- Infiltrate further local anaesthetic deeper in the tissues, down to the synovial membrane of the suprapatellar pouch

Procedure
- Insert an 18G needle attached to a 20-mL syringe at the same point where you infiltrated local anaesthetic.
   - O As you advance pull back on the syringe.
- When you reach the joint space, aspirate fluid. Continue until dryness

Post procedure
- Apply dressing
- Send aspirated fluid for: Gram stain, microscopy, C&S, cell count

21. Fracture manipulation

Introduction

Rapid reduction of a displaced fracture may be required to restore circulation or reduce pressure on affected nerves or skin.

Indications

- Neurovascular compromise (distal sensation and circulation, but also tight, tented, blanched skin at site of fracture)
- Simple fracture which is angulated or displaced
- Fracture is expected to be straightforward to reduce

Contraindications

- Current position acceptable
- Open fractures requiring operative debridement (unless neurovascular compromise)

Complications

- Pain
- Failure to reduce the fracture
- Conversion of closed fracture to open fracture
- Nerve or skin damage

Notes

It is essential that the patient is comfortable throughout the procedure and a number of methods may be considered either in isolation or in combination, including opiate analgesia, inhaled O_2 and nitrous oxide (N_2O) gas mixture, regional or local anaesthetic, or sedation.

It should be noted that different fracture patterns require specific techniques for optimum reduction: a list of these is beyond the scope of this book and direct supervision by someone experienced in these techniques is required. One method of Colles fracture reduction is as follows:

- After appropriate analgesia/nerve block, apply traction to the hand with dorsal angulation in order to disimpact the fracture
- Whilst maintaining traction, push the distal fragment distally and flex the wrist along with the application of ulna deviation. The wrist position should therefore be 20–30° of flexion, 15° ulna deviation, and 20° pronation
- Hold this position whilst a plaster slab is applied

Further reading

Standards for the management of open fractures of the lower limb. British Association of Plastic and Reconstructive Surgeons and British Orthopaedic Association. https://www2.aofoundation.org, 2009.

Algorithm for fracture manipulation

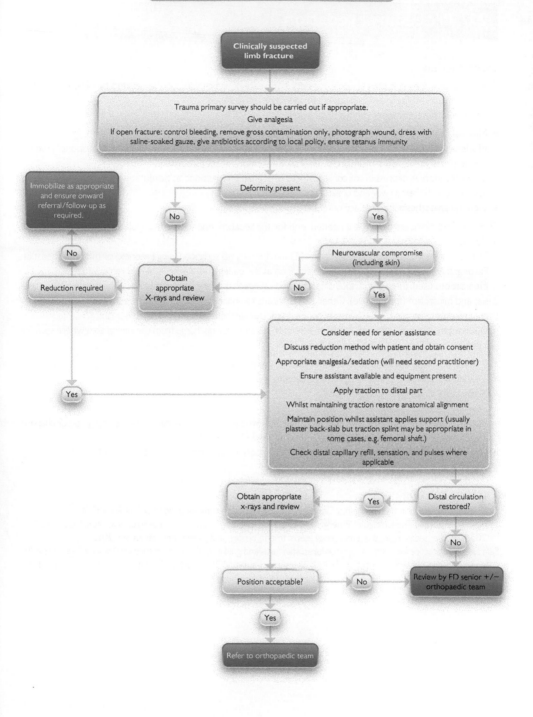

22. Procedural sedation

Introduction

This guidance is for adult patients only. Patients <18 years of age should only be sedated by clinicians skilled in paediatric airway management and advanced paediatric resuscitation.

There are different kinds of depths of sedation:

- **Minimal sedation**. Patients respond normally to voice and command
- **Moderate sedation** (or 'conscious sedation'). A depression of consciousness where patients respond to voice. Spontaneous ventilation is maintained. Their airway remains intact throughout
- **Deep sedation**. A depression of consciousness where patients respond to painful stimuli. Patients may require assistance with their airway and breathing
- **General anaesthesia**. Patients are unrousable

Three trained members of staff are needed: one for the sedation, one for the manipulation, and one to monitor the patient.

During reduction of a dislocated joint in the ED, aim for minimal sedation (using Entonox) or moderate sedation.

Fasting: this is not required for moderate sedation as the patient's airway reflexes will remain intact.

Medications used: there are various different medications that can be used. One example is morphine (for analgesia) and midazolam (for sedative). Other examples are ketamine (causing 'dissociative sedation') and propofol—these are **only** to be used in the hands of senior trained anaesthetists or emergency physicians.

Discharge: patients should be formally assessed for suitability for discharge from the clinical area where sedation has taken place. Discharge criteria are as follows:

- The patient has returned to their baseline level of consciousness
- Vital signs are within normal limits for that patient
- Respiratory status is not compromised
- Pain and discomfort have been addressed
- Patients meeting discharge criteria following sedation who go on to be discharged home should be discharged into the care of a suitable third party
- Patients need to be advised not to drive and not to operate heavy machinery in the next 24 hours
- Verbal and written instructions should be given

Further reading

Safe sedation of adults in the Emergency Department. Report and Recommendations by The Royal College of Anaesthetists and The College of Emergency Medicine, November 2012. https://rcem.ac.uk/wp-content/uploads/2021/10/safe_sedation_in_the_emergency_department_report_and_recommendations.pdf, 2012.

Safe sedation practice for healthcare procedures: standards and guidance. Academy of Medical Royal Colleges. https://www.evidence.nhs.uk/document?id=1629012&returnurl=search%3fq%3dsafe%2bpractice&q=safe+practice, 2013.

Algorithm for procedural sedation

Decision made to reduce a fracture/
dislocation in ADULTS in the ED
Assess neurovascular state prior to reduction
Aim for **MODERATE** sedation

Obtain Consent
Ideally written consent.
If unable, then verbal consent

Pre-assess patient
Procedure to be performed in the resuscitation room
Take care with sedating patients with co-morbidities
eg liver, lung, heart disease, obesity and those in shock
If patient has significant comorbidities or is critically
unwell-ensure senior support is present

Monitor patient
IV access (ideally 2)
Oxygen (be warned-oxygen will correct
hypoxia but may mask hypoventilation)
ECG and non-invasive BP cuff
Oxygen saturations
Ideally capnography
Resuscitation room facilities, including
difficult airway trolley

Example of medications used:
IV morphine
Start at 2.5 mg.
Titrate until analgesia obtained
(up to 10 mg)

IV midazolam
Start at 2 mg in a fit adult. Start
at 0.5–1 mg in the elderly
Titrate until moderate sedation
achieved
Total dose may be up to 10mg

Prepare equipment:
Analgesic (eg morphine)
Sedative (eg midazolam)
Antidotes-ensure that you are
familiar with dose if needed

Antidotes:
Morphine-**naloxone**
Start at 400 micrograms IV
May need further boluses

Midazolam-**flumazenil**
Start at 200 micrograms IV
over 30 seconds
Repeat after 1 minute
May need up to 1 mg

Perform procedure
Keep communication with
patient at all times

Recovery and discharge/admission where appropriate
Ensure full documentation of procedure
Verbal and written advice leaflet given

SECTION 2

Airway and breathing

1. Anaphylaxis

Introduction

Anaphylaxis is an acute, severe, life threatening type 1 hypersensitivity reaction. The clinical manifestations relate to four systems:

- Skin: flushing, pruritus, urticarial, angioedema
- Respiratory: upper and/or lower tract, upper airway swelling, bronchospasm
- Cardiovascular: vasodilatation, hypotension
- Gastrointestinal (GI): abdominal pain, nausea, vomiting, diarrhoea

Recognition

Anaphylaxis is likely with any **one** of the following:

- Acute onset:
  - Skin or mucosal involvement **and** respiratory distress **or** hypotension
- Two or more of:
  - Skin involvement
  - Respiratory distress
  - Hypotension
  - GI symptoms
- Hypotension after allergen exposure

Most cases occur within 1 hour of exposure but can be delayed up to 12 hours.

Treatment

- See Algorithm
- Additional treatment: consider IV glucagon (1 mg) for patients on B blockers. B blockers may cause persistent hypotension in patients with anaphylaxis
- Fluid: use crystalloid: 500–1000 mL in an adult, 20 mL/kg in a child

Investigations

- Mast cell degranulation causes an increase in serum tryptase, which can be measured. Ideally take three samples—at 1, 4, and 24 hours—after onset of symptoms
- Consider measuring electrolytes if at risk of renal failure and FBC (may see a raised eosinophil level)

Follow-up

- Patients need to be observed for at least 6 hours to monitor for biphasic reaction
- Consider 3 days of oral prednisolone and antihistamines
- Ensure that patient follows up with their GP to consider immunology referral
- Discharge with an EpiPen® with clear instructions of how and when to use it
- Stop any angiotensin-converting enzyme (ACE) inhibitors

Further reading

Soar J, Deakin CD, Nolan JP, Perkins GD, Yeung J, Couper K, . . . Hampshire S. *Adult advanced life support guidelines*. Retrieved from https://www.resus.org.uk/library/2021-resuscitation-guidelines/adult-advanced-life-support-guideli nes, 2021.

Algorithm for anaphylaxis

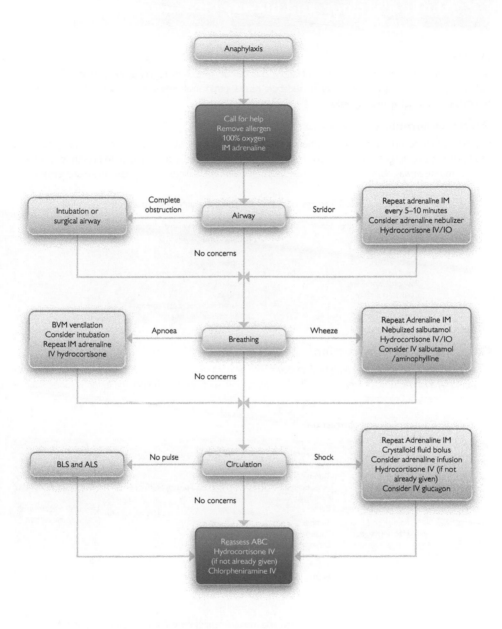

2. Apnoea, stridor and airway obstruction

Apnoea

Apnoea is defined as the cessation of ventilation. This can be secondary to airway obstruction. Other causes include poisoning, iatrogenic secondary to sedation, raised intracranial pressure, respiratory failure, high spinal trauma, and obstructive sleep apnoea.

Partial vs complete airway obstruction

It is important to recognize the difference between partial and complete obstruction (Table 2.1). Complete airway obstruction is an emergency; it needs early recognition and early definitive management to prevent death. When acute complete airway obstruction is recognized, a surgical airway is indicated as the definitive management.

Table 2.1 Clinical features of partial vs. complete airway obstruction

Partial airway obstruction	Complete airway obstruction
Ventilation may be maintained	Unable to breathe or talk
Stridor	Unable to cough
Use of accessory muscles	Apnoea
Drooling	Paradoxical chest movements
Positional worsening	Desaturation
Conscious initially	Cyanosis
	Reduced consciousness/coma
	Failed assisted ventilation

Causes of airway obstruction

Causes of airway obstruction can be broken down into anatomical location (Table 2.2). This can be within the airway, luminal, intramural, or extramural. This can be further specified by whether the lesion is supraglottic, laryngeal, tracheal, or bronchial.

Table 2.2 Causes of airway obstruction

Causes of obstruction	Luminal	Intramural	Extramural	Other
Upper airway	Foreign body Epiglottitis Haemorrhage	Tumour Angioedema Anaphylaxis Burns	Tumour Traumatic/postoperative neck haematoma	Congenital abnormality Reduced consciousness Poisoning Laryngeal fracture with airway transection
Lower airway	Foreign body Haemorrhage	Tumour Bacterial tracheitis Laryngotracheitis Angioedema Anaphylaxis Burns	Tumour	

Further reading

Herth FJF. Clinical presentation, diagnostic evaluation, and management of central airway obstruction in adults. https://www.uptodate.com/contents/clinical-presentation-diagnostic-evaluation-and-management-of-central-airway-obstruction-in-adults, 2021.

Algorithm for apnoea and airway obstruction

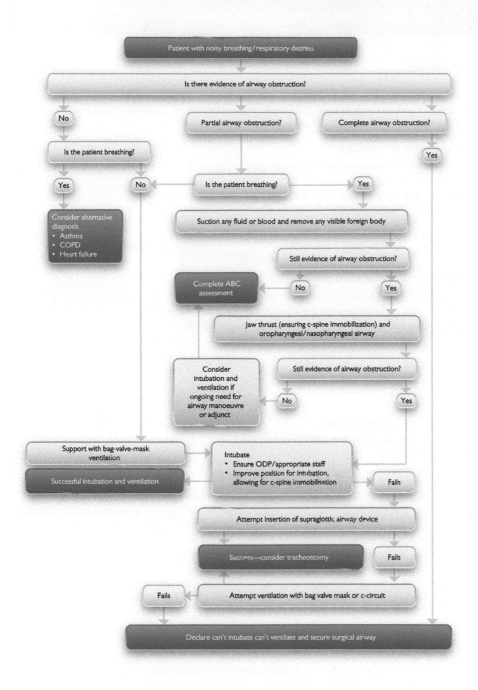

Algorithms for Emergency Medicine

3. Pneumothorax/haemothorax

Introduction
- Thoracic trauma has a high morbidity and mortality (25% of traumatic deaths)
- Chest injuries occur in roughly 60% of polytrauma cases
- Pneumothorax (PTX) is a significant global health problem (incidence 18–28 cases/100,000/year for men)
- 12% risk in smokers vs 0.1% risk in non-smokers for PTX

Tension pneumothorax
- Tension PTX is an **emergency** and requires immediate treatment by needle thoracocentesis. A formal chest drain can then be sited
- Diagnosis is **not** radiological but from clinical signs of respiratory distress:
  - Cyanosis/low SpO_2/low PaO_2
  - Hypotension/shock
  - Tracheal deviation away from side of other signs
  - Silent, resonant hemithorax

Spontaneous pneumothorax
- The size of a pneumothorax is less important than the degree of clinical compromise
  - Patients with significant breathlessness should undergo active intervention
- Large PTX has a visible rim of >2 cm between lung margin and chest wall
- Aspirate in second intercostal space, mid-clavicular line with a 18G cannula
- Stop aspiration if
  - More than 2.5 L aspirated
  - Resistance is felt
  - Excessive coughing

Traumatic pneumothorax
- Chest drains are required for any history of chest trauma
- A repeat chest radiograph should always be obtained

Haemothorax
- 400–500 mL of blood required to obliterate costophrenic angle on upright CXR
- All haemothoraces, regardless of size, should be considered for drainage with a tube thoracostomy (usually 36–42 Fr)
- Criteria indicating the necessity to proceed with urgent thoracotomy:
  - >1,500 mL of blood immediately evacuated by tube thoracostomy
  - Persistent bleeding of 150–200 mL/hour for 2–4 hours
  - Persistent blood transfusion is required to maintain haemodynamic stability

Discharge
- Patients with small primary spontaneous PTX, without breathlessness, with early outpatient (O/P) review
- Clear written advice to return immediately if less well or more breathless
- Air travel should be avoided until full resolution (contact airline)
- Diving contraindicated unless patient undergoes bilateral surgical pleurectomy
- PTX recurrence risk up to 50% within 4 years

Further reading
MacDuff A, Arnold A, Harvey J. Management of spontaneous pneumothorax: British Thoracic Society pleural disease guidelines 2010. *Thorax* 2010;65(Suppl 2):ii18–31.

Mowery NT, Gunter OL, Collier BR, et al. Practice management guidelines for management of haemothorax and occult pneumothorax. *J Trauma* 2011;70(2):510–518.

Algorithm for pneumothorax/haemothorax

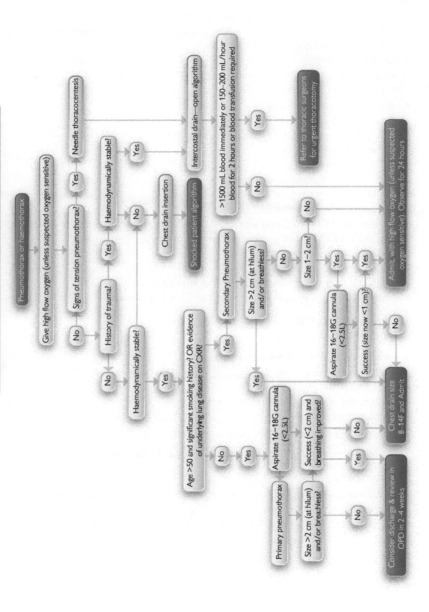

Pneumothorax or haemothorax

Give high flow oxygen (unless suspected oxygen sensitive)

Signs of tension pneumothorax?

Yes → Needle thoracocentesis

No → History of trauma?

Yes → Haemodynamically stable?

Yes → Chest drain insertion

No → Shocked patient algorithm

Intercostal drain—open algorithm

>1500 mL blood immediately or 150–200 mL/hour blood for 2 hours or blood transfusion required

Yes → Refer to thoracic surgeons for urgent thoracotomy

No → Admit, with high flow oxygen (unless suspected oxygen sensitive). Observe for 24 hours

No → Haemodynamically stable?

Yes → Age >50 and significant smoking history? OR evidence of underlying lung disease on CXR?

Yes → Secondary Pneumothorax

Size >2 cm (at hilum) and/or breathless?

Yes → Aspirate 16–18G cannula (<2.5L)

Success (size now <1 cm)?

Yes → Admit, with high flow oxygen (unless suspected oxygen sensitive). Observe for 24 hours

No → Chest drain size 8–14F and Admit

No → Size 1–2 cm?

Yes → Aspirate 16–18G cannula (<2.5L)

Yes → Admit, with high flow oxygen...

No → Admit, with high flow oxygen...

No → Primary pneumothorax

Size >2 cm (at hilum) and/or breathless?

Yes → Aspirate 16–18G cannula (<2.5L)

Success (<2 cm) and breathing improved?

Yes → Consider discharge & review in OPD in 2–4 weeks

No → Chest drain size 8–14F and Admit

No → Consider discharge & review in OPD in 2–4 weeks

4. Asthma and chronic obstructive pulmonary disease

Introduction

- Both asthma and COPD are obstructive pulmonary diseases
  - If patient is symptomatic, spirometry should show an obstructive pattern with forced expiratory volume (FEV1)/forced vital capacity (FVC) <70%
- Asthma is inflammation of the airways, leading to reversible airflow obstruction
  - Either FEV1 or FVC improves with the use of a bronchodilator
  - Prevalence of 3.85 million people in the UK
- Some examples of classic triggers of asthma include:
  - Exercise and cold air
  - Upper respiratory tract infections
  - Animal fur/pollen/mould
  - Tobacco smoke
- Asthma is often associated with atopy
- COPD is airflow obstruction that is not fully reversible
  - It accounts for 1 in 8 emergency admissions in the UK
  - Reduction in FEV1/FVC ratio with minimal or no improvement after inhaled bronchodilator
- Diagnosis of COPD should be considered in patients >35 years old with:
  - Risk factors (predominantly smoking)
  - Exertional breathlessness
  - Chronic cough or wheeze and regular sputum production
- Exacerbations requiring hospital admissions carry 3–4% mortality rate

Diagnosis and evaluation

Factors implying hospital admission:

- Inability to cope at home/confined to bed
- Severe breathlessness
- Cyanosis
- Impaired level of consciousness/acute confusion
- Significant comorbidities

A key aspect of asthma is variability in airflow obstruction.

- A peak flow meter is useful to monitor exacerbations of established disease

Treatment

- Treat with a combination of quick relief (beta agonist inhaler, such as salbutamol) and controller medications (IV corticosteroids or steroid inhaler)
- Educate patients to avoid triggers and maintain a clean living environment
- Smoking cessation is essential
- Frequent use of systemic corticosteroids, nocturnal symptoms, Emergency Department visits, and previous intubations all suggest poor control and portend a poorer prognosis
- Non-invasive ventilation (NIV) should be used for persistent hypercapnic ventilatory failure not responding to medical therapy

Further reading

British Thoracic Society. SIGN Guideline 158. British guideline on the management of asthma 2019. https://www.brit-thoracic.org.uk/document-library/guidelines/asthma/btssign-guideline-for-the-management-of-asthma-2019/

Mushlin S, Greene H. Decision Making in Medicine, An Algorithmic Approach, 3rd edn. Amsterdam: Mosby Elsevier, 2010.

National Institute for Health and Care Excellence. Clinical Guideline 101. Chronic obstructive pulmonary disease in over 16s. https://www.nice.org.uk/guidance/cg101, 2010.

Algorithm for asthma and COPD

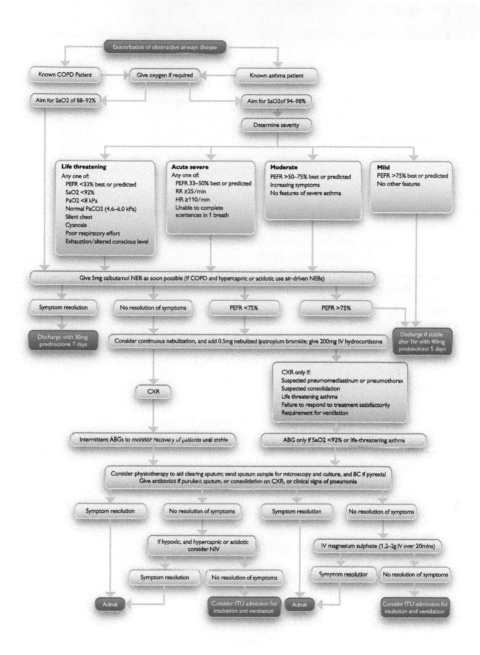

Exacerbation of obstructive airways disease

Known COPD Patient · Give oxygen if required · Known asthma patient

Aim for SaO2 of 88–92%

Aim for SaO2of 94–98%

Determine severity

Life threatening
Any one of:
PEFR <33% best or predicted
SaO2 <92%
PaO2 <8 kPa
Normal PaCO2 (4.6–6.0 kPa)
Silent chest
Cyanosis
Poor respiratory effort
Exhaustion/altered conscious level

Acute severe
Any one of:
PEFR 33–50% best or predicted
RR ≥25/min
HR ≥110/min
Unable to complete
scentences in 1 breath

Moderate
PEFR >50–75% best or predicted
Increasing symptoms
No features of severe asthma

Mild
PEFR >75% best or predicted
No other features

Give 5mg salbutamol NEB as soon possible (if COPD and hypercapnic or acidotic use air-driven NEBs)

Symptom resolution · No resolution of symptoms · PEFR <75% · PEFR >75%

Discharge with 30mg prednisolone 7 days

Consider continuous nebulization, and add 0.5mg nebulized ipatropium bromide; give 200mg IV hydrocortisone

Discharge if stable after 1hr with 40mg prednisolone 5 days

CXR only if:
Suspected pneumomediastinum or pneumothorax
Suspected consolidation
Life threatening asthma
Failure to respond to treatment satisfactorily
Requirement for ventilation

CXR

Intermittent ABGs to monitor recovery of patients until stable · ABG only if SaO2 <92% or life-threatening asthma

Consider physiotherapy to aid clearing sputum; send sputum sample for microscopy and culture, and BC if pyrexial
Give antibiotics if purulent sputum, or consolidation on CXR, or clinical signs of pneumonia

Symptom resolution · No resolution of symptoms · Symptom resolution · No resolution of symptoms

If hypoxic, and hypercapnic or acidotic consider NIV

IV magnesium sulphate (1.2–2g IV over 20mins)

Symptom resolution · No resolution of symptoms · Symptom resolution · No resolution of symptoms

Admit · Consider ITU admission for intubation and ventilation · Admit · Consider ITU admission for intubation and ventilation

5. Pulmonary embolism

Introduction
- Major risk factors include the following (relative risk 5–20):
  - Venous stasis or immobilization • Surgery and trauma • Pregnancy
  - Malignancy • Previous proven thromboembolism

Signs and symptoms
- Classically, abrupt onset of pleuritic chest pain, shortness of breath, and hypoxia
- PE should be suspected in patients with respiratory symptoms unexplained by an alternative diagnosis

Diagnosis
- ECG: right axis deviation, right bundle branch block (RBBB), S1Q3T3, sinus tachycardia
- Two-level Wells score to aid diagnosis (Box 2.1)
- Negative predictive value (NPV) of D-dimers useful in low-risk patients (89–96%)
- CTPA or V/Q scan if renal failure/contrast allergy

Box 2.1 Two-level Wells score

Clinically suspected DVT (3)	Previous DVT/PE (1.5)
PE most likely diagnosis (3)	Haemoptysis (1)
Heart rate >100 (1.5)	Malignancy <6 months (1)
Immobile >3 days/surgery <4 weeks (1.5)	**Total score >4 = high risk**

Management
Anticoagulation and thrombolysis
- Thrombolysis is the first-line treatment for massive PE, and may be instituted on clinical grounds alone if cardiac arrest is imminent (see Box 2.2 for agents)—may take 90 minutes
- For non-massive PE, low molecular weight heparin (LMWH) is recommended over unfractionated heparin
  - Thrombolysis should not be used as first-line treatment in non-massive PE.

Box 2.2 Thrombolytic agents licensed for PE

Alteplase
- Accelerated regimen: 50 mg bolus
- 10 mg over 1–2 minutes, followed by 90 mg over 2 hours

Streptokinase
- Accelerated regimen: 1.5 million IU over 2 hours
- 250,000 units over 30 minutes, then 100,000 units/hour over 12–72 hours

Urokinase
- Accelerated regimen: 3 million IU over 2 hours
- 4400 units/kg over 10–20 minutes, then 4400 units/kg/hour for 12 hours

---

Surgical options
- If thrombolysis has failed or is contraindicated, surgical management options include:
  - Catheter embolectomy and fragmentation • Surgical embolectomy

Further reading
British Thoracic Society Standards of Care Committee, Pulmonary Embolism Guideline Development Group. BTS guidelines for the management of suspected acute pulmonary embolism. *Thorax* 2003;58:470–484.

National Institute for Health and Care Excellence. Clinical Guideline 144. Venous thromboembolic diseases. https://www.nice.org.uk/guidance/cg144, 2012.

Algorithm for pulmonary embolism

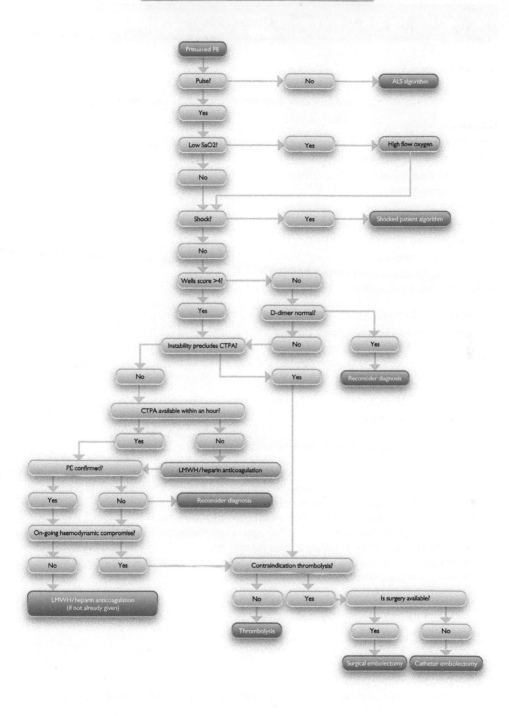

6. Acute heart failure

Introduction

In heart failure the heart does not pump enough blood to meet all the needs of the body. Heart failure may present as a first occurrence or as a consequence of acute decompensation of chronic heart failure.

Causes

It may be caused by primary cardiac dysfunction or be precipitated by extrinsic factors. Among the most frequent causes of acute heart failure are:

- Acute myocardial dysfunction (ischaemic, inflammatory, or toxic)
- Acute valve insufficiency
- Pericardial tamponade

Decompensation of chronic heart failure can occur

- Infection
- Uncontrolled hypertension
- Rhythm disturbances
- Non-adherence with drugs/diet.

Clinical manifestations

- Progressive dypnoea, cough, pink frothy sputum
- Symptoms of peripheral and abdominal congestion—ankle swelling, abdominal fullness
- Abdominal tenderness due to hepatic congestion and patient may complain of nausea and anorexia

Physical signs

- Elevated jugular venous pressure (JVP)/positive hepatojugular reflex
- Reduced air entry at lung bases
- Leg oedema
- Cardiac examination may be normal or can show displaced apex and third heart sound

Investigations

- Bloods—U&E, bicarbonate, lactate, troponin T, N-terminal pro B-type natriuretic peptide (NT-pro BNP)
- ABGs—if patient hypoxic and likely to need ventilatory support
- ECG—checking specifically for evidence of ischaemia or dysrhythmia
- CXR—this may (in 20% of cases) be normal; other signs include mild pulmonary vascular redistribution to marked cardiomegaly and extensive bilateral interstitial markings
- Echocardiogram—recommended for patients with new diagnosis of heart failure. The urgency of this depends upon the acuity of presentation

Management

- Diuresis (choice and dose of diuretic according to local protocols). Furosemide +/– other diuretics with urine output monitoring
- Supplemental oxygen +/– assisted ventilation if needed
- Vasodilator therapy
- Arrhythmia management (if present)

Venous thromboembolism prophylaxis is indicated for all patients hospitalized with acute heart failure.

Further reading

Colucci WS. Treatment of acute decompensated heart failure: Specific therapies. https://www.uptodate.com/contents/treatment-of-acute-decompensated-heart-failure-specific-therapies, 2022

Algorithm for acute heart failure

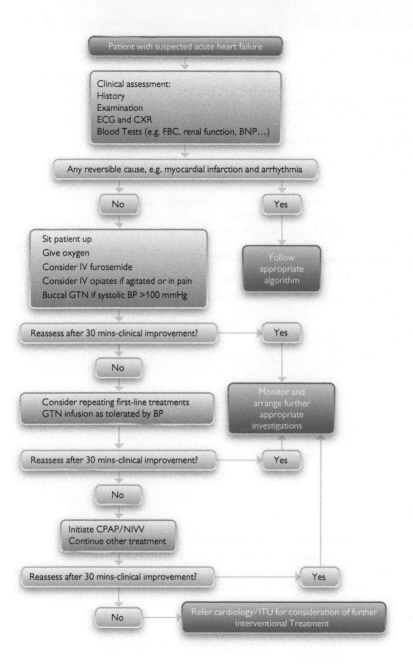

Patient with suspected acute heart failure

Clinical assessment:
History
Examination
ECG and CXR
Blood Tests (e.g. FBC, renal function, BNP…)

Any reversible cause, e.g. myocardial infarction and arrhythmia

No

Yes

Sit patient up
Give oxygen
Consider IV furosemide
Consider IV opiates if agitated or in pain
Buccal GTN if systolic BP >100 mmHg

Follow appropriate algorithm

Reassess after 30 mins-clinical improvement?

Yes

No

Consider repeating first-line treatments
GTN infusion as tolerated by BP

Monitor and arrange further appropriate investigations

Reassess after 30 mins-clinical improvement?

Yes

No

Initiate CPAP/NIVV
Continue other treatment

Reassess after 30 mins-clinical improvement?

Yes

No

Refer cardiology/ITU for consideration of further Interventional Treatment

7. Cough

Duration of symptoms

For ease of assessment and management it is best to establish how long a patient has had a cough. A cough of <3 weeks duration is deemed an acute cough, 3–8 weeks is subacute, and >8 weeks is termed a chronic cough. These are arbitrary cut-off points but generally accepted. For the purposes of assessment and investigation in an Emergency Department, an intermediate and a chronic cough are approached in much the same way.

Clinical features suggesting admission likely

- Respiratory rate (RR) >30
- Heart rate (HR) >130
- Significant hypotension: systolic blood pressure (SBP) <90; diastolic blood pressure (DBP) <60
- Oxygen saturations <92% on air (unless normal for patient, e.g. known COPD)
- Central cyanosis (if no history of chronic hypoxia)
- Peak expiratory flow rate (PEFR) <33% predicted (if asthmatic)
- Reduced Glasgow Coma Scale (GCS)
- Significant respiratory effort/exhaustion
- Clinical features of PE, pneumothorax, or aspirated foreign body (FB)

Clinical features suggesting admission should be considered

- Tachycardia
- Hypotension
- Fever (temperature >38.5°C)
- Peak expiratory flow rate (PEFR) <50% predicted
- Age >65 years

Clinical features suggestive of lung cancer

- Haemoptysis
- Any of the following that are unexplained and persist >3 weeks:
  - Chest/shoulder pain
  - Breathlessness
  - Weight loss
  - Hoarseness
  - Finger clubbing
  - Cervical or supraclavicular lymphadenopathy

Clinical features suggestive of foreign body aspiration

- Sudden onset of cough, possibly associated with history suggestive of inhaled FB
- Stridor if FB in upper airway
- Signs of lung or lobar collapse if FB in lower airways

Pertussis

Suspect if:

- Cough has lasted more than 14 days, with paroxysms of coughing or vomiting after coughing or cough associated with inspiratory 'whoop'
- Cough develops within 2 weeks of contact with someone with confirmed pertussis

Clinical features suggestive of TB

- Chronic cough with associated sputum, breathlessness, or haemoptysis
- Weight loss

Further reading

National Institute for Health and Care Excellence. Clinical Knowledge Summary—Cough. https://cks.nice.org.uk/topics/cough/, 2021.

Algorithm for cough

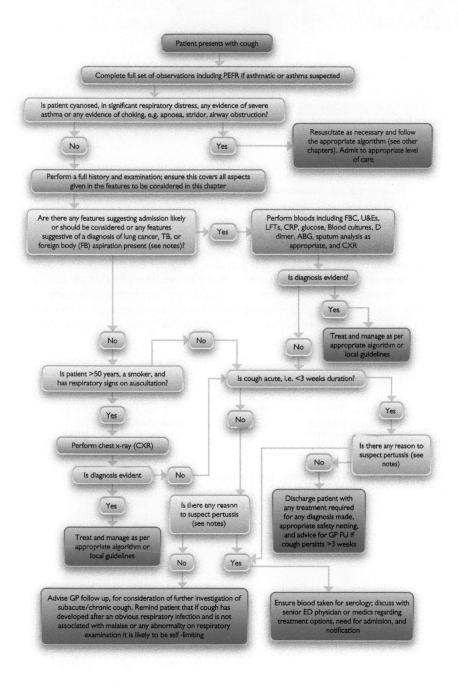

Patient presents with cough

Complete full set of observations including PEFR if asthmatic or asthma suspected

Is patient cyanosed, in significant respiratory distress, any evidence of severe asthma or any evidence of choking, e.g. apnoea, stridor, airway obstruction?

No

Yes → Resuscitate as necessary and follow the appropriate algorithm (see other chapters). Admit to appropriate level of care

Perform a full history and examination; ensure this covers all aspects given in the features to be considered in this chapter

Are there any features suggesting admission likely or should be considered or any features suggestive of a diagnosis of lung cancer, TB, or foreign body (FB) aspiration present (see notes)?

Yes → Perform bloods including FBC, U&Es, LFTs, CRP, glucose, Blood cultures, D dimer, ABG, sputum analysis as appropriate, and CXR

Is diagnosis evident?

Yes

No → Treat and manage as per appropriate algorithm or local guidelines

No

No

Is patient >50 years, a smoker, and has respiratory signs on auscultation?

Is cough acute, i.e. <3 weeks duration?

Yes

No

Yes

Perform chest x-ray (CXR)

Is there any reason to suspect pertussis (see notes)

No

Is diagnosis evident

No

Is there any reason to suspect pertussis (see notes)

Discharge patient with any treatment required for any diagnosis made, appropriate safety netting, and advice for GP FU if cough persists >3 weeks

Yes

Treat and manage as per appropriate algorithm or local guidelines

No

Yes

Advise GP follow up, for consideration of further investigation of subacute/chronic cough. Remind patient that if cough has developed after an obvious respiratory infection and is not associated with malaise or any abnormality on respiratory examination it is likely to be self-limiting

Ensure blood taken for serology; discuss with senior ED physician or medics regarding treatment options, need for admission, and notification

8. Cyanosis

Introduction

It is worth noting at the start that there is significant inter-observer variability in the identification of cyanosis.

It should also be noted that below approximately 5 g/dL of haemoglobin, cyanosis is not clinically detectable, irrespective of the level of hypoxaemia. Likewise, in less severe cases of anaemia, the level of hypoxaemia required to produce detectable cyanosis is greater that in patients with higher haemoglobin concentrations (i.e. cyanosis appears at a higher oxygen saturation level in patients with normal haemoglobin levels).

Causes

- In cyanosis due to acute hypoxaemia (e.g. caused by infection or pulmonary oedema) optimal medical treatment should be started immediately, with supplementary oxygen. Failure to improve warrants consideration of non-invasive or invasive respiratory support.
- Many cases have been reported in the literature of skin staining, e.g. from blue socks, giving the appearance of cyanosis!
- Cyanosis-like skin discoloration may also be seen as a side effect of medications, e.g. amiodarone.
- It is also common to see peripheral vasoconstriction, usually brought on by cold temperatures, resulting in cyanotic changes to the distal limbs. More seriously, this may be seen in peripheral vascular occlusion.
- Patients with congenital cyanotic heart disease or severe COPD or heart failure may be chronically hypoxaemic. These patients frequently know their 'normal' oxygen saturations, and if available there are likely to be previous PaO_2 results in their medical records for comparison. Further causes of reversible hypoxia should still be sought.

Notes

Methaemoglobinaemia causes interference to normal light absorption utilized by pulse oximetry. As such, in patients with methaemoglobinaemia, pulse oximetry reading typically displays around 85%; however, this does not correlate with their PaO_2. Most cases occur after drug use such as nitrites. Management advice can be obtained from the National Poisons Information Service (NPIS) (UK telephone 0344 892 0111) or via the TOXBASE® website (www.toxbase.org).

Further reading

McMullen S, Ward P. Cyanosis. *Am J Med* 2013;126(3):210–212.

Algorithm for cyanosis

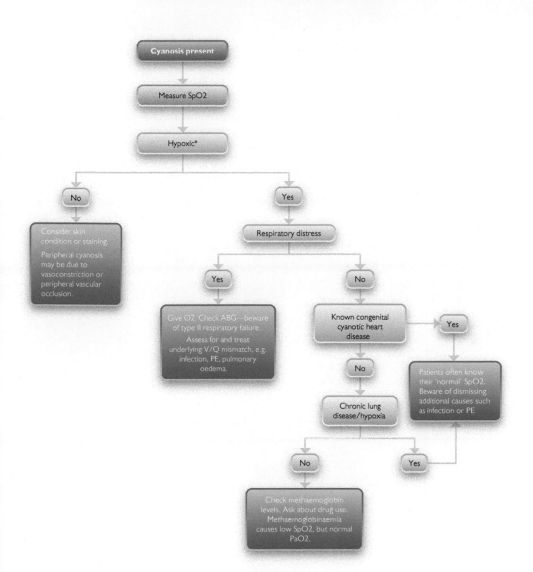

Cyanosis present

Measure SpO2

Hypoxic*

No

Consider skin condition or staining.
Peripheral cyanosis may be due to vasoconstriction or peripheral vascular occlusion.

Yes

Respiratory distress

Yes

Give O2. Check ABG—beware of type II respiratory failure.
Assess for and treat underlying V/Q mismatch, e.g. infection, PE, pulmonary oedema.

No

Known congenital cyanotic heart disease

Yes

Patients often know their 'normal' SpO2. Beware of dismissing additional causes such as infection or PE

No

Chronic lung disease/hypoxia

No

Yes

Check methaemoglobin levels. Ask about drug use. Methaemoglobinaemia causes low SpO2, but normal PaO2.

SECTION 3

Cardiovascular

1. Cardiorespiratory arrest—adult life support (ALS)

Introduction
- VF/VT is the first monitored rhythm in approximately 25% of cardiac arrests
  - Also seen in approximately 25% of cases with initial rhythm of asystole or pulseless electrical activity (PEA)
- Survival following cardiac arrest with asystole or PEA is unlikely unless a reversible cause can be treated effectively

During CPR
- Ensure high-quality CPR: rate, depth, recoil
  - Change individual every 2 minutes to prevent tiring
- Plan actions before interrupting CPR
  - Emphasis on minimally interrupted high-quality chest compressions
  - Chest compressions are continued whilst defibrillator is charged
  - Pads are safer and enable a shock to be delivered more rapidly than paddles
- Give oxygen (remove source during defibrillation)
- Consider advanced airway and capnography
  - Continuous chest compressions when advanced airway in place
- Vascular access (IV, IO)
- Give 1 mg adrenaline (1 in 10,000) every 3–5 minutes
  - 1st adrenalin given immediately if non-shockable rhythm
  - 1st adrenalin given just after 3rd shock for VF/pulseless VT
  - 300 mg amiodarone also given just after 3rd shock for VF/pulseless VT
- Correct reversible causes

Reversible causes (4 Hs and 4 Ts)
- Hypoxia
- Hypovolaemia
- Hyper/hypokalaemia/metabolic
  - IV calcium chloride indicated in presence of hyperkalaemia, hypocalcaemia, and calcium channel-blocking drug overdose
- Hypothermia
  - Use low-reading thermometer, especially in drowning
- Tamponade—cardiac
- Thrombosis—coronary or pulmonary
  - Consider immediate thrombolysis if likely cause (may require 90 minutes of CPR)
- Toxins
- Tension pneumothorax

Management
- Three stacked shocks are recommended for VF/pulseless VT in witnessed arrest
- Initial shock should be at least 150 J (biphasic) or 360 J (monophasic)
- Delivery of drugs via ET tube is no longer recommended
  - If IV access cannot be achieved, give drugs IO
- Do not interrupt chest compressions if organized rhythm seen within 2-minute period, unless patient shows signs of life
- If any doubt about existence of a pulse, resume CPR

Further reading
Resuscitation Council UK. Resuscitation Guidelines 2010. http://www.resus.org.uk/pages/gl2010.pdf.

Algorithm for adult life support (ALS)

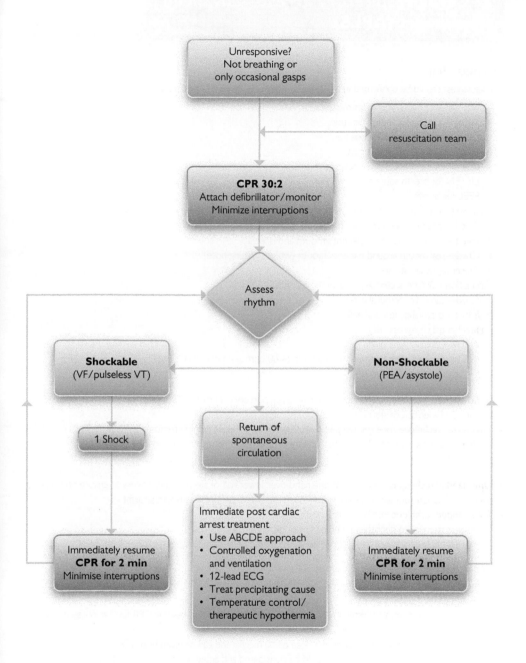

2. Cardiorespiratory arrest—advanced paediatric life support (APLS)

Introduction

Cardiac arrest should be confirmed in a collapsed child by following the ABC approach:

- Airway (A): Use head tilt/chin lift manoeuvre
  - Infant—head tilt to neutral position
  - Child—head tilt to sniffing position
  - If no improvement—jaw thrust
  - LOOK for chest/abdominal movement
  - LISTEN for breath sounds
  - FEEL for breath
- Breathing (B): If normal breathing starts after airway manoeuvres, place in recovery position
  - If no breathing—give 5 rescue breaths
  - Infant—seal mouth around patient's mouth and nose
  - Child—seal mouth around patient's mouth (whilst pinching nose)
  - Observe the chest rise
- Circulation (C): Check central pulse for 10 seconds:
  - Child—carotid or femoral artery
  - Infant—brachial or femoral artery
  - Start chest compressions if:
    - There are no signs of life
    - There is no pulse or there is a slow pulse (<60 bpm and poor perfusion)

Infant

- **Hand-encircling technique** (two or more rescuers): partially encircle/encircle chest with hands and place thumbs on lower half of sternum
- **Two-finger technique** (one rescuer): two fingers placed on lower half of sternum
- Compress chest at rate of 100–120 per minute in a ratio of 15 compressions to 2 breaths (15:2)

Child

- **One-handed technique**: place heel of one hand over lower half of sternum. Lift fingers to ensure no pressure over ribs. Position yourself vertically above child's chest and compress with arm straight
- **Two-handed technique**: use both hands with fingers interlocked
- Compress sternum to depress it by one-third of depth of chest
- Compress chest at rate of 100–120 per minute in a ratio of 15 compressions to 2 breaths (15:2)

Defibrillation

Attach defibrillator pads and assess the patient's rhythm. Determine if the rhythm is shockable (VF/pulseless VT) or non-shockable (PEA/asystole).

If in a shockable rhythm, administer shock of 4 J/kg and then immediately resume CPR for 2 minutes. If in a non-shockable rhythm immediately resume CPR for 2 minutes.

Adrenaline is given every 3–5 minutes at a dose of 10 mcg/kg and can be given IV or IO.

The reversible causes (4 Hs and 4 Ts) should be considered and acted upon as appropriate. (Please see appropriate chapters for management.)

Further reading

Advanced Life Support Group. Advanced Paediatric Life Support: A Practical Approach to Emergencies (APLS), 6th edn. Wiley-Blackwell, 2016.

Algorithm for advanced paediatric life support (APLS)

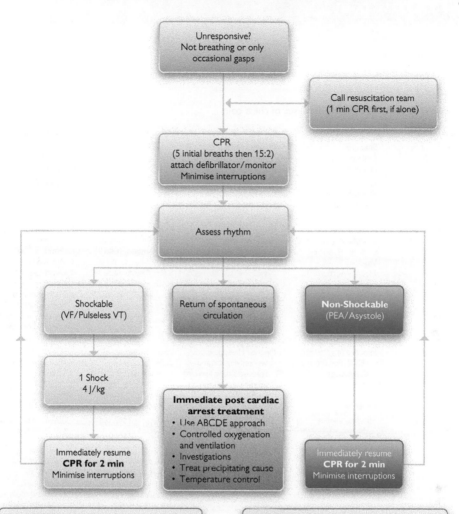

Unresponsive?
Not breathing or only
occasional gasps

Call resuscitation team
(1 min CPR first, if alone)

CPR
(5 initial breaths then 15:2)
attach defibrillator/monitor
Minimise interruptions

Assess rhythm

Shockable
(VF/Pulseless VT)

**Return of spontaneous
circulation**

Non-Shockable
(PEA/Asystole)

1 Shock
4 J/kg

**Immediate post cardiac
arrest treatment**
• Use ABCDE approach
• Controlled oxygenation
  and ventilation
• Investigations
• Treat precipitating cause
• Temperature control

Immediately resume
CPR for 2 min
Minimise interruptions

Immediately resume
CPR for 2 min
Minimise interruptions

During CPR

• Ensure high-quality CPR: rate, depth, recoil
• Plan actions before interrupting CPR
  Give oxygen
• Vascular access (intravenous, intraosseous)
• Give adrenaline every 3–5 min
• Consider advanced airway and capnography
• Continous chest compressions when advanced
  airway in place
• Correct reversible causes
• Consider amiodarone after 3 and 5 shocks

Reversible Causes

• Hypoxia
• Hypovolaemia
• Hyper/hypokalaemia, metabolic
• Hypothermia
• Thrombosis (coronary or pulmonary)
• Tension pneumothorax
• Tamponade (cardiac)
• Toxic/therapeutic disturbances

3. Chest pain

Introduction

Table 3.1 shows risk factors, typical presenting features, examination findings and investigations that can help diagnose various causes of chest pain.

Table 3.1 Features of different causes of chest pain

Diagnosis	Risk factors/cause	Typical history	Examination	Investigations
MI	Smoking Diabetes Hypertension	Persistent heavy tight chest pain, radiating to jaw, arms, or neck	May be normal May look clammy, pale, sweaty, and unwell	ECG may be normal or may show signs of ischaemia
Angina	Hypercholesterol Family history Previous MI	Exertional pain relieved by rest. Pain may be neck, arms, back, jaw, or chest		CXR and ECG may be normal Serial troponins may be normal
Aortic dissection	Hypertension Vascular disease Collagen disorders Vasculitis Bicuspid aortic valve	Classically *sudden onset* severe interscapular tearing pain May present with syncope, stroke, heart failure, pericardial effusion, or anterior chest pain	Radial-radial delay BP difference in arms >20 mmHg (L<R) Signs of heart failure Signs of tamponade Heart murmur Neurological deficits Signs of haemothorax	ECG may show inferior ischaemia CXR may show: • Widened mediastinum • Depression of L mainstem bronchus • Obliteration of the aortic knob CT aortagram to diagnose D-dimer to rule out if low risk
Myocarditis/pericarditis	Infective (e.g. mumps, (EBV), *Pneumococcus*, Coxsackie) Cancer Rheumatic fever Uraemia	Pleuritic chest pain, worse lying flat and relieved sitting forward Preceding viral illness common	Look for pericardial rub Look for signs of pericardial effusion or tamponade (raised JVP, quiet heart sounds, hypotension)	ECG—classically saddle-shaped widespread ST elevation and PR depression ESR, CRP, and troponins may be raised
Pulmonary embolus	Previous venous thromboembolism Family history Hypercoagulable disorders Pregnancy or pueperium Recent immobility or operation (especially pelvic or abdominal)	Clinical DVT Haemoptysis Syncope Breathlessness	Tachycardia, tachypnoea, hypoxia Exam may be normal Look for DVT Look for R ventricular heave, raised JVP, and signs of acute right heart failure	ECG—may have any tachydysrhythmia CXR may show wedge-shaped infarct or pleural effusion ECHO—right heart strain CTPA (gold standard) or V/Q scan
Pneumonia	Smoking, pre-existing lung or cardiac disease Immunosuppression Causes include *Pneumococcus*, *Staphylococcus aureus*, *Haemophilus*, *Mycoplasma*	Cough, sputum, chest pain, fevers, breathlessness, anorexia, haemoptysis	Tachycardia, tachypnoea, hypoxia Crepitations and bronchial breathing on auscultation, increased vocal resonance, pleural rub	CXR, FBC, CRP, U&E, consider ABG
Musculoskeletal	**Beware:** this should be a diagnosis of exclusion once the other life-threatening causes of chest pain have been ruled out via history, examination, and investigations			

Notes

MI can present with a normal ECG and chest wall tenderness and be relieved by antacids. It can also present in patients aged <30. If in any doubt, admit patients for further tests, including serial troponins, and discussion with senior colleagues.

Further reading

Soar J, Deakin CD, Nolan JP, Perkins GD, Yeung J, Couper K, . . . Hampshire S. Adult advanced life support guidelines. Retrieved from https://www.resus.org.uk/library/2021-resuscitation-guidelines/adult-advanced-life-support-guidelines, 2021.

Algorithm for chest pain

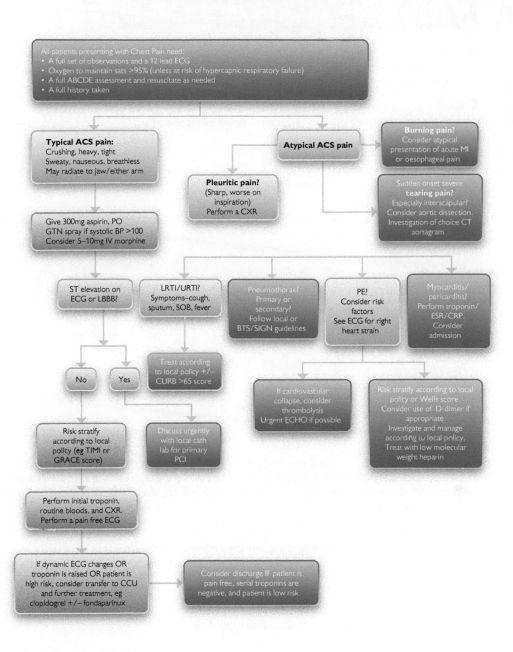

All patients presenting with Chest Pain need:
- A full set of observations and a 12 lead ECG
- Oxygen to maintain sats >95% (unless at risk of hypercapnic respiratory failure)
- A full ABCDE assessment and resuscitate as needed
- A full history taken

Typical ACS pain:
Crushing, heavy, tight
Sweaty, nauseous, breathless
May radiate to jaw/either arm

Atypical ACS pain

Burning pain?
Consider atypical presentation of acute MI or oesophageal pain

Pleuritic pain?
(Sharp, worse on inspiration)
Perform a CXR

Sudden onset severe **tearing pain?**
Especially interscapular?
Consider aortic dissection.
Investigation of choice CT aortagram

Give 300mg aspirin, PO
GTN spray if systolic BP >100
Consider 5–10mg IV morphine

ST elevation on ECG or LBBB?

LRTI/URTI?
Symptoms–cough, sputum, SOB, fever

Pneumothorax?
Primary or secondary?
Follow local or BTS/SIGN guidelines

PE?
Consider risk factors
See ECG for right heart strain

Myocarditis/pericarditis?
Perform troponin/ESR/CRP.
Consider admission

No

Yes

Treat according to local policy +/− CURB >65 score

If cardiovascular collapse, consider thrombolysis
Urgent ECHO if possible

Risk stratify according to local policy or Wells score.
Consider use of D-dimer if appropriate
Investigate and manage according to local policy.
Treat with low molecular weight heparin

Risk stratify according to local policy (eg TIMI or GRACE score)

Discuss urgently with local cath lab for primary PCI

Perform initial troponin, routine bloods, and CXR.
Perform a pain free ECG

If dynamic ECG changes OR troponin is raised OR patient is high risk, consider transfer to CCU and further treatment, eg clopidogrel +/− fondaparinux

Consider discharge IF patient is pain free, serial troponins are negative, and patient is low risk

4. Palpitations

Introduction

Palpitations are a subjective awareness of one's heartbeat. It is essential to clarify exactly what each patient means by this term: asking them to tap out what they feel can give invaluable information with regard to rate and rhythm.

Causes

Although many causes of palpitations are benign, more serious causes do exist, and high-risk features should always be looked for (Box 3.1).

Box 3.1 High-risk features

Associated syncope
Precipitated by exercise
History of sudden cardiac death
Second or third AV block on ECG
Prolonged QT interval
Heart murmur

Precipitants include caffeine, alcohol, amphetamine, and other illicit drug use, along with a number of commonly prescribed medications (Box 3.2).

Box 3.2 Modifiable causes

Alcohol
Caffeine
Anxiety
Prescribed or non-prescribed drug use
Suspected thyroid disease

A group of rare but significant causes are the inherited cardiac diseases: any history of a relative with sudden cardiac death, unexplained death under age 40, or 'epilepsy' (which may be a misdiagnosed arrhythmia) should be taken seriously.

A number of non-cardiac causes may present with palpitations, including electrolyte abnormalities, thyroid disease, anaemia, and anxiety.

Management

All cases of atrial fibrillation (AF) (paroxysmal and permanent) carry a thromboembolic risk, and CHA_2DS_2-VASc score (Table 3.2) should be recorded and consideration given to long-term anticoagulation if >0. *Note*: acute-onset AF may be suitable for early cardioversion. Discuss with senior ED clinician.

Table 3.2 CHA_2DS_2-VASc score

Congestive heart failure (ejection fraction <41%)	1
Hypertension	1
Age 65–74	1
Age ≥75	2
Diabetes	1
Stroke/transient ischaemic attack (TIA)/thromboembolism	2
Vascular disease	1
Female sex	1
Total	

Further reading

Wolff A, Cowan C. 10 steps before your refer for palpitations. *Br J Cardiol* 2009;16:182–186.

Algorithm for palpitations

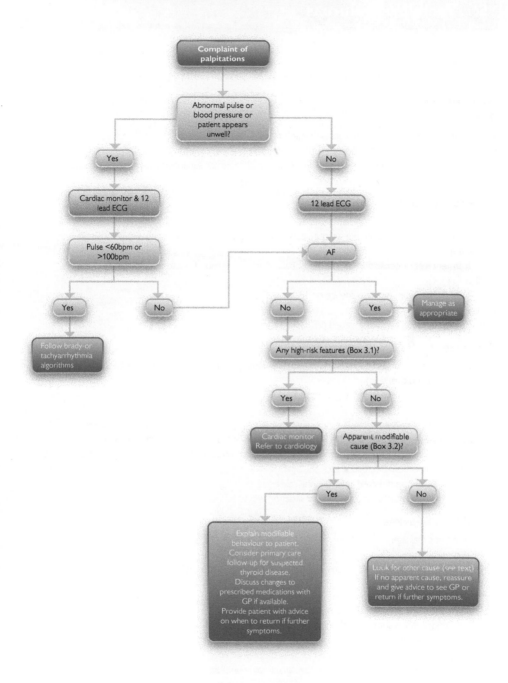

Complaint of palpitations

Abnormal pulse or blood pressure or patient appears unwell?

Yes

Cardiac monitor & 12 lead ECG

Pulse <60bpm or >100bpm

Yes

Follow brady- or tachyarrhythmia algorithms

No

No

12 lead ECG

AF

No

Yes

Manage as appropriate

Any high-risk features (Box 3.1)?

Yes

Cardiac monitor Refer to cardiology

No

Apparent modifiable cause (Box 3.2)?

Yes

Explain modifiable behaviour to patient. Consider primary care follow-up for suspected thyroid disease. Discuss changes to prescribed medications with GP if available. Provide patient with advice on when to return if further symptoms.

No

Look for other cause (see text). If no apparent cause, reassure and give advice to see GP or return if further symptoms.

5. Tachyarrhythmias

Introduction
Tachyarrhythmias are relatively common in the peri-arrest period. They may precipitate VF.

Assessment
Determine two factors:

- Condition of the patient (stable versus unstable)
- Nature of arrhythmia (from 12-lead ECG)
  - Broad complex is QRS duration of >0.12 seconds (three small squares on standard ECG paper speed of 25 mm/s)

Adverse features
- Shock
  - Hypotension (BP <90 mmHg systolic), pallor, sweating, cold, confusion
- Syncope
  - Transient loss of consciousness due to global reduction in blood flow to the brain
- MI
  - Typical chest pain and/or evidence on 12-lead ECG
- Heart failure
  - Pulmonary oedema and/or raised JVP

Treatment
- Dependent on nature and condition, immediate treatment is categorized under four headings:
  - Electrical (cardioversion)
  - Simple clinical interventions (e.g. vagal manoeuvres)
  - Pharmacological
  - No treatment needed
- If tachyarrhythmia is due to an underlying condition, ensure that condition is treated appropriately
- Sinus tachycardia (regular narrow complex) is not an arrhythmia but a physiological response to exercise, anxiety, pain, infection, blood loss, etc.
- Treatment should be directed at underlying cause
- Trying to slow sinus tachycardia may make situation worse

Vagal manoeuvres
- Carotid sinus massage
- Valsalva manoeuvre
- Successful in up to 25% of paroxysmal supraventricular tachycardia (SVT)

Cardioversion
- Perform under general anaesthesia or conscious sedation
- Ensure defibrillator is set to synchronized mode
- Provide increasing increments of energy if fails to convert
  - Commence at 120–150 J biphasic for broad-complex or AF
  - 70–120 J biphasic for atrial flutter or regular narrow complex

Further reading
Resuscitation Council UK. Resuscitation Guidelines 2010. http://www.resus.org.uk/pages/gl2010.pdf.

Algorithm for tachyarrhythmias

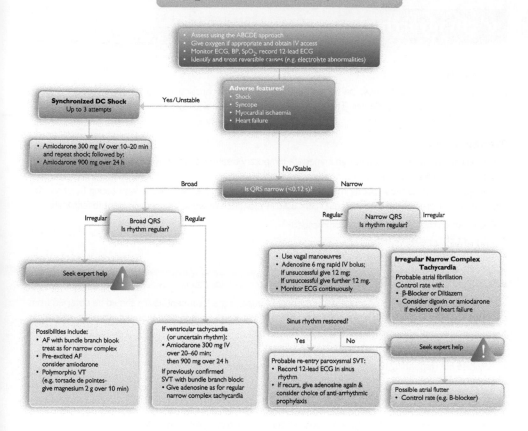

- Assess using the ABCDE approach
- Give oxygen if appropriate and obtain IV access
- Monitor ECG, BP, SpO₂, record 12-lead ECG
- Identify and treat reversible causes (e.g. electrolyte abnormalities)

Adverse features?
- Shock
- Syncope
- Myocardial ischaemia
- Heart failure

Yes/Unstable

Synchronized DC Shock
Up to 3 attempts

- Amiodarone 300 mg IV over 10–20 min
  and repeat shock; followed by:
- Amiodarone 900 mg over 24 h

No/Stable

Is QRS narrow (<0.12 s)?

Broad | Narrow

Broad QRS
Is rhythm regular?

Irregular | Regular

Narrow QRS
Is rhythm regular?

Regular | Irregular

Seek expert help ⚠

Possibilities include:
- AF with bundle branch block
  treat as for narrow complex
- Pre-excited AF
  consider amiodarone
- Polymorphio VT
  (e.g. torsade de pointes-
  give magnesium 2 g over 10 min)

If ventricular tachycardia
(or uncertain rhythm):
- Amiodarone 300 mg IV
  over 20–60 min;
  then 900 mg over 24 h
If previously confirmed
SVT with bundle branch block:
- Give adenosine as for regular
  narrow complex tachycardia

- Use vagal manoeuvres
- Adenosine 6 mg rapid IV bolus;
  If unsuccessful give 12 mg;
  If unsuccessful give further 12 mg.
- Monitor ECG continuously

Sinus rhythm restored?

Yes | No

Probable re-entry paroxysmal SVT:
- Record 12-lead ECG in sinus
  rhythm
- If recurs, give adenosine again &
  consider choice of anti-arrhythmic
  prophylaxis

**Irregular Narrow Complex
Tachycardia**
Probable atrial fibrillation
Control rate with:
- β-Blocker or Diltiazem
- Consider digoxin or amiodarone
  if evidence of heart failure

Seek expert help ⚠

Possible atrial flutter
- Control rate (e.g. B-blocker)

6. Bradyarrhythmias

Introduction

Potential underlying causes must be sought and treated whilst managing cardiovascular compromise using Resuscitation Council UK guidelines. These include heart block, sick sinus syndrome, hypothermia, and toxicity from, for example, beta-blockers.

Management

In the peri-arrest setting, fist pacing is an immediate temporary treatment option which can be used whilst arranging drug or electrical treatment.

Emergency transcutaneous pacing may be performed using a suitable defibrillator with pacing function. You must ensure you are familiar with the equipment used in your place of work. The generic steps to follow are:

- Place pads on chest (AP position recommended)
- Connect ECG leads
- Set pacemaker mode to demand
- Set rate to required value (typically 70–80 bpm)
- Start pacing and increase mA until pacing rate captured on monitor (confirm by palpating peripheral pulse).

Where toxicity (deliberate or accidental) is suspected, appropriate treatment advice should be obtained from the National Poisons Information Service. Common causative agents include beta-blockers, digoxin (especially in the presence of hypokalaemia), and calcium channel blockers.

Early cardiology involvement is required in the following:

- Any case not responding to interventions listed in the algorithm
- Suspected MI
- Complete heart block
- Presence of prolonged PR interval associated with either new bifascicular block (RBBB +LAD or RBBB + RAD) or with complete LBBB: this may suddenly deteriorate to complete heart block.

Notes

Transcutaneous pacing can be life-saving but is often intolerable for the patient. Analgesia +/– sedation is required. Beware of deterioration to PEA with paced complexes remaining on the monitor.

Further reading

Nickson C. *Transcutaneous Pacing.* https://litfl.com/transcutaneous-pacing/, 2020.

Soar J, Deakin CD, Nolan JP, Perkins GD, Yeung J, Couper K, . . . Hampshire S. *Adult advanced life support guidelines.* Retrieved from https://www.resus.org.uk/library/2021-resuscitation-guidelines/adult-advanced-life-support-guidelines, 2021.

Algorithm for bradyarrhythmias

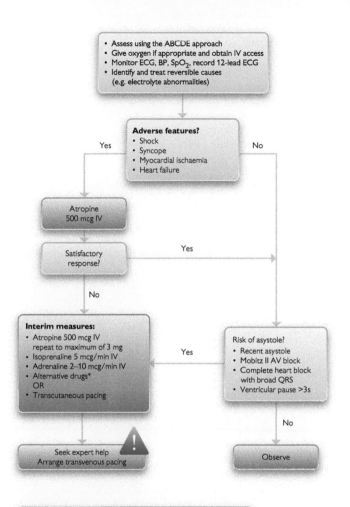

- Assess using the ABCDE approach
- Give oxygen if appropriate and obtain IV access
- Monitor ECG, BP, SpO$_2$, record 12-lead ECG
- Identify and treat reversible causes
  (e.g. electrolyte abnormalities)

Adverse features?
- Shock
- Syncope
- Myocardial ischaemia
- Heart failure

Yes

No

Atropine
500 mcg IV

Satisfactory
response?

Yes

No

Interim measures:
- Atropine 500 mcg IV
  repeat to maximum of 3 mg
- Isoprenaline 5 mcg/min IV
- Adrenaline 2–10 mcg/min IV
- Alternative drugs*
  OR
- Transcutaneous pacing

Yes

Risk of asystole?
- Recent asystole
- Mobitz II AV block
- Complete heart block
  with broad QRS
- Ventricular pause >3s

No

Seek expert help
Arrange transvenous pacing

Observe

*Alternatives include:
- Aminophylline
- Dopamine
- Glucagon (if beta-blocker or calcium channel blocker overdose)
- Glycopyrrolate can be used instead of atropine

SECTION 4

Abdominal

1. Acute abdominal pain

Definition

Acute abdominal pain is a common clinical presentation in the Emergency Department. The clinician addressing the patient with acute abdominal pain ideally should eliminate acute medical causes of abdominal pain as well as acute surgical causes.

Acute versus chronic pain

While a 12-week arbitrary interval can be used to separate acute from chronic abdominal pain, there is no strict time period that will classify the differential diagnosis. A clinical judgement must be made that considers whether this is an accelerating process, one that has reached a plateau, or one that is longstanding but intermittent.

Pain in a sick or unstable patient should generally be managed as acute, since patients with chronic abdominal pain may present with an acute exacerbation of a chronic problem or a new and unrelated problem.

Important points to consider when managing patients

- A normal WBC count does not rule out appendicitis or other acute inflammatory conditions
- Normal-looking CXR does not rule out the presence of pneumoperitoneum (if you see it, it's there; if you don't see it, it doesn't mean it's not there)
- Analgesia should not be withheld to patients with abdominal pain for the fear of obscuring clinical findings. Oligoanalgesia is not acceptable practice
- Plain abdominal X-ray (AXR) should not be taken unless bowel obstruction is suspected
- Avoid overzealous resuscitation in patients with suspected abdominal aortic aneurysm (AAA) rapture and immediate vascular referral should be made. AAA should be suspected in any patient >65 years of age
- It is hazardous making a diagnosis of renal colic in an elderly patient without considering the diagnosis of a leaking AAA
- Medical causes for abdominal pain should not be overlooked, like MI, basal pneumonia, and diabetic ketoacidosis (DKA)
- The diagnosis of mesenteric ischaemia should be considered, particularly in patients with the classic finding of pain out of proportion to physical findings or risk factors such as congestive heart failure, recent MI, hypotension, hypovolaemia, sepsis, cardiac surgery, or requirement for dialysis.

Further reading

Hardy A, Butler B, Crandall M. The evaluation of the acute abdomen. In: Common Problems in Acute Care Surgery (pp. 19–31). New York: Springer, 2013.

Algorithm for acute abdominal pain

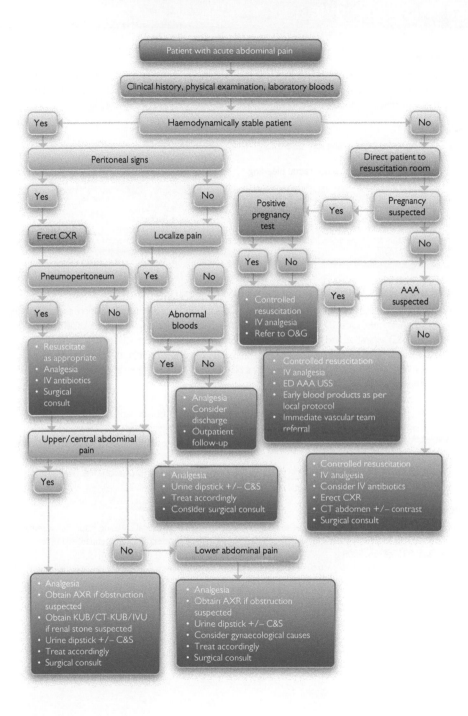

2. Rectal bleeding

Definition

Lower gastrointestinal bleeding (LGIB) is defined as bleeding derived from a source distal to the ligament of Treitz.

Haematochesia is the passage of fresh or altered blood per rectum usually due to colonic bleeding. Occasionally profuse upper gastrointestinal bleeding (UGIB) or small bowel bleeding can be responsible.

Causes

For causes of acute rectal bleeding see Table 4.1.

Table 4.1 Causes of acute rectal bleeding

Common	Less common
• Diverticular disease	• Angiodysplasia
• Ischaemic colitis	• Rectal varices
• Neoplasia	• Coagulopathies
• Benign anorectal disease (e.g. haemorrhoid, anal fissure)	• Radiation proctitis
• Massive UGIB	• Endometriosis
• Inflammatory bowel disease (Crohn's disease, ulcerative colitis)	• Trauma (possible sexual abuse)

Important points in initial management and resuscitation

- Consider a UGIB source in patients with haemodynamic instability, orthostatic hypotension, and an elevated urea-to-creatinine ratio, since 10–15% of patients with severe haematochesia will have a UGIB source
- Nasogastric (NG) aspiration and lavage may help identify patients with upper GI bleeding. Findings that suggest UGIB include the presence of coffee-ground material or bright-red blood in the lavage fluid
- A haemodynamically normal patient with per rectal bleeding which has stopped and normal haemoglobin might be considered for discharge with surgical outpatient follow-up
- Colorectal malignancy should be suspected in:
  - Patients aged ≥40 years reporting rectal bleeding with a change of bowel habit towards looser stools and/ or increased stool frequency persisting for ≥6 weeks
  - Patients aged ≥60 years with rectal bleeding persisting for ≥6 weeks without a change in bowel habit and without anal symptoms
  - Patients aged ≥60 years with a change in bowel habit to looser stools and/or more frequent stools persisting for ≥6 weeks without rectal bleeding

Further reading

Scottish Intercollegiate. SIGN Management of acute upper and lower gastrointestinal bleeding. https://www.semantic scholar.org/paper/sign-management-of-acute-upper-and-lower-bleeding-intercollegiate/4eebda884511e9c61e63d d038c38a589957c4955, 2008.

Strate L. Approach to acute lower gastrointestinal bleeding in adults. http://www.uptodate.com/contents/approach-to-acute-lower-gastrointestinal-bleeding-in-adults, 2021.

Algorithm for rectal bleeding

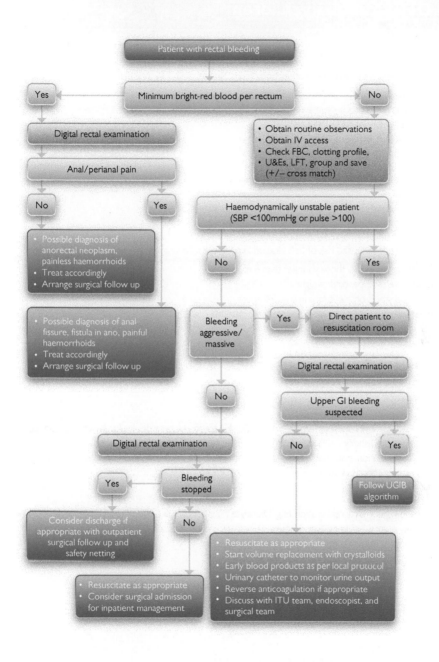

Patient with rectal bleeding

Minimum bright-red blood per rectum

Yes

No

Digital rectal examination

- Obtain routine observations
- Obtain IV access
- Check FBC, clotting profile, U&Es, LFT, group and save (+/– cross match)

Anal/perianal pain

No

Yes

Haemodynamically unstable patient (SBP <100mmHg or pulse >100)

- Possible diagnosis of anorectal neoplasm, painless haemorrhoids
- Treat accordingly
- Arrange surgical follow up

No

Yes

- Possible diagnosis of anal fissure, fistula in ano, painful haemorrhoids
- Treat accordingly
- Arrange surgical follow up

Bleeding aggressive/ massive

Yes

Direct patient to resuscitation room

Digital rectal examination

No

Upper GI bleeding suspected

Digital rectal examination

No

Yes

Bleeding stopped

Follow UGIB algorithm

Yes

Consider discharge if appropriate with outpatient surgical follow up and safety netting

No

- Resuscitate as appropriate
- Start volume replacement with crystalloids
- Early blood products as per local protocol
- Urinary catheter to monitor urine output
- Reverse anticoagulation if appropriate
- Discuss with ITU team, endoscopist, and surgical team

- Resuscitate as appropriate
- Consider surgical admission for inpatient management

3. Dehydration in children

Aetiology

Occurs with excess loss of water and other body fluids, due to:

- Decreased intake
- Increased output (renal, GI, or insensible losses)
- Shift of fluid (ascites or effusions)
- Capillary leak of fluid (burns or sepsis)

Causes

- Gastroenteritis or GI obstruction (e.g. pyloric stenosis)
- Pain limiting oral intake (e.g. mouth ulcers or tonsillitis)
- DKA, febrile illness, or burns

Assessment

Children who are at increased risk of dehydration include the following:

- <1 year of age, especially those younger than 6 months
- Infants who were of low birth weight
- >5 diarrhoeal stools or >2 vomits in past 24 hours
- Not been offered or not been able to tolerate oral fluids
- Stopped breastfeeding during the illness
- Signs of malnutrition

Calculation of deficit

- No significant dehydration (<3%)
  - No signs
- Clinical dehydration (3–8%)
  - Dry mucous membranes, sunken eyes, reduced skin turgor, tachycardia, looks unwell, drowsiness, irritability
- Severe dehydration/shock (>8%)
  - Acidotic respiration, poor perfusion (capillary refill time (CRT) >2 seconds), circulatory collapse, deteriorating conscious level

Treatment

- Mild to moderate = Oral rehydration (e.g. Dioralyte™) whenever possible
  - 50 mL/kg in small volumes over 4 hours
  - If vomiting persists, try smaller volumes more frequently
  - Consider NG fluids if refusing
- Severe = Replace deficit (50 mL/kg) plus maintenance over 24 hours
  - If signs of shock, give 10–20 mL/kg 0.9% saline as IV bolus and repeat as necessary

Maintenance fluids

These should be given at a rate of:

- <10 kg: 100 mL/kg/day
- 10–20kg: 1000 mL plus 50 mL/kg/day for every kg >10 kg
- >20 kg: 1500 mL plus 20 mL/kg/day for every kg >20 kg

Further reading

National Institute for Health and Care Excellence. Clinical Guideline 84. Diarrhoea and vomiting in children under 5. www.nice.org.uk/cg84, 2009.

National Patient Safety Agency. Reducing the risk of hyponatraemia when administering intravenous infusions to children. http://www.nrls.npsa.nhs.uk/resources/?entryid45=59809, 2007.

Algorithm for dehydration in children

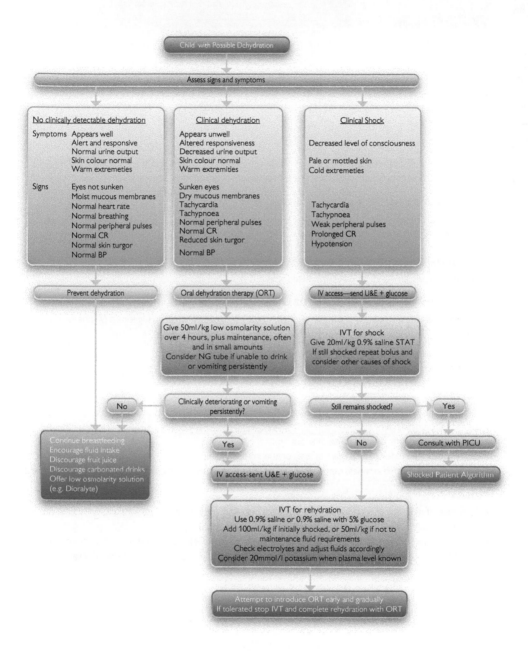

Child with Possible Dehydration

Assess signs and symptoms

No clinically detectable dehydration

Symptoms	Appears well
	Alert and responsive
	Normal urine output
	Skin colour normal
	Warm extremeties
Signs	Eyes not sunken
	Moist mucous membranes
	Normal heart rate
	Normal breathing
	Normal peripheral pulses
	Normal CR
	Normal skin turgor
	Normal BP

Clinical dehydration

Appears unwell
Altered responsiveness
Decreased urine output
Skin colour normal
Warm extremities

Sunken eyes
Dry mucous membranes
Tachycardia
Tachypnoea
Normal peripheral pulses
Normal CR
Reduced skin turgor
Normal BP

Clinical Shock

Decreased level of consciousness

Pale or mottled skin
Cold extremities

Tachycardia
Tachypnoea
Weak peripheral pulses
Prolonged CR
Hypotension

Prevent dehydration

Oral dehydration therapy (ORT)

IV access—send U&E + glucose

Give 50ml/kg low osmolality solution over 4 hours, plus maintenance, often and in small amounts
Consider NG tube if unable to drink or vomiting persistently

IVT for shock
Give 20ml/kg 0.9% saline STAT
If still shocked repeat bolus and consider other causes of shock

No

Clinically deteriorating or vomiting persistently?

Still remains shocked?

Yes

Continue breastfeeding
Encourage fluid intake
Discourage fruit juice
Discourage carbonated drinks
Offer low osmolality solution
(e.g. Dioralyte)

Yes

No

Consult with PICU

IV access-sent U&E + glucose

Shocked Patient Algorithm

IVT for rehydration
Use 0.9% saline or 0.9% saline with 5% glucose
Add 100ml/kg if initially shocked, or 50ml/kg if not to maintenance fluid requirements
Check electrolytes and adjust fluids accordingly
Consider 20mmol/l potassium when plasma level known

Attempt to introduce ORT early and gradually
If tolerated stop IVT and complete rehydration with ORT

4. Diarrhoea

Definition

The following definitions have been suggested according to the duration of diarrhoea:

- Acute diarrhoea: ≤14 days in duration
- Persistent diarrhoea: >14 days in duration
- Chronic diarrhoea: >30 days in duration

Causes

Most cases of acute diarrhoea are due to infections with viruses and bacteria and are self-limiting. Non-infectious aetiologies become more common as the diarrhoea persists and becomes chronic.

Important points in patient evaluation

- Duration of illness
- Frequency and characteristics of the stool
- Associated signs and symptoms of systemic illness such as fever, anorexia, weight loss, and volume depletion
- Evaluate for hypovolaemia (e.g. decreased skin turgor, orthostatic hypotension)
- Abdominal pain and presence of peritoneal signs

Indications for diagnostic evaluation

A diagnostic evaluation is indicated in patients with relatively severe illness, as suggested by one or more of the following:

- Profuse watery diarrhoea with signs of hypovolaemia
- Passage of many small-volume stools containing blood and mucus
- Bloody diarrhoea
- Temperature ≥38.5°C (101.3°F)
- Passage of ≥6 unformed stools per 24 hours or a duration of illness >48 hours
- Severe abdominal pain
- Hospitalized patients or recent use of antibiotics
- Diarrhoea in the elderly (≥70 years of age) or the immunocompromised
- Systemic illness with diarrhoea, especially in pregnant women (in which case listeriosis should be suspected)

Notes

- Presence of either WBCs or RBCs in stool implies infection with invasive organisms and/or inflammatory bowel disease
- Empiric antibiotic therapy should be avoided, as patient might develop haemolytic–uraemic syndrome if infected with enterohaemorrhagic *Escherichia coli* (increase in the production or release of Shiga toxin)

Further reading

LaRocque R, Harris JB. Approach to the adult with acute diarrhoea in resource-rich settings. https://www.uptodate.com/contents/approach-to-the-adult-with-acute-diarrhea-in-resource-rich-settings, 2021.

Guerrant RL. Practice guidelines for the management of infectious diarrhoea. *Clin Infect Dis* 2001;32(3):331.

Algorithm for diarrhoea

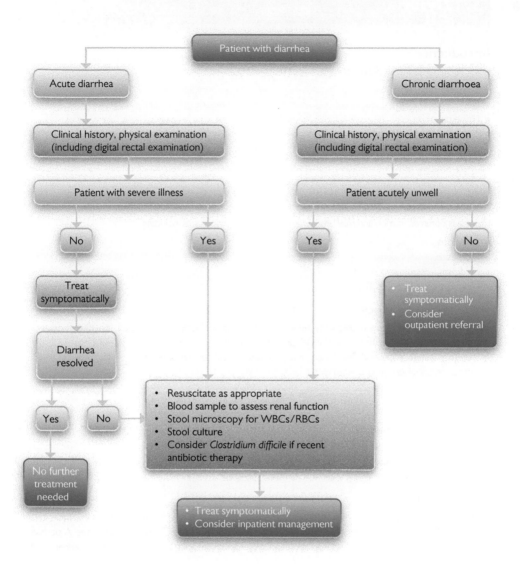

Patient with diarrhea

Acute diarrhea

Clinical history, physical examination (including digital rectal examination)

Patient with severe illness

No → Treat symptomatically → Diarrhea resolved

Yes → No

Yes → No further treatment needed

No → Resuscitate as appropriate
- Blood sample to assess renal function
- Stool microscopy for WBCs/RBCs
- Stool culture
- Consider *Clostridium difficile* if recent antibiotic therapy

Yes →

- Resuscitate as appropriate
- Blood sample to assess renal function
- Stool microscopy for WBCs/RBCs
- Stool culture
- Consider *Clostridium difficile* if recent antibiotic therapy

- Treat symptomatically
- Consider inpatient management

Chronic diarrhoea

Clinical history, physical examination (including digital rectal examination)

Patient acutely unwell

No →
- Treat symptomatically
- Consider outpatient referral

5. Dysuria

Introduction

Physical examination in a patient complaining of dysuria should include:

- Temperature
- General well-being
- Urine dipstick
- Examination of lymph nodes
- Consider blood culture if systemically unwell (temperature >38°C)

Patients with risk factors for sexually transmitted infection should be offered or referred for screening, including HIV.

Dysuria in men

Dysuria is common in men and may be a symptom of various conditions including:

- Urethritis
- Prostatitis
- Epididymitis/epididymo-orchitis
- Urinary tract infection (UTI)

Dysuria in pregnancy

Bacteriuria is very common in pregnancy, especially in the first trimester. If not treated, 30–40% of cases will go on to develop a symptomatic UTI. In the UK, pregnant women are screened at 12–16 weeks—by urine dip (and microscopy, culture, and sensitivity (MC&S) if appropriate). *E. coli* remains the most common organism.

Untreated bacteriuria is associated with:

- Preterm birth
- Low birth weight
- Perinatal mortality

Ascending urinary tract infection

Acute pyelonephritis is usually associated with systemic upset, high temperature, and loin or back pain. Patients often require admission for IV antibiotics, IV fluids, and analgesia.

Urine dipstick

A urine test strip or dipstick is a basic diagnostic tool used to determine pathological changes in a patient's urine. It checks urine acidity, specific gravity, protein, sugar, ketones, bilirubin, WBCs, RBCs, and nitrates. A positive test for nitrates indicates a possible urine infection caused by nitrate-reducing bacteria, and a high number of WBCs indicates urinary infection.

Further reading

Cohen MS, Seña AC. Approach to infectious causes of dysuria in the adult man. https://www.uptodate.com/contents/approach-to-infectious-causes-of-dysuria-in-the-adult-man, 2021.

Hooton MS, Gupta K. Urinary tract infections and asymptomatic bacteriuria in pregnancy. https://www.uptodate.com/contents/urinary-tract-infections-and-asymptomatic-bacteriuria-in-pregnancy, 2021.

Ramrakha P, Moore K, Sam A. Oxford Handbook of Acute Medicine. Oxford, UK: Oxford University Press. Retrieved 2 May, 2022, from https://oxfordmedicine.com/view/10.1093/med/9780198797425.001.0001/med-9780198797425, 2019–11.

Wyatt J, Taylor R, de Wit K, Hotton E. Oxford Handbook of Emergency Medicine. Oxford, UK: Oxford University Press. Retrieved 2 May, 2022, from https://oxfordmedicine.com/view/10.1093/med/9780198784197.001.0001/med-9780198784197, 2020–08.

Algorithm for dysuria

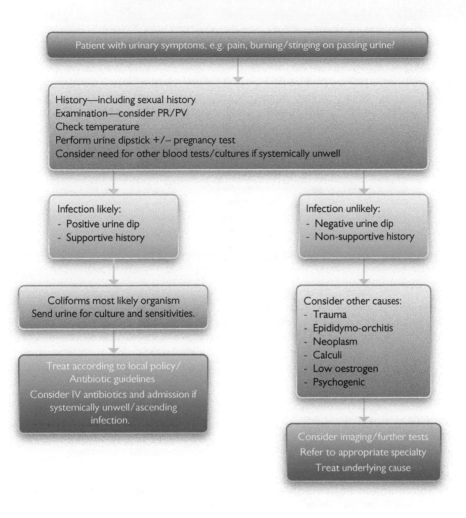

Patient with urinary symptoms, e.g. pain, burning/stinging on passing urine?

↓

History—including sexual history
Examination—consider PR/PV
Check temperature
Perform urine dipstick +/− pregnancy test
Consider need for other blood tests/cultures if systemically unwell

Infection likely:
- Positive urine dip
- Supportive history

Coliforms most likely organism
Send urine for culture and sensitivities.

Treat according to local policy/
Antibiotic guidelines
Consider IV antibiotics and admission if
systemically unwell/ascending
infection.

Infection unlikely:
- Negative urine dip
- Non-supportive history

Consider other causes:
- Trauma
- Epididymo-orchitis
- Neoplasm
- Calculi
- Low oestrogen
- Psychogenic

Consider imaging/further tests
Refer to appropriate specialty
Treat underlying cause

6. Ectopic pregnancy

Introduction

Ectopic pregnancies occur in approximately 1% of all pregnancies, and 97% occur as a tubal implantation.

It is imperative that a pregnancy test is performed in **all** patients presenting with any of the symptoms or signs shown in Table 4.2. A urine or serum beta-human chorionic gonadotropin (β-HCG) test is needed. It is important to recognize and treat an ectopic pregnancy promptly to improve morbidity and mortality. Early assistance from seniors, the gynaecology team, and anaethetists is recommended.

Table 4.2 Risk factors, symptoms, and signs of ectopic pregnancy

Risk factors	Symptoms	Signs
Pelvic inflammatory disease	Abdominal/pelvic pain	Pelvic or abdominal tenderness
In vitro fertilization (IVF)	Amenorrhoea	Adnexal tenderness
Previous pelvic/tubal surgery	Vaginal bleeding	Cervical excitation
Previous ectopic	Dizziness/syncope	Peritonitis
Intra-uterine device	Shoulder-tip pain	Signs of 'shock'
	Rectal 'pressure'	Cervical os usually closed

Symptoms and Signs

The 'classical' history is one of lower abdominal pain and per vagina (PV) bleeding; however, the symptoms are varied and an open mind is needed to diagnose ectopic pregnancies.

If the patient is haemodynamically unstable, an urgent laparotomy is needed to clamp the bleeding artery. If gynaecology is not on site, immediate discussion with the senior surgeon is required.

Anti-D immunoglobulin

Anti-D immunoglobulin (Ig) should be given to all rhesus-negative women who need a surgical procedure to manage an ectopic pregnancy. Patients with a medically managed ectopic pregnancy may not need anti-D—discuss this with the gynaecology team.

Anti-D is given IM via the deltoid muscle at 250 IU.

There is no clinical need to perform a Kleihauer test to quantify feto-maternal haemorrhage.

Further reading

National Institute for Health and Care Excellence. Ectopic pregnancy and miscarriage: diagnosis and initial management [NG126]. Available from: https://www.nice.org.uk/guidance/126, 2019 [Accessed 17 February 2022].

Algorithm for ectopic pregnancy

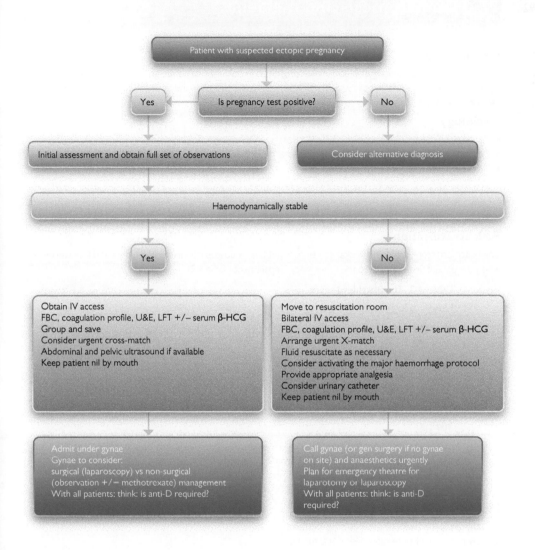

Patient with suspected ectopic pregnancy

Is pregnancy test positive?
- Yes
- No

Initial assessment and obtain full set of observations

Consider alternative diagnosis

Haemodynamically stable
- Yes
- No

Yes:
Obtain IV access
FBC, coagulation profile, U&E, LFT +/− serum β-HCG
Group and save
Consider urgent cross-match
Abdominal and pelvic ultrasound if available
Keep patient nil by mouth

No:
Move to resuscitation room
Bilateral IV access
FBC, coagulation profile, U&E, LFT +/− serum β-HCG
Arrange urgent X-match
Fluid resuscitate as necessary
Consider activating the major haemorrhage protocol
Provide appropriate analgesia
Consider urinary catheter
Keep patient nil by mouth

Yes (continued):
Admit under gynae
Gynae to consider:
surgical (laparoscopy) vs non-surgical
(observation +/− methotrexate) management
With all patients: think: is anti-D required?

No (continued):
Call gynae (or gen surgery if no gynae
on site) and anaesthetics urgently
Plan for emergency theatre for
laparotomy or laparoscopy
With all patients: think: is anti-D
required?

7. Haematemesis and melaena

Introduction

Haematemesis is the vomiting of blood, either bright red in colour or of coffee-ground material (altered blood). Melaena is the passage of black tarry stools. The tarriness is characteristic and distinguishes melaena from the passage of black stools due to dietary agents, including the ingestion of iron.

Aetiology

- Peptic ulcer disease (commonest—50% of cases) • Oesophago-gastric varices
- Gastritis, esophagitis, duodenitis • Oesophageal (Mallory–Weiss) tear
- Tumour • Arteriovenous malformation

At the time of first assessment, this should focus on trying to identify the cause of the bleeding, assess the haemodynamic status of the patient, and define factors that predict outcome (risk stratification). A history of previous ulcer disease, aspirin, or NSAID use is common in patients with bleeding peptic ulcer.

Risk stratification

The Blatchford score, unlike the Rockall score, does not take endoscopic findings into account and thus can be used when the patient first presents to the Emergency Department (Table 4.3).

Table 4.3 The Blatchford score

	Score value		Score value
Blood urea (mmol/L)		Other markers	
6.5–7.9	2	Pulse ≥100/minute	1
8.0–9.9	3	Presentation with melaena	1
10.0–25.0	4	Presentation with syncope	2
>25.0	6	Hepatic disease	2
Haemoglobin for men (g/L)		Cardiac failure	2
120–129	1		
100–119	3		
<100	6		

Low risk = Score of 0. Any score higher than 0 is 'high risk'.

Data from Blatchford et al. A risk score to predict need for treatment for upper gastrointestinal haemorrhage, Early Report, Volume 356, Issue 9238, pp. 1318–1321, October 14, 2000.

Features of a major bleed

- Tachycardia (be aware of patients on β-blockers)
- Tachypnea • Hypotension (SBP <100 mmHg)
- Presence of significant postural drop in BP • Reduced conscious level • History of syncope

Important points in initial management and resuscitation

- Transfuse patients with massive bleeding with blood, platelets, and clotting factors
- Offer platelet transfusion to patients who are actively bleeding and have a platelet count of $<50 \times 10^9$ L
- Offer prothrombin complex concentrate (e.g. Beriplex® 30 units/kg) to patients who are taking warfarin with high INR and actively bleeding
- Give terlipressin acetate (2 mg IV qds) to patients with suspected variceal bleeding
- Antibiotic therapy should be commenced in patients with chronic liver disease: e.g. IV aztreonam 2 g bd and IV metronidazole 500 mg tds
- Proton pump inhibitor (PPI) should not routinely be used prior to diagnosis by endoscopy

Further reading

National Institute for Health and Care Excellence. Clinical Guideline 141. Acute upper gastrointestinal bleeding in over 16s. https://www.nice.org.uk/guidance/cg141, 2012.

Saltzman JR. Approach to acute upper gastrointestinal bleeding in adults. http://www.uptodate.com/contents/approach-to-acute-upper-gastrointestinal-bleeding-in-adults, 2012.

Algorithm for haematemesis and melaena

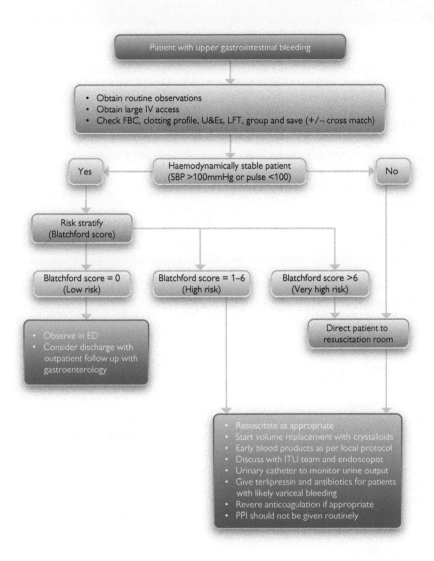

Patient with upper gastrointestinal bleeding

- Obtain routine observations
- Obtain large IV access
- Check FBC, clotting profile, U&Es, LFT, group and save (+/− cross match)

Haemodynamically stable patient
(SBP >100mmHg or pulse <100)

Yes

No

Risk stratify
(Blatchford score)

Blatchford score = 0
(Low risk)

Blatchford score = 1–6
(High risk)

Blatchford score >6
(Very high risk)

Direct patient to
resuscitation room

- Observe in ED
- Consider discharge with
  outpatient follow up with
  gastroenterology

- Resuscitate as appropriate
- Start volume replacement with crystalloids
- Early blood products as per local protocol
- Discuss with ITU team and endoscopist
- Urinary catheter to monitor urine output
- Give terlipressin and antibiotics for patients
  with likely variceal bleeding
- Revere anticoagulation if appropriate
- PPI should not be given routinely

8. Jaundice

Definition

Jaundice is not a diagnosis per se but rather a physical manifestation of elevated serum bilirubin, usually not clinically apparent unless the serum total bilirubin is >50 µmol/L. It is not a common chief complaint. Instead, the jaundiced patient often presents with a related symptom (e.g. abdominal pain, pruritis, vomiting, or substance ingestion).

Differential diagnosis

The differential diagnosis of jaundice is broad, and a precise diagnosis is not always possible. For this reason, the emergency physician has two primary responsibilities: to identify and stabilize patients with life-threatening conditions and to provide an appropriate work-up for non-emergency cases.

The critical and emergency causes of jaundice include:

- Massive hemolysis
- Acute cholangitis
- Acute liver failure
- Acute fatty liver of pregnancy
- Neonatal hyperbilirubinaemia

Unstable jaundiced patient

Clues to a potentially critical unstable patient with jaundice include:

- Altered mental status
- Hypotension
- Fever
- Abdominal pain
- Coagulopathy, multiple bruises

Laboratory tests

Initial laboratory tests for a jaundiced patient should include bilirubin, alkaline phosphatase, aminotransferases (aspartate transaminase (AST), alanine transaminase (ALT)), prothrombin time/INR, and albumin.

- With normal alkaline phosphatase and aminotransferases, jaundice is likely not due to hepatic injury or biliary tract disease. In such patients, haemolysis or inherited disorders of bilirubin metabolism may be responsible for the hyperbilirubinaemia
- Predominant aminotransferase elevation suggests that jaundice is caused by intrinsic hepatocellular disease
- Predominant alkaline phosphatase elevation, out of proportion to serum aminotransferases, suggests biliary obstruction or intrahepatic cholestasis

Further reading

Roy-Chowdhury N, Roy-Chowdhury J. Bilirubin metabolism. http://www.uptodate.com/contents/bilirubin-metabol ism, 2020.
Wheatley M, Heilpern KL. Jaundice: An Emergency Department approach to diagnosis and management. *Emerg Med* 2008;10(3).

Algorithm for jaundice

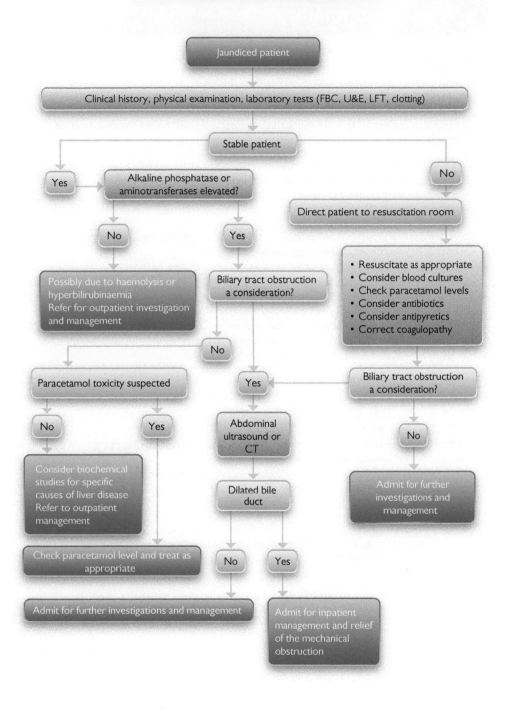

Jaundiced patient

Clinical history, physical examination, laboratory tests (FBC, U&E, LFT, clotting)

Stable patient

Yes

Alkaline phosphatase or aminotransferases elevated?

No

Direct patient to resuscitation room

No

Yes

Possibly due to haemolysis or hyperbilirubinaemia
Refer for outpatient investigation and management

Biliary tract obstruction a consideration?

- Resuscitate as appropriate
- Consider blood cultures
- Check paracetamol levels
- Consider antibiotics
- Consider antipyretics
- Correct coagulopathy

No

Paracetamol toxicity suspected

Yes

Biliary tract obstruction a consideration?

No

Yes

Abdominal ultrasound or CT

No

Consider biochemical studies for specific causes of liver disease
Refer to outpatient management

Admit for further investigations and management

Dilated bile duct

Check paracetamol level and treat as appropriate

No

Yes

Admit for further investigations and management

Admit for inpatient management and relief of the mechanical obstruction

9. Nausea and vomiting

Definition

Nausea is a subjective unpleasant sensation of being about to vomit.

Vomiting is the physical event that results in rapid, forceful expulsion of gastric contents and it should be differentiated from regurgitation.

Regurgitation is a passive act by which gastric contents are brought back into the mouth without the abdominal and diaphragmatic muscular activity that characterizes vomiting.

Causes

In most cases, the cause of nausea and vomiting can be determined from the history and physical examination and additional testing is not required.

Salient points in the history

- Abdominal pain with vomiting often indicates an organic etiology (e.g. cholelithiasis)
- Abdominal distension and tenderness suggest bowel obstruction
- Vomiting of food eaten several hours earlier and a succussion splash detected on abdominal examination suggest gastric obstruction or gastroparesis
- Vomiting in the morning is typically related to pregnancy, uraemia, alcohol ingestion, or increased intracranial pressure
- The quality of vomiting may be helpful. A feculent odor to the vomitus is a feature of intestinal obstruction suggestive of bacterial degradation of stagnant intestinal contents
- Heartburn with nausea often indicates gastroesophageal reflux disease

Management

As a general rule, the following four steps should be considered in patients with persistent nausea and vomiting:

- Etiology should be sought, taking into account whether the patient has acute nausea and vomiting or chronic symptoms (at least 1 month in duration)
- The consequences or complications of nausea and vomiting (e.g. fluid depletion, hypokalaemia, and metabolic alkalosis) should be identified and corrected
- Targeted therapy should be provided, when possible (e.g. surgery for bowel obstruction or malignancy). In other cases, the symptoms should be treated
- In women of childbearing age, a pregnancy test must be done

Further reading

Longstreth GF. Approach to the adult with nausea and vomiting. http://www.uptodate.com/contents/approach-to-the-adult-with-nausea-and-vomiting, 2020.

Algorithm for nausea and vomiting

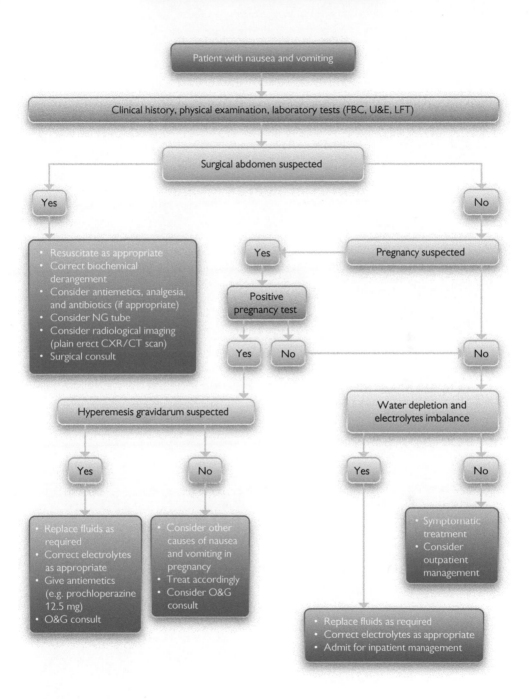

SECTION 5

Neurological

1. The unconscious patient

Introduction

Conscious level is determined using the GCS. The adult score ranges from a minimum of 3 to a maximum of 15 and is calculated as shown in Table 5.1. 'Unconsciousness' is generally taken to mean no eye response and a GCS ≤8.

Table 5.1 The Glasgow Come Score

Eye response	Open spontaneously	4
	Open to verbal command	3
	Open to pain	2
	No response	1
Verbal response	Talking and oriented	5
	Confused/disoriented	4
	Inappropriate words	3
	Incomprehensible sounds	2
	No response	1
Motor response	Obeys commands	6
	Localizes to pain	5
	Flexion/withdrawal	4
	Abnormal flexion	3
	Extension	2
	No response	1

MDCalc. 2015. *Glasgow Coma Scale/Score (GCS) - MDCalc.* [online] Available at: <http://www.mdcalc.com/glasgow-coma-scale-score/> [Accessed May 2022].

Causes

In the absence of trauma there are a number of different causes of a low GCS:

- Vascular (stroke/subarachnoid haemorrhage (SAH))
- Infection
- Neoplasm
- Seizures
- Metabolic disturbance

History

A thorough history is vital in determining the cause of 'unconsciousness'. This includes information obtained from paramedics, the patient's relatives and friends, and information from old medical records/Emergency Department attendances.

Examination

Thorough neurological examination may help to determine the cause:

- Coma without lateralizing signs is often due to poisoning, a postictal state, or hepatic failure
- Tricyclic antidepressant overdose causes coma with dilated pupils, increased tone, jerky limb movements, and ECG abnormalities
- Ocular nerve palsy with coma could indicate Wernicke's encephalopathy and requires treatment with IV thiamine

Further reading

Wyatt JP, Illingworth RN, Graham CA, Hogg K, Robertson C, Clancy M. Oxford Handbook of Emergency Medicine, 4th edn. Oxford: Oxford University Press, 2012.

Algorithm for the unconscious patient

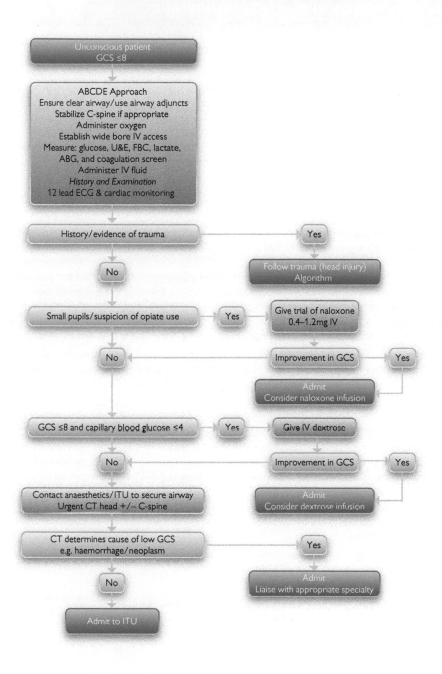

Unconscious patient
GCS ≤8

ABCDE Approach
Ensure clear airway/use airway adjuncts
Stabilize C-spine if appropriate
Administer oxygen
Establish wide bore IV access
Measure: glucose, U&E, FBC, lactate,
ABG, and coagulation screen
Administer IV fluid
History and Examination
12 lead ECG & cardiac monitoring

History/evidence of trauma — Yes

No

Follow trauma (head injury)
Algorithm

Small pupils/suspicion of opiate use — Yes — Give trial of naloxone
0.4–1.2mg IV

No

Improvement in GCS — Yes

Admit
Consider naloxone infusion

GCS ≤8 and capillary blood glucose ≤4 — Yes — Give IV dextrose

No

Improvement in GCS — Yes

Admit
Consider dextrose infusion

Contact anaesthetics/ITU to secure airway
Urgent CT head +/– C-spine

CT determines cause of low GCS
e.g. haemorrhage/neoplasm — Yes

No

Admit
Liaise with appropriate specialty

Admit to ITU

2. Aggressive/disturbed behaviour

Initial approach

There are many causes of agitation and it is important to use a methodical approach.

The initial priorities are to ensure that any life-threatening problem is identified and treated promptly (e.g. hypoxia, hypovolaemia, hypoglycaemia). The next step is to ensure that a thorough history (including a collateral history) and examination is undertaken. In these situations, good communication and explanation to the patient and relatives are imperative. These verbal and non-verbal skills are often sufficient to de-escalate the situation and help to treat the aggressive behaviour. A calm manner, non-critical approach, and active listening provide patients with reassurance and will reduce the need for pharmacological intervention.

Your personal safety and those of staff and patients around you is paramount. Ask for assistance early from seniors, security staff, or the police if needed.

Treatment options

- **Treat the underlying cause**. It is imperative that the cause for this behaviour is found and treated appropriately (e.g. aggressive treatment of sepsis, or treatment of encephalopathy, or correction of hypoxia or hypoglycaemia)
- **Nursing techniques**. Patients should be nursed in a well-lit, quiet room. It is important that good verbal and non-verbal communication skills are used to explain to the patient and reassure the patient about diagnosis and treatment options. De-escalation techniques can be used to ensure that patients are reassured
- **Medication**. When de-escalation techniques have failed or if they are inappropriate, medication can be given to patients who are at risk of harming themselves or harming others due to their agitated behaviour

Medication is, however, a last resort and should be given in discussion with senior support. Medication must be given with reference to the Mental Health Act and the Mental Capacity Act with respect to those patients who cannot consent to this treatment option. The aim is to minimize the risk of harm to the patient and to others around them.

- Oral therapy is preferred; however, this may not be possible in a violent and aggressive patient
- Ensure that the British National Formulary (BNF) is used prior to administering
- Allow sufficient time in between first dose and subsequent dose
- It is important to be aware of possible complications from lorazepam (e.g. respiratory depression) and haloperidol (e.g. acute dystonia) and know how to treat these (e.g. 5–10 mg IV procyclidine for haloperidol-induced dystonia)
- Avoid IV sedation for agitation if possible
- Care should be taken with the elderly or those with multiple comorbidities, and an appropriate reduced dose should be considered

Table 5.2 offers suggestions for possible choice of medications.

Table 5.2 Medication options

Route	Non-psychotic patient	Psychotic patient
Oral	Lorazepam 1–2 mg	Lorazepam 1–2 mg + haloperidol 2.5 mg
Intramuscular	Lorazepam 2–4 mg	Lorazepam 2–4 mg + haloperidol 5 mg

Further reading

National Institute for Health and Care Excellence. Clinical Guideline 103. Delirium: prevention, diagnosis and management. www.nice.org.uk/guidance/cg103, 2019.

National Institute for Health and Care Excellence. NICE Guideline 10. Violence and aggression: short term management in mental health, health and community settings. www.nice.org.uk/guidance/ng10, 2015.

National Institute for Health and Care Excellence. Quality Standard 63. Delirium in adults. www.nice.org.uk/guidance/qs63, 2014.

Algorithm for aggressive/disturbed behaviour

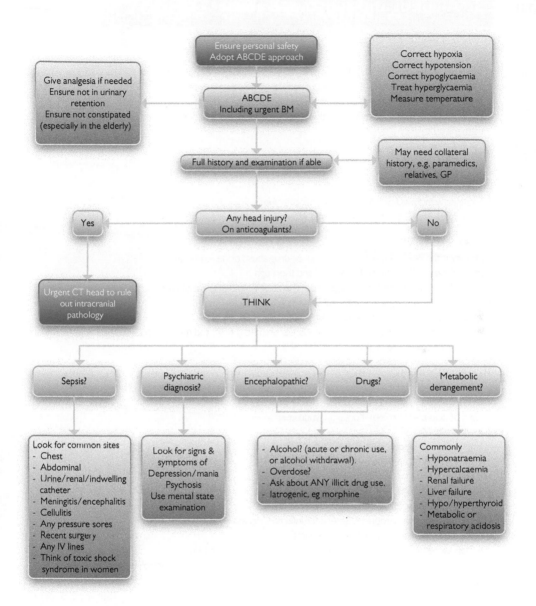

Ensure personal safety
Adopt ABCDE approach

Give analgesia if needed
Ensure not in urinary
retention
Ensure not constipated
(especially in the elderly)

ABCDE
Including urgent BM

Correct hypoxia
Correct hypotension
Correct hypoglycaemia
Treat hyperglycaemia
Measure temperature

Full history and examination if able

May need collateral
history, e.g. paramedics,
relatives, GP

Yes

Any head injury?
On anticoagulants?

No

Urgent CT head to rule
out intracranial
pathology

THINK

Sepsis?

Psychiatric
diagnosis?

Encephalopathic?

Drugs?

Metabolic
derangement?

Look for common sites
- Chest
- Abdominal
- Urine/renal/indwelling
  catheter
- Meningitis/encephalitis
- Cellulitis
- Any pressure sores
- Recent surgery
- Any IV lines
- Think of toxic shock
  syndrome in women

Look for signs &
symptoms of
Depression/mania
Psychosis
Use mental state
examination

- Alcohol? (acute or chronic use,
  or alcohol withdrawal).
- Overdose?
- Ask about ANY illicit drug use.
- Iatrogenic, eg morphine

Commonly
- Hyponatraemia
- Hypercalcaemia
- Renal failure
- Liver failure
- Hypo/hyperthyroid
- Metabolic or
  respiratory acidosis

3. Alcohol and substance abuse

Introduction

- Alcohol dependence and withdrawal has significant morbidity and mortality
- People admitting to >10 units/day are likely to have withdrawal symptoms
- Delirium tremens is rare at a consumption of <15 units/day
- Hypoglycaemia, hypokalaemia, hypocalcaemia, and fever may predispose patients to seizures or delirium tremens (DTs)

Presentation

- Acute intoxication
- Withdrawal DTs
- Seizures: withdrawal or intoxication, or hypoglycaemia
- Associated problem, e.g. pneumonia, rhabdomyolysis

Patient workup

- History is the key to a diagnosis of alcohol or drug abuse or dependence
- Physical examination should be detailed and thorough
  - Cirrhosis, ascites, oedema, and jaundice characterize end-stage alcoholism
- Laboratory screening can be informative
  - Look for elevations in AST, ALT, and γ-glutamyltransferase (GGT)
  - FBC often shows elevated mean corpuscular volume (MCV) and mean corpuscular haemoglobin (MCHb) with prolonged use of alcohol

Management

- Pabrinex® required if nil by mouth (NBM), or actual or incipient Wernicke's encephalopathy
  - Note: risk of anaphylaxis (**must** give before glucose)
- Signs of possible Wernicke–Korsakov syndrome:
  - Acute confusion
  - Reduced conscious level
  - Memory problems
  - Ataxia
  - Ophthalmoplegia
  - Hypoglycaemia
- Treat any associated problems. Screen for infection including CXR
- Remember spontaneous bacterial peritonitis
  - Tap ascites and send for culture, urgent Gram stain, and cell count
- Common precipitating causes of encephalopathy are infection, GI bleed, electrolyte disturbance, and constipation

Substance abuse

- NPIS is commissioned by the Health Protection Agency to contribute to the TOXBASE® website (www.toxbase.org), providing:
  - Guidance on management of poisoning
- A 24-hour telephone line (tel. 0344 892 0111) with information for more complex poisoning cases

Further reading

Smith Connery H, Kleber HD. Guideline Watch (April 2007): Practice guideline for the treatment of patients with substance use disorders, 2nd edn. *Am J Psychiatry* 2006;163:8.

Algorithm for alcohol and substance abuse

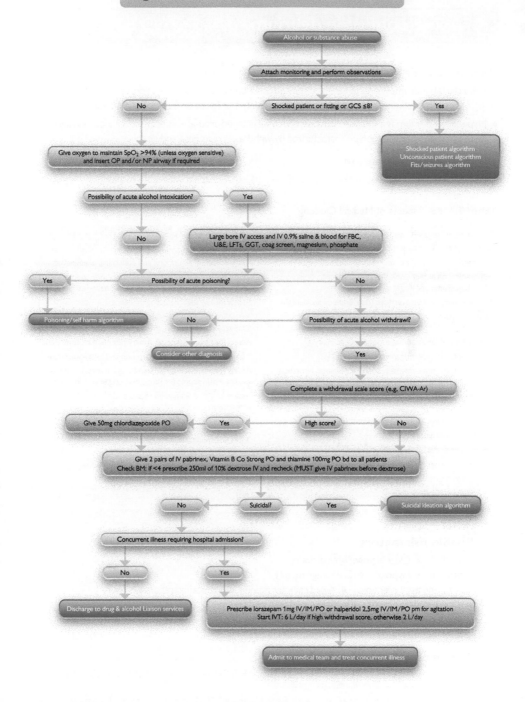

Alcohol or substance abuse

Attach monitoring and perform observations

Shocked patient or fitting or GCS ≤8?

No → Give oxygen to maintain SpO₂ >94% (unless oxygen sensitive) and insert OP and/or NP airway if required

Yes → Shocked patient algorithm / Unconscious patient algorithm / Fits/seizures algorithm

Possibility of acute alcohol intoxication?

Yes → Large bore IV access and IV 0.9% saline & blood for FBC, U&E, LFTs, GGT, coag screen, magnesium, phosphate

No

Possibility of acute poisoning?

Yes → Poisoning/self harm algorithm

No → Possibility of acute alcohol withdrawl?

No → Consider other diagnosis

Yes → Complete a withdrawal scale score (e.g. CIWA-Ar)

High score?

Yes → Give 50mg chlordiazepoxide PO

No

Give 2 pairs of IV pabrinex, Vitamin B Co Strong PO and thiamine 100mg PO bd to all patients
Check BM: if <4 prescribe 250ml of 10% dextrose IV and recheck (MUST give IV pabrinex before dextrose)

Suicidal?

Yes → Suicidal ideation algorithm

No → Concurrent illness requiring hospital admission?

No → Discharge to drug & alcohol Liaison services

Yes → Prescribe lorazepam 1mg IV/IM/PO or haloperidol 2.5mg IV/IM/PO prn for agitation
Start IVT: 6 L/day if high withdrawal score, otherwise 2 L/day

Admit to medical team and treat concurrent illness

4. Acute confusion/delirium

Definition of delirium

This is a clinical syndrome characterized by disturbed consciousness, cognitive function, or perception. It usually has an acute onset and a fluctuating course. It may be hyperactive or hypoactive or occasionally both.

- Hyperactive delirium is a subtype characterized by heightened arousal, restlessness, agitation, and aggression
- Hypoactive delirium is a subtype characterized by withdrawal, quietness, and sleepiness

History and examination

Table 5.3 shows the key aspects to be covered in the clerking of a patient with acute confusion.

Table 5.3 Key Aspects of Medical Clerking

Salient points to cover in the history	Important aspects to cover in the examination
Onset and course of confusion	Usual vital signs
Past medical history and comorbidities	Cardiovascular, respiratory, and abdominal examination
Full medication history (including recent changes, prescription, over-the-counter and illegal substances)	Assessment of cognitive function, e.g. abbreviated Mental Test Score (MTS), six-item Cognitive Impairment Test (6-CIT)
Any possibility of drug overdose (deliberate or accidental)	Assess for any focal neurological deficit
Alcohol history	Assess for evidence of raised intracranial pressure (ICP) or meningeal irritation
Any history of falls/trauma, especially head injury	Assess for any evidence of urinary retention or constipation
Any symptoms suggesting infection	Assess skin for any signs of infection and hydration status
Any symptoms suggesting raised ICP or meningeal irritation (headache, photophobia, neck stiffness)	Assess for any evidence of pain using if necessary one of the validated pain scores for those with cognitive impairment
Any preceding loss of consciousness or seizure activity	Assess for any evidence of effects of drug overdose or alcohol withdrawal
Recent oral intake (evidence of malnutrition or dehydration)	
Bladder/bowel function	
Previous episodes of acute/chronic confusion	
Any history of sensory impairments and aids used	
Premorbid cognitive and functional status	
Any psychiatric history	
Social history	

Modifiable risk factors

- Familiar staff • Clear signage/lighting/clocks
- Fluid balance • Hypoxia • Encourage mobility
- Search for and treat infections • Avoid catheterization • Medication reconciliation
- Assess for and manage pain (look for non-verbal clues)
- Resolve any reversible causes of sensory impairment, e.g. impacted ear wax
- Encourage normal sleep patterns (reduce noise levels)

Further reading

Healthcare of Older Australians Standing Committee (HCOASC) Guideline. Clinical Practice Guidelines for the Management of Delirium in Older People. 2006

National Institute for Health and Care Excellence. Clinical Guideline 103. Delirium: prevention, diagnosis and management. www.nice.org.uk/guidance/cg103, 2019.

Algorithm for acute confusion/delirium

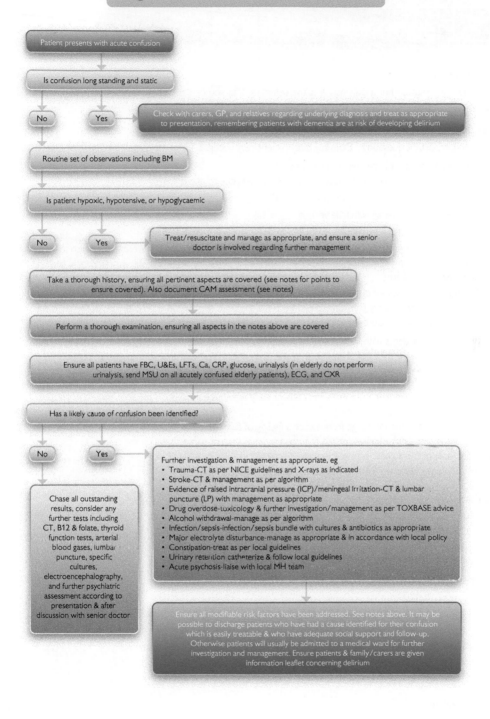

Patient presents with acute confusion

Is confusion long standing and static

No

Yes → Check with carers, GP, and relatives regarding underlying diagnosis and treat as appropriate to presentation, remembering patients with dementia are at risk of developing delirium

Routine set of observations including BM

Is patient hypoxic, hypotensive, or hypoglycaemic

No

Yes → Treat/resuscitate and manage as appropriate, and ensure a senior doctor is involved regarding further management

Take a thorough history, ensuring all pertinent aspects are covered (see notes for points to ensure covered). Also document CAM assessment (see notes)

Perform a thorough examination, ensuring all aspects in the notes above are covered

Ensure all patients have FBC, U&Es, LFTs, Ca, CRP, glucose, urinalysis (in elderly do not perform urinalysis, send MSU on all acutely confused elderly patients), ECG, and CXR

Has a likely cause of confusion been identified?

No

Yes → Further investigation & management as appropriate, eg
- Trauma-CT as per NICE guidelines and X-rays as indicated
- Stroke-CT & management as per algorithm
- Evidence of raised intracranial pressure (ICP)/meningeal irritation-CT & lumbar puncture (LP) with management as appropriate
- Drug overdose-toxicology & further investigation/management as per TOXBASE advice
- Alcohol withdrawal-manage as per algorithm
- Infection/sepsis-infection/sepsis bundle with cultures & antibiotics as appropriate
- Major electrolyte disturbance-manage as appropriate & in accordance with local policy
- Constipation-treat as per local guidelines
- Urinary retention-catheterize & follow local guidelines
- Acute psychosis-liaise with local MH team

Chase all outstanding results, consider any further tests including CT, B12 & folate, thyroid function tests, arterial blood gases, lumbar puncture, specific cultures, electroencephalography, and further psychiatric assessment according to presentation & after discussion with senior doctor

Ensure all modifiable risk factors have been addressed. See notes above. It may be possible to discharge patients who have had a cause identified for their confusion which is easily treatable & who have adequate social support and follow-up. Otherwise patients will usually be admitted to a medical ward for further investigation and management. Ensure patients & family/carers are given information leaflet concerning delirium

5. Dizziness and vertigo

Definition

Vertigo is a symptom not a diagnosis. It is the sensation that you or the environment around you is moving or spinning in the absence of any physical movement.

Types

The first important question is: 'Does my dizzy patient have vertigo?' There are three basic forms of dizziness:

- Presyncope or light-headedness—see Chapter 8
- Unsteadiness or the feeling of imbalance or unsteadiness due to ataxia
- Vertigo

This chapter deals primarily with true vertigo.

The second important question is: 'Is the vertigo central or peripheral in origin?'

- Peripheral vertigo is caused by altered activity in the balance organs of the inner ear, from which the brain detects a sensation of movement (e.g. benign paroxysmal positional vertigo, vestibular neuronitis, labyrinthitis, and Ménière's disease)
- Central vertigo is caused by disturbance of the visual–vestibular interaction centres in the brainstem and cerebellum, or to sensory pathways to and from the thalamus (e.g. migraine, stroke, TIA, posterior fossa tumour, and multiple sclerosis)

Nystagmus in patients with vertigo is usually rotatory. If it is sustained, this is suggestive of a central cause; if it fatigues, it is suggestive of a peripheral cause. If the nystagmus is vertical (rare), this suggests a central cause.

Salient points in the history

- Duration, onset, frequency, severity, and details of any previous episodes
- Aggravating/precipitating factors
- Hearing loss, tinnitus, discharge from ear, or a feeling of fullness
- Headache, visual disturbance, speech disturbance, weakness, or paraesthesia
- Nausea, vomiting, sweating, or palpitations
- Recent upper respiratory tract infection or ear infection
- Recent head injury/direct trauma to the ear
- Cardiovascular risk factors
- Past medical history including any previous cancers
- Medications taken
- Alcohol intake and illicit drug use
- Family history of Ménière's disease

Salient areas for examination

- Facial asymmetry
- Ears including tympanic membrane and hearing
- Central nervous and cerebellar function
- Eyes including movements, examining for nystagmus, fields, and ophthalmoscopy
- Neurological examination of limbs
- Cardiovascular examination
- Gait
- Hallpike's test
- Consider Romberg's test

Further reading

NICE Clinical Knowledge Summaries Vertigo April 2010.

National Institute for Health and Care Excellence. Clinical Knowledge Summary. Vertigo: prevention. https://cks.nice.org.uk/topics/vertigo/, 2020.

Algorithm for dizziness and vertigo

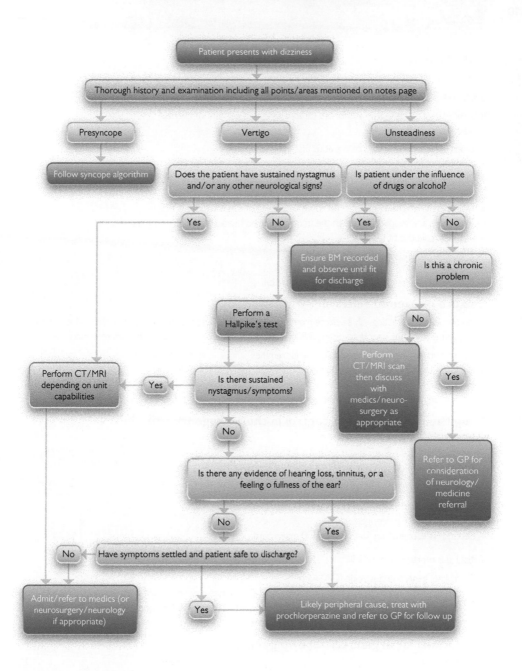

6. Fits/seizures

Introduction

This chapter is concerned with both primary and secondary generalized seizures.

Salient points in the history

It is imperative to make every effort to capture a witness account of events.
  Salient points include:

- Does patient have history of previous fits?
- Condition of patient prior to fit, unwell in any way/trauma prior to fit
- Did the patient have any prodrome or warning of the fit?
- Was there any trigger for the fit?
- Was there any focal element prior to development of the tonic clonic fit?
- Was there any headache prior to the fit or prolonged headache after?
- How long did the fit last?
- Was any medication given to terminate the fit?
- Was there any urinary incontinence?
- Was there any tongue biting or buccal mucosa biting?

Seizure or pseudo seizure?

It can be difficult to distinguish a seizure from a pseudo seizure, and the default position should be to treat a possible seizure if you are unable to distinguish the two. Some possible clues to aid the differentiation are:

- Uncoordinated failing movements of the extremities
- Evidence of consciousness, such as talking during an apparent tonic clonic fit
- Babinski sign is absent in a pseudo seizure
- Tongue biting does not occur (although patients have been known to bite the mucosa of the cheek)

Drug therapy for seizure control in the emergency situation

First-line: benzodiazepine can be

- Diazepam 10–20 mg per rectum
- Midazolam 10 mg buccal
- Lorazepam 4 mg IV

This can be repeated after 10–15 minutes if seizure continues.
  If seizure is more prolonged:

- Second- line: phenytoin 15 mg/kg at 100 mg/minute

If seizure is more prolonged still:

- Third-line: general anaesthetic (GA) with
  - Propofol 1–2 mg/kg bolus, then titrate to effect (2–10 mg/kg/hour)
  - Midazolam 0.1–0.2 mg/kg bolus, then titrate to effect (0.05–0.5 mg/kg/hour)
  - Thiopentone 3–5 mg/kg bolus, then titrate to effect (3–5 mg/kg/hour)

Indications for urgent CT following seizure

- Post head injury
- Associated sudden onset or persistent headache
- Associated focal neuro deficit (Todd's paresis)
- Patient has history of (h/o) cancer, HIV, or stroke
- Associated fever
- Focal onset
- Patient is anticoagulated
- Patient will not be compliant with follow-up

Further reading

NICE guidelines CG137 The Epilepsies: the diagnosis and management of the epilepsies in adults and children in primary and secondary care January 2012

National Institute for Health and Care Excellence. NICE Guideline 217. Epilepsies in children, young people and adults. www.nice.org.uk/guidance/ng217, 2022.

Algorithm for fits/seizures

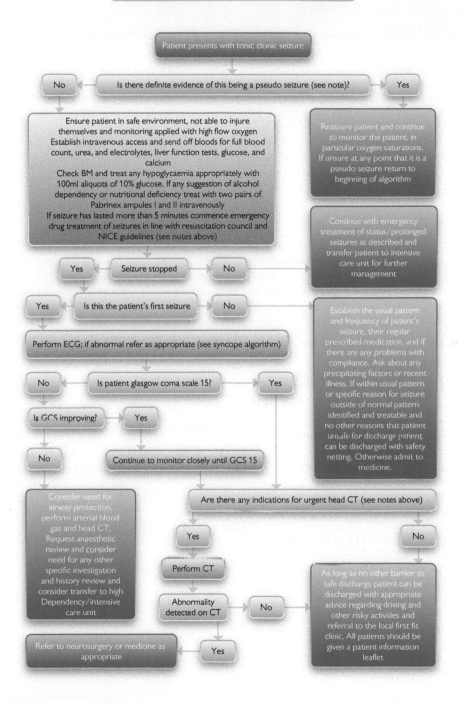

Patient presents with tonic clonic seizure

No ← Is there definite evidence of this being a pseudo seizure (see note)? → Yes

Ensure patient in safe environment, not able to injure themselves and monitoring applied with high flow oxygen
Establish intravenous access and send off bloods for full blood count, urea, and electrolytes, liver function tests, glucose, and calcium
Check BM and treat any hypoglycaemia appropriately with 100ml aliquots of 10% glucose. If any suggestion of alcohol dependency or nutritional deficiency treat with two pairs of Pabrinex ampules I and II intravenously
If seizure has lasted more than 5 minutes commence emergency drug treatment of seizures in line with resuscitation council and NICE guidelines (see notes above)

Reassure patient and continue to monitor the patient, in particular oxygen saturations. If unsure at any point that it is a pseudo seizure return to beginning of algorithm

Yes ← Seizure stopped → No

Continue with emergency treatment of status/prolonged seizures as described and transfer patient to intensive care unit for further management

Yes ← Is this the patient's first seizure → No

Establish the usual pattern and frequency of patient's seizure, their regular prescribed medication, and if there are any problems with compliance. Ask about any precipitating factors or recent illness. If within usual pattern or specific reason for seizure outside of normal pattern identified and treatable and no other reasons that patient unsafe for discharge patient can be discharged with safety netting. Otherwise admit to medicine.

Perform ECG; if abnormal refer as appropriate (see syncope algorithm)

No ← Is patient glasgow coma scale 15? → Yes

Is GCS improving? → Yes

No

Continue to monitor closely until GCS 15

Consider need for airway protection, perform arterial blood gas and head CT. Request anaesthetic review and consider need for any other specific investigation and history review and consider transfer to high Dependency/intensive care unit

Are there any indications for urgent head CT (see notes above)

Yes

No

Perform CT

As long as no other barrier to safe discharge patient can be discharged with appropriate advice regarding driving and other risky activities and referral to the local first fit clinic. All patients should be given a patient information leaflet

Abnormality detected on CT → No

Refer to neurosurgery or medicine as appropriate ← Yes

7. Headache

Primary headache

Primary headaches are classified according to the symptoms experienced; their diagnosis is reliant upon recognition of a clinical pattern. Most are episodic, but some, especially tension headache and sometimes migraine, can become chronic. Primary headaches can be positively diagnosed and do not require imaging for reassurance purposes alone. In the Emergency Department, primary headache should be a diagnosis of exclusion. As the diagnosis of primary headache is based on recurrence, one should be wary of diagnosing primary headache on a first presentation to the Emergency Department. No primary headache is caused by demonstrable organic disease or structural neurologic abnormality. Most common types of primary headache include:

- Migraine
- Tension-type
- Cluster and other trigeminal autonomic cephalagias

Secondary headache

Secondary headaches are classified according to their aetiology. They are usually of recent onset and associated with abnormalities on clinical examination. The diagnosis is confirmed by laboratory testing or imaging. The recognition of secondary headaches is vital, as treatment of the underlying cause will usually eradicate the headache, and more importantly some of the underlying conditions are life threatening. Although some important differential diagnoses are mentioned in the algorithm, these are by no means an exhaustive list.

Salient points in the history

- Impaired conscious level
- New-onset cognitive dysfunction (delirium)
- Fever
- Photophobia, neck stiffness
- New neurological deficit
- Sudden onset, maximal within 5 minutes
- Severity, worsening
- Recent (within 3 months) head trauma
- Change in personality
- Triggered by cough, valsalva, or sneeze
- Triggered by exercise
- Orthostatic headache (triggered by changes in posture)
- Symptoms suggestive of giant cell arteritis
- Symptoms and signs of acute narrow-angle glaucoma
- Substantial change in characteristic of patient's headache
- Compromised immunity
- Age <20 years and a history of malignancy
- History of malignancy known to metastasize to brain
- Vomiting without obvious cause
- Early morning headache
- New-onset daily headache (without other symptoms) lasting at least 1 month

Further reading

Kriegler JS. Headache. Cleveland Clinic. https://www.clevelandclinicmeded.com/medicalpubs/diseasemanagement/neurol ogy/headache-syndromes/, 2021.

National Institute for Health and Care Excellence. Clinical Guideline 150. Headaches in over 12s: diagnosis and management. www.nice.org.uk/guidance/cg150, 2021.

Shah SM, Kelly KM (Eds). Emergency Neurology. Cambridge: Cambridge University Press, 1999.

Algorithm for headache

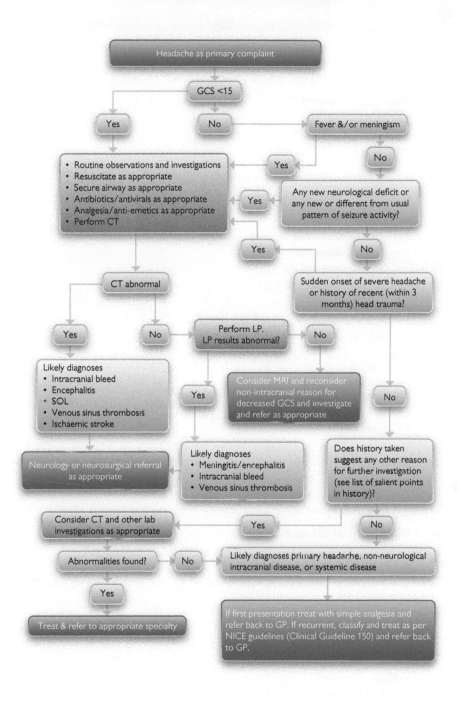

Headache as primary complaint

GCS <15

Yes

No → Fever &/or meningism

- Routine observations and investigations
- Resuscitate as appropriate
- Secure airway as appropriate
- Antibiotics/antivirals as appropriate
- Analgesia/anti-emetics as appropriate
- Perform CT

Yes

No

Yes → Any new neurological deficit or any new or different from usual pattern of seizure activity?

Yes

No

CT abnormal

Sudden onset of severe headache or history of recent (within 3 months) head trauma?

Yes

No

Perform LP. LP results abnormal?

No

Yes

Likely diagnoses
- Intracranial bleed
- Encephalitis
- SOL
- Venous sinus thrombosis
- Ischaemic stroke

Yes

Consider MRI and reconsider non-intracranial reason for decreased GCS and investigate and refer as appropriate

No

Neurology or neurosurgical referral as appropriate

Likely diagnoses
- Meningitis/encephalitis
- Intracranial bleed
- Venous sinus thrombosis

Does history taken suggest any other reason for further investigation (see list of salient points in history)?

Consider CT and other lab investigations as appropriate

Yes

No

Abnormalities found?

No → Likely diagnoses primary headache, non-neurological intracranial disease, or systemic disease

Yes

Treat & refer to appropriate specialty

If first presentation treat with simple analgesia and refer back to GP. If recurrent, classify and treat as per NICE guidelines (Clinical Guideline 150) and refer back to GP.

8. Syncope and pre-syncope

Definition
Syncope is the spontaneous, transient loss of consciousness with complete recovery.

Salient points in the history
- Circumstances of event
- Posture immediately before loss of consciousness
- Prodromal symptoms
- Appearance: eyes open/shut, colour of patient
- Presence/absence of movement during event (and duration)
- Tongue biting (side or tip of tongue)
- Injury occurring during event (site and severity)
- Duration of event
- **Presence/absence of confusion during recovery (red flag)**
- **Weakness down one side during recovery (red flag)**
- **Family history of sudden death (red flag)**

Abnormalities to look for on ECG
- Inappropriate, persistent bradycardia
- Any ventricular arrhythmia (including ventricular ectopics)
- Long QT (cQT >450 ms) and short QT (cQT <350 ms)
- Brugada syndrome
- Ventricular pre-excitation
- Left or right ventricular hypertrophy
- Abnormal T wave inversion
- Pathological Q waves
- Atrial arrhythmias (sustained)
- Paced rhythm

Features suggestive of simple vasovagal syncope (the three Ps)
- Posture: prolonged standing or similar episodes that have been prevented by lying down
- Provoking factors (such as pain or medical procedure)
- Prodromal symptoms (e.g. sweating or feeling warm/hot)

Features suggestive of seizure activity
- Bitten tongue
- Head or eyes turning to one side during transient loss of consciousness
- No memory of abnormal behaviour that was witnessed before, during, or after the transient loss of consciousness by someone else
- Unusual posturing
- Prolonged limb jerking (note that brief seizure-like activity can often occur during uncomplicated vasovagals)
- Confusion following the event
- Prodromal déjà vu or jamais vu

Further reading
Del Rosso A, Ungar A, Maggi R, et al. Clinical predictors of cardiac syncope at initial evaluation in patients referred urgently to a general hospital: the EGSYS Score. Heart 2008;94(12):1620–1626.

National Institute for Health and Care Excellence. Clinical Guideline 109. Transient loss of consciousness ('blackouts') in over 16s. www.nice.org.uk/guidance/cg109, 2014.

Algorithm for syncope and pre-syncope

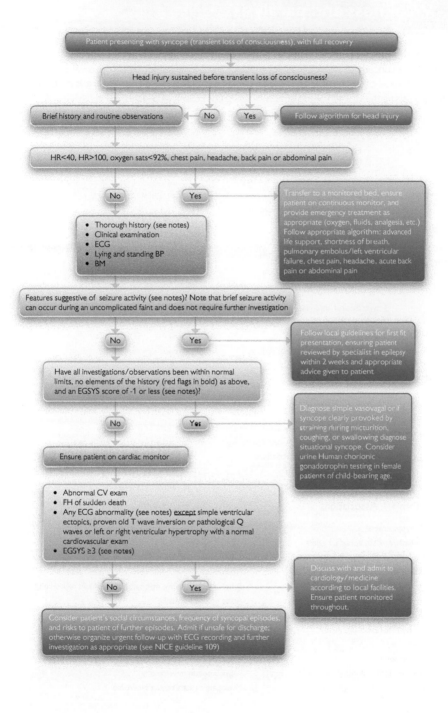

Patient presenting with syncope (transient loss of consciousness), with full recovery

Head injury sustained before transient loss of consciousness?

Brief history and routine observations ← No | Yes → Follow algorithm for head injury

HR<40, HR>100, oxygen sats<92%, chest pain, headache, back pain or abdominal pain

No | Yes

Yes → Transfer to a monitored bed, ensure patient on continuous monitor, and provide emergency treatment as appropriate (oxygen, fluids, analgesia, etc.) Follow appropriate algorithm: advanced life support, shortness of breath, pulmonary embolus/left ventricular failure, chest pain, headache, acute back pain or abdominal pain

No:
- Thorough history (see notes)
- Clinical examination
- ECG
- Lying and standing BP
- BM

Features suggestive of seizure activity (see notes)? Note that brief seizure activity can occur during an uncomplicated faint and does not require further investigation

No | Yes

Yes → Follow local guidelines for first fit presentation, ensuring patient reviewed by specialist in epilepsy within 2 weeks and appropriate advice given to patient

No: Have all investigations/observations been within normal limits, no elements of the history (red flags in bold) as above, and an EGSYS score of -1 or less (see notes)?

No | Yes

Yes → Diagnose simple vasovagal or if syncope clearly provoked by straining during micturition, coughing, or swallowing diagnose situational syncope. Consider urine Human chorionic gonadotrophin testing in female patients of child-bearing age

No: Ensure patient on cardiac monitor

- Abnormal CV exam
- FH of sudden death
- Any ECG abnormality (see notes) except simple ventricular ectopics, proven old T wave inversion or pathological Q waves or left or right ventricular hypertrophy with a normal cardiovascular exam
- EGSYS ≥3 (see notes)

No | Yes

Yes → Discuss with and admit to cardiology/medicine according to local facilities. Ensure patient monitored throughout.

No: Consider patient's social circumstances, frequency of syncopal episodes, and risks to patient of further episodes. Admit if unsafe for discharge; otherwise organize urgent follow-up with ECG recording and further investigation as appropriate (see NICE guideline 109)

Algorithms for Emergency Medicine

9. Weakness and paralysis

Introduction

The algorithm is concerned only with patients with true muscle weakness; it does not cover patients presenting with general malaise or fatigue. In order to assess a patient for true muscle weakness it is necessary to have a system for assessing the strength of the various muscle groups examined (Table 5.4).

Table 5.4 Medical Research Council grading system for muscle weakness

0	No muscle contraction
1	Flicker or trace of muscle contraction
2	Limb or joint movement possible only with gravity eliminated
3	Limb or joint movement against gravity only
4	Power decreased but limb or joint movement possible against resistance
5	Normal power against resistance

Establishing patterns

The second step in the assessment of patients with weakness is establishing the pattern of weakness. This may be in terms of site, onset, or signs (Table 5.5).

Table 5.5 Pattern of signs

Lower motor neurone syndrome	Upper motor neurone syndrome
Flaccid paralysis	Spastic paralysis
Areflexia	Hyperreflexia
Later—muscle wasting and fasciculation	Positive Babinski sign

Salient points in the history

The following tables list the most important aspects of the history to be elicited (Table 5.6) and (Table 5.7).

Table 5.6 Distribution

Proximal	Muscular dystrophies, myopathies, neuromuscular junction disorders
Distal	Polyneuropathies
Generalized	Myopathies
Localized	Radiculopathy, plexopathy, peripheral mononeuropathy

Table 5.7 Associations

Pain, tenderness	Myopathy
Aphasia, agnosia, apraxia, neglect	Cortical stroke
Diplopia	Neuromuscular junction disorder, brainstem process
Bulbar symptoms	Neuromuscular junction disorder, brainstem process
Alcoholism	Peripheral neuropathy, myopathy, entrapment neuropathy
Drug abuse (cocaine, amphetamines)	Acute myopathy, stroke
Vomiting/diarrhoea, diuretic use	Electrolyte-induced myopathy
Heavy metal exposure (lead)	Polyneuropathy or mononeuropathy
Rash	Dermatomyositis
Tick exposure	Tick paralysis
Recent infective illness (*Campylobacter*, viral)	Polyneuropathy, myelopathy
Bladder or bowel symptoms	Myelopathy, cauda equina syndrome

Further reading

Asimos AW. Evaluation of the adult with acute weakness in the Emergency Department. https://www.uptodate.com/contents/evaluation-of-the-adult-with-acute-weakness-in-the-emergency-department?search=evaluation-of-the-adult-with-acute-weakness-in-the-emergency-department, 2021.

Emergency Medicine Practice. Weakness: a systematic approach to acute non-traumatic neurological and neuromuscular causes. Andrew W Asimos, MD. December 2002 volume 4 number 12.

Algorithm for weakness and paralysis

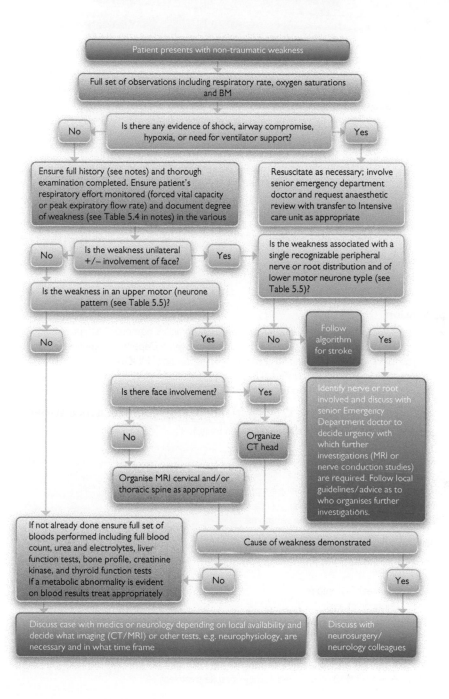

Patient presents with non-traumatic weakness

Full set of observations including respiratory rate, oxygen saturations and BM

No ← Is there any evidence of shock, airway compromise, hypoxia, or need for ventilator support? → Yes

Ensure full history (see notes) and thorough examination completed. Ensure patient's respiratory effort monitored (forced vital capacity or peak expiratory flow rate) and document degree of weakness (see Table 5.4 in notes) in the various

Resuscitate as necessary; involve senior emergency department doctor and request anaesthetic review with transfer to Intensive care unit as appropriate

No ← Is the weakness unilateral +/− involvement of face? → Yes → Is the weakness associated with a single recognizable peripheral nerve or root distribution and of lower motor neurone typle (see Table 5.5)?

Is the weakness in an upper motor (neurone pattern (see Table 5.5)?

No

Yes

No → Follow algorithm for stroke ← Yes

Is there face involvement? → Yes

No

Organize CT head

Identify nerve or root involved and discuss with senior Emergency Department doctor to decide urgency with which further investigations (MRI or nerve conduction studies) are required. Follow local guidelines/advice as to who organises further investigations.

Organise MRI cervical and/or thoracic spine as appropriate

If not already done ensure full set of bloods performed including full blood count, urea and electrolytes, liver function tests, bone profile, creatinine kinase, and thyroid function tests
If a metabolic abnormality is evident on blood results treat appropriately

Cause of weakness demonstrated

No

Yes

Discuss case with medics or neurology depending on local availability and decide what imaging (CT/MRI) or other tests, e.g. neurophysiology, are necessary and in what time frame

Discuss with neurosurgery/ neurology colleagues

10. Stroke

Introduction

The potentially difficult but vital first step is to identify the person presenting with an acute stroke.

There are various tools available to aid this process, including the well-publicized Face Arm Speech Test (FAST) screen often used by the emergency services. The ROSIER (recognition of stroke in the emergency room) scale is more suitable for hospital use, with a score of >0 indicating that the diagnosis of stroke is likely (Table 5.8).

Table 5.8 ROSIER scale

ROSIER scale	Score for Yes	Score for No
Has there been LOC/syncope	−1	0
Has there been seizure activity	−1	0
Has there been new **acute** onset (including on wakening from sleep) of:		
Asymmetric facial weakness	+1	0
Asymmetric arm weakness	+1	0
Asymmetric leg weakness	+1	0
Speech disturbance	+1	0
Visual field deficit	+1	0

Application

There is sometimes confusion between a TIA and stroke. For practical purposes, if symptoms and signs have not completely resolved by the time the patient is seen in the Emergency Department, continue down the stroke algorithm. This algorithm deals with patients presenting with stroke, not TIA. If the patient meets the requirements for thrombolysis he/she should be transferred to the nearest hospital with these facilities as soon as possible at the direction of the stroke physician at that hospital.

Indications for immediate CT in patients presenting with acute stroke

- Indications for thrombolysis or early anticoagulation treatment
- On anticoagulation treatment
- A known bleeding tendency
- Decreased GCS (<13)
- Unexplained progressive or fluctuating symptoms
- Papilloedema, neck stiffness, or fever
- Severe headache at onset of stroke symptoms

Exclusions for thrombolysis

- ≥4 hours since onset
- GCS ≤8
- Seizure since onset of symptoms
- Previously reliant on others
- Ischaemic stroke within last 6 weeks
- Haemorrhagic stroke in the past
- GI or genitourinary bleed or major surgery in last 3 weeks
- On warfarin and INR >1.7, or on new anticoagulant
- Blood pressure >185/110 on repeated readings, despite treatment

Further reading

NICE CG 68 Stroke: Diagnosis and initial management of acute stroke and transient ischaemic attack July 2008
National Institute for Health and Care Excellence. NICE Guideline 128. Stroke and transient ischaemic attack in over 16s: diagnosis and initial management. 128, 2022.
Guidance and Protocol on Diagnosis and Initial Management of Stroke/Transient Ischaemic Attack by the Accident and Emergency, On-Call Acute Medicine and Back of House Teams Northumbria Healthcare Trust Mark Sudlow June 2013

Algorithm for stroke

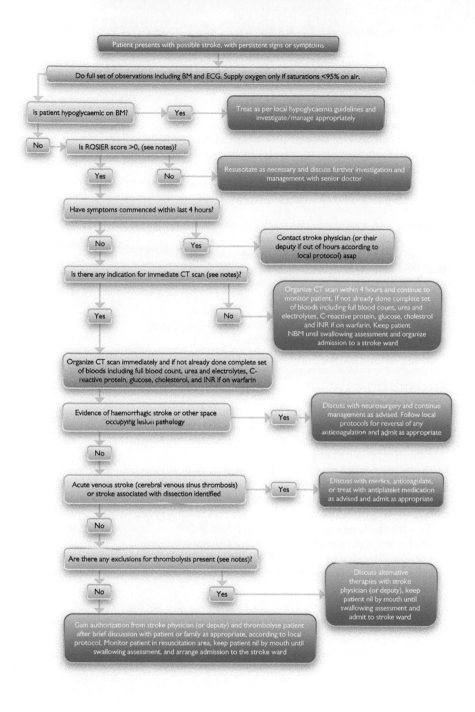

Patient presents with possible stroke, with persistent signs or symptoms

Do full set of observations including BM and ECG. Supply oxygen only if saturations <95% on air.

Is patient hypoglycaemic on BM? → **Yes** → Treat as per local hypoglycaemia guidelines and investigate/manage appropriately

No

Is ROSIER score >0, (see notes)?

Yes | **No** → Resuscitate as necessary and discuss further investigation and management with senior doctor

Have symptoms commenced within last 4 hours?

No | **Yes** → Contact stroke physician (or their deputy if out of hours according to local protocol) asap

Is there any indication for immediate CT scan (see notes)?

Yes | **No** → Organize CT scan within 4 hours and continue to monitor patient. If not already done complete set of bloods including full blood count, urea and electrolytes, C-reactive protein, glucose, cholestrol and INR if on warfarin. Keep patient NBM until swallowing assessment and organize admission to a stroke ward

Organize CT scan immediately and if not already done complete set of bloods including full blood count, urea and electrolytes, C-reactive protein, glucose, cholesterol, and INR if on warfarin

Evidence of haemorrhagic stroke or other space occupying lesion pathology → **Yes** → Discuss with neurosurgery and continue management as advised. Follow local protocols for reversal of any anticoagulation and admit as appropriate

No

Acute venous stroke (cerebral venous sinus thrombosis) or stroke associated with dissection identified → **Yes** → Discuss with medics, anticoagulate, or treat with antiplatelet medication as advised and admit as appropriate

No

Are there any exclusions for thrombolysis present (see notes)?

No | **Yes** → Discuss alternative therapies with stroke physician (or deputy), keep patient nil by mouth until swallowing assessment and admit to stroke ward

Gain authorization from stroke physician (or deputy) and thrombolyse patient after brief discussion with patient or family as appropriate, according to local protocol. Monitor patient in resuscitation area, keep patient nil by mouth until swallowing assessment, and arrange admission to the stroke ward

11. Subarachnoid haemorrhage

Introduction

- Acute headache is the chief complaint in as many as 5% of patients visiting the Emergency Department
- UK incidence of 8–12 per 100,000 per year
- Three- to seven-fold increased risk in first-degree relatives
- Mortality rate up to 40% in first week; 50% in first 6 months
  - More than 1/3 of survivors have major neurological deficits
- Sudden onset of severe headache ('thunderclap') and no history of head trauma requires a full neurologic evaluation and head CT scan
  - Imaging can be negative in up to 15% of cases, so an LP is often required

Pathology

- Acute bleed into subarachnoid space; this may also be an intracerebral component
  - 85%: aneurysmal
  - 10%: no known vascular cause (perimesencephalic)
  - 5%: arteriovenous malformations (AVMs), tumours, etc.
- 10–40% of patients get sentinel bleeds (headaches)

Presentation

- Acute onset (severe) headache (maximal instantly or within a few minutes)
  - 20% of cases of SAH present with headache alone
- Transient or persisting loss of consciousness
- Seizures (roughly 7%) or focal neurological signs
- Vomiting, hypertension, and tachycardia

Management

- Manage patient 30° head-up if possible
- Laryngoscopy can cause severe hypertension and may precipitate rebleeding
- CT brain should be performed early
  - 93–98% sensitivity on first day, falling to 85% on day 3
  - If negative, LP must be performed (unless contraindicated)
  - Xanthochromia only detected 6–12 hours after symptom onset (used to differentiate from traumatic LP)
- PO nimodipine 60 mg 4-hourly (if hypotension, reduce dose to 30 mg or omit)
  - Aim for <160 mmHg to reduce hypertension, but maintain CPP
- Tight control of temperature, glucose, and fluid balance for better outcomes
- Rebleeding: up to 20% in first 24 hours and 40% in first month if left untreated
  - Definitive treatment is to occlude the aneurysm by endovascular 'coiling', or sometimes neurosurgical 'clipping'

Further reading

Hankey GJ, Nelson MR. Subarachnoid haemorrhage. *BMJ* 2009;339:b2874.

Steiner T, Juvela S, Unterberg A, et al. European Stroke Organization guidelines for the management of intracranial aneurysms and subarachnoid haemorrhage. *Cerebrovasc Dis* 2013;35:93–112.

Van Gjin J, Rinkel GJ. Subarachnoid haemorrhage: diagnosis, causes and management. *Brain* 2001;124(Pt2):249–278.

Algorithm for subarachnoid haemorrhage

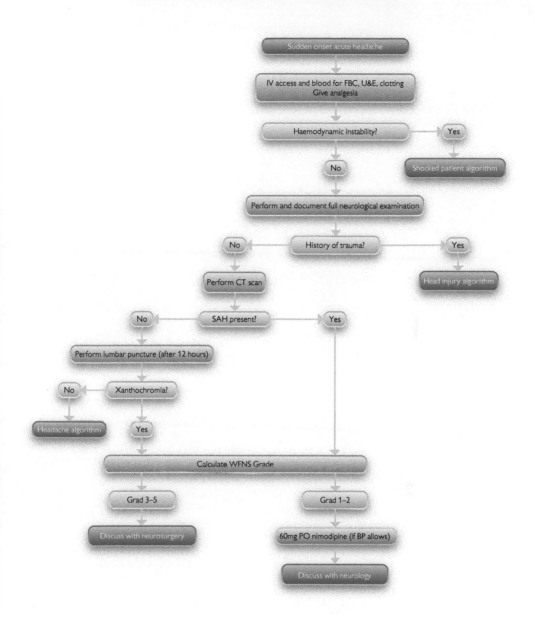

Sudden onset acute headache

IV access and blood for FBC, U&E, clotting
Give analgesia

Haemodynamic instability? — Yes → Shocked patient algorithm

No

Perform and document full neurological examination

No ← History of trauma? → Yes → Head injury algorithm

Perform CT scan

No ← SAH present? → Yes

Perform lumbar puncture (after 12 hours)

No ← Xanthochromia?

Headache algorithm

Yes

Calculate WFNS Grade

Grad 3–5 | Grad 1–2

Discuss with neurosurgery | 60mg PO nimodipine (if BP allows)

Discuss with neurology

SECTION 6

Trauma

1. Primary survey

Assessment

In trauma, it is essential to undertake a rapid assessment of patients as they arrive to the Emergency Department. This follows ABCDE assessment. In an ideal situation, the trauma team leader should stand at the foot end of the bed and direct the team. If enough clinicians are present, each team member should assess and treat A, B, and C simultaneously (the so-called *horizontal* approach). If there are few clinicians present, the *vertical* approach should be adopted (assess A, *then* B, *then* C).

Identification and treatment

It is important to identify and treat problems as you find them during the primary survey (Table 6.1).

Table 6.1 Life threatening conditions that must be addressed during primary survey

Problem	Identification/recognition	Treatment
Airway obstruction	Stridor Facial burns See-saw breathing	Airway opening manoeuvres (jaw thrust as trauma—do not do chin lift/head tilt) Airway adjuncts (oropharyngeal airway) Intubation if simple manoeuvres/adjuncts failing Consider needle or surgical cricothyroidotomy if needed
Tension PTX	Distended neck veins (may be absent in hypovolaemia) High RR and low O_2 saturation Decreased AE and hyper-resonant PN on side of PTX Cardiovascular collapse Deviated trachea away from PTX (late sign) May have surgical emphysema	Needle thoracocentesis in fifth intercostal space, mid axillary line on the same side off the PTX Definitive treatment is ICD
Open PTX	Bubbling wound on thoracic cage Surgical emphysema	Dressing taped on three sides Will need urgent ICD
Massive HTX	Decreased AE on same side as HTX Dull PN on same side as HTX High RR and low O_2 saturation Cardiovascular collapse	Bilateral IV access Urgent ICD Consider discussion with thoracic surgeon (if >1500 mL immediately drained or persistent blood loss over the next few hours)
Flail chest	Paradoxical movement during breathing Surgical emphysema Palpable fractured ribs	Analgesia Consider intercostal nerve blocks Consider intubation
Cardiac tamponade	Hypotension Muffled heart sounds Raised JVP (may be absent in hypovolaemia) Use diagnostic ultrasound	Needs immediate consideration for resuscitative thoracotomy

Assessment

In cases of major trauma, rapid transfer of the patient to CT is imperative to identify major injuries, even in some cases of haemodynamic instability; the resuscitation team should be prepared to accompany the patient to CT with ongoing resuscitation. The decision when to transfer the patient to CT or straight to theatre is a team decision.

Adjuncts to primary survey

Consider, ECG monitoring, urinary catheter and gastric catheter.

Radiology

Consider, CXR and pelvis X-ray in resus, USS (extended focused assessment with sonography (eFAST)), Rapid transfer to CT for whole-body CT and interventional radiology.

Further reading

American College of Surgeons. Committee on Trauma. Advanced trauma life support: Student course manual, 10th edn. Chicago, IL: American College of Surgeons, 2018.

Algorithm for primary survey

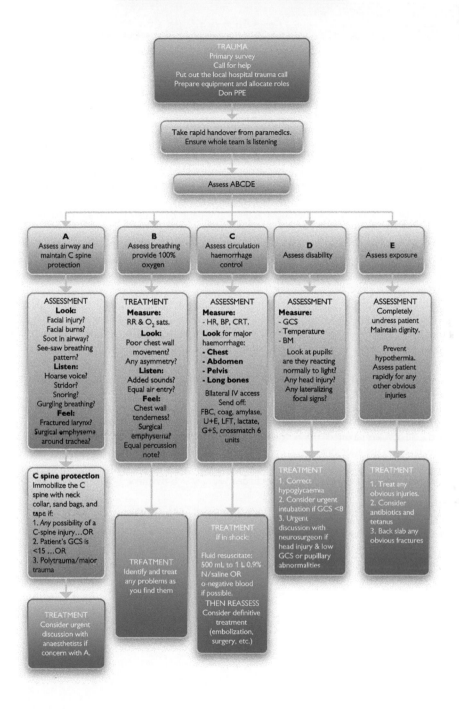

TRAUMA
Primary survey
Call for help
Put out the local hospital trauma call
Prepare equipment and allocate roles
Don PPE

Take rapid handover from paramedics.
Ensure whole team is listening

Assess ABCDE

A
Assess airway and maintain C spine protection

B
Assess breathing provide 100% oxygen

C
Assess circulation haemorrhage control

D
Assess disability

E
Assess exposure

ASSESSMENT
Look:
Facial injury?
Facial burns?
Soot in airway?
See-saw breathing pattern?
Listen:
Hoarse voice?
Stridor?
Snoring?
Gurgling breathing?
Feel:
Fractured larynx?
Surgical emphysema around trachea?

TREATMENT
Measure:
RR & O$_2$ sats.
Look:
Poor chest wall movement?
Any asymmetry?
Listen:
Added sounds?
Equal air entry?
Feel:
Chest wall tenderness?
Surgical emphysema?
Equal percussion note?

ASSESSMENT
Measure:
- HR, BP, CRT.
Look for major haemorrhage:
- **Chest**
- **Abdomen**
- **Pelvis**
- **Long bones**
Bilateral IV access
Send off:
FBC, coag, amylase, U+E, LFT, lactate, G+S, crossmatch 6 units

ASSESSMENT
Measure:
- GCS
- Temperature
- BM
Look at pupils:
are they reacting normally to light?
Any head injury?
Any lateralizing focal signs?

ASSESSMENT
Completely undress patient
Maintain dignity.

Prevent hypothermia.
Assess patient rapidly for any other obvious injuries

C spine protection
Immobilize the C spine with neck collar, sand bags, and tape if:
1. *Any* possibility of a C-spine injury…OR
2. Patient's GCS is <15 …OR
3. Polytrauma/major trauma

TREATMENT
1. Correct hypoglycaemia
2. Consider urgent intubation if GCS <8
3. Urgent discussion with neurosurgeon if head injury & low GCS or pupillary abnormalities

TREATMENT
1. Treat any obvious injuries.
2. Consider antibiotics and tetanus
3. Back slab any obvious fractures

TREATMENT
Identify and treat any problems as you find them

TREATMENT
If in shock:
Fluid resuscitate: 500 mL to 1 L 0.9% N/saline OR o-negative blood if possible.
THEN REASSESS
Consider definitive treatment (embolization, surgery, etc.)

TREATMENT
Consider urgent discussion with anaesthetists if concern with A.

2. Secondary survey

Introduction

The secondary survey is a head to toe assessment of the patient for other injuries not found in the primary survey. It is important to ensure the primary survey and any intervention that is required is completed prior to commencing the secondary survey. If at any point during the assessment there is deterioration or change in clinical status, go back to the primary survey and reassess.

Important points to consider

- The AMPLE history will allow you to gather important information to aid your management. Comorbidities will help you to understand physiological response to trauma and the mechanism of injury will help with injury prediction
- It is important to assess the eyes thoroughly, as developing periorbital swelling can often inhibit this assessment later. Eye examination should include pupillary size and reaction, visual acuity, visual fields, ocular movements, fundoscopy, and inspection for hyphema and penetrating globe injury
- Whilst assessing for CSF leakage, it is important to consider other signs of a base of skull fracture. These include post-auricular bruising (Battle's sign), panda eyes (bruising around the eyes), bleeding from the ears, haemotympanum, and cranial nerve palsy
- Be aware of facial instability when assessing for facial fractures. When assessing for maxillary movement there is a risk of provoking haemorrhage, which in turn could affect the patient's airway patency
- If the patient is unconscious, it will be difficult to assess the more subjective aspects of the secondary survey. This is particularly true when assessing for any bony and abdominal tenderness or neurological status of a limb. It is important to consider this when assessing these areas, and therefore injury cannot be ruled out based on the lack of tenderness in an unconscious patient. Equally, the patient cannot have their cervical spine cleared clinically until they are conscious
- Ensure the whole of the patient is visualised to ensure missing posterior injuries. If the patient is immobilised, they must be log rolled to ensure spinal immobilisation remains intact when assessing for posterior injuries
- You should not insert a catheter prior to assessing for urethral injury, as outlined in the genito-urinary and perineum box in the algorithm
- Limb injuries that aren't neurovascularly intact should not take priority over the primary survey. However, once the patient has stabilised it is important to deal with any limb-threatening injuries early

Further reading

American College of Surgeons. Committee on Trauma. Advanced trauma life support: Student course manual, 10th edn. Chicago, IL: American College of Surgeons, 2018.

Algorithm for secondary survey

Stable trauma patient post primary survey

Take an AMPLE history.
- Allergies
- Medications
- Past medical history
- Last meal
- Events leading to injury

Assess the head and face for:
- Lacerations and bruising
- Feel for any bony tenderness and depressions suggestive of fractures
- Full eye examination
- Assess ears for presence of CSF leak, haemotympanum, and active bleeding
- Assess nose for deformity, active bleeding, septal haematoma, and CSF leak
- Full oral inspection for mucosal, tongue, palate, and dental injury

Assess the neck for:
- Cervical spine tenderness
- Subcutaneous emphysema
- Tracheal deviation
- Carotid artery bruit and neck vein distention
- Bruising and swelling
- Lacerations and penetrating injuries
- Soft tissue tenderness
- Laryngeal tenderness and crepitus

Assess the chest for:
- External evidence of open pneumothorax, flail segment, penetrating injuries, occult blood loss and contusions
- Bony tenderness by palpating all bony structures including clavicles, ribs, and sternum
- Equal air entry by auscultating and percussing both lungs

Assess the abdomen and pelvis for:
- Bruising, distention, penetrating injuries or laceration by inspection
- Tenderness, particularly over the spleen, liver, kidneys, and bladder
- Pelvic tenderness by gentle palpation

Assess the genito-urinary system and perineum for:
- Perineum and genitalia contusions, lacerations, and haematomas
- Urethral and vaginal bleeding
- High riding prostate, rectal wall injury and anal tone by PR examination
- Vaginal bleeding, vaginal vault injury and laceration by PV examination.

Assess the spine, lower and upper limbs for:
- Bony and soft tissue tenderness and joint instability
- Deformity, bruising and wounds
- Neurovascular injury

3. Head injury

Definition

Head injuries are traumatic injuries which range from superficial skin and soft tissue injuries to skull fractures and intracranial haemorrhage. They are one of the commonest presentations to the Emergency Department.

It is important to remember that a head injury may be part of multisystem trauma and the patient should be assessed in the standard ABCDE approach.

Mechanism of injury

Understanding the mechanism of an injury can help to predict injury pattern and severity of injury. The mechanisms in Table 6.2 are considered dangerous and are classified as one of the risk factors in the secondary assessment for CT indication.

Secondary indications for CT

In adult patients who do not meet the initial NICE criteria for CT, if they have had loss of conscious or amnesia since the injury they should be assessed for the following features:

- Age 65 or older
- History of bleeding or clotting disorders
- Dangerous mechanism
- More than 30 minutes' retrograde amnesia of events immediately before the head injury

If any of these are present, the patient should have a CT head scan within 8 hours of the injury.

Secondary indications in the paediatric population are outlined in the algorithm.

Management

It is important to promptly refer all patients with acute intracranial pathology to the neurosurgical team as these are potentially time-critical injuries. It is important to minimise secondary brain injury by avoiding hypotension, hypoxia, hypoventilation, and hyperthermia.

Table 6.2 Dangerous mechanisms of injury—NICE guidance

Adults patients	Paediatric patients
• Pedestrian or cycle struck by a motor vehicle • Occupant ejected from a motor vehicle • Fall from a height of >1 m or 5 stairs	• High-speed road traffic accident as a pedestrian, cyclist, or vehicle occupant • Fall from a height of >3 m • High-speed injury from a projectile or other object

Further reading

NICE head injury: assessment and early management. Clinical guideline [CG176] https://www.nice.org.uk/guidance/cg176

Algorithm for head injury

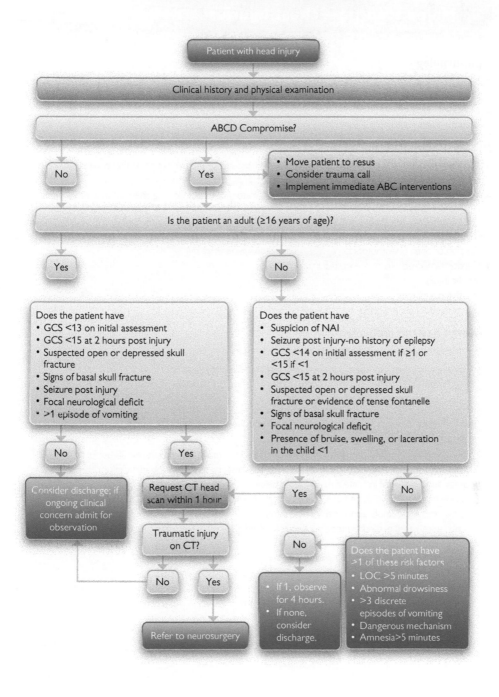

4. Major trauma—chest injuries

Epidemiology

- Road traffic collisions represent the most common cause of major thoracic injury among Emergency Department patients
- Increased mortality and morbidity is associated with multiple rib fractures, increased age, and higher injury severity scores

Initial management

- Clinicians first assess and stabilise the patient's airway, breathing, and circulation, in that order (ABCs; i.e. primary survey)
- The one caveat to this principle in patients with respiratory distress following chest trauma is that breathing may take priority over airway

Immediate life-threatening injuries

- Tension or open pneumothorax
- Cardiac tamponade from myocardial injury
- Aortic injury
- Massive haemothorax
- Tracheobronchial disruption

Emergency thoracotomy

In the setting of blunt trauma, ED thoracotomy rarely results in successful resuscitation:

- Neurologically intact survival in approximately less than 5% of those in shock
- 1% of those without vital signs upon arrival to the Emergency Department
- None of those without signs of life pre-hospital

Chest X-ray

- CXR is the initial test for all patients who warrant imaging
- CXR is inexpensive, non-invasive, and easy to obtain, and, in many instances, it reveals useful information
- Although no single finding on CXR possesses high sensitivity or specificity for aortic injury, the following findings on a plain CXR indicate a need for further investigation:
  - Wide mediastinum (supine CXR >8 cm; upright CXR >6 cm)
  - Obscured aortic knob; abnormal aortic contour
  - Left 'apical cap' (i.e. pleural blood above apex of left lung)
  - Large left haemothorax
  - Deviation of nasogastric tube rightward
  - Deviation of trachea rightward and/or right mainstem bronchus downward
- A widened mediastinum is a sensitive but non-specific sign of aortic injury. Such injuries account for about 20% of abnormal mediastinal widening on CXR after blunt trauma

Further reading

Uptodate. https://www.uptodate.com/contents/initial-evaluation-and-management-of-blunt-thoracic-trauma-in-adults

Algorithm for chest injuries

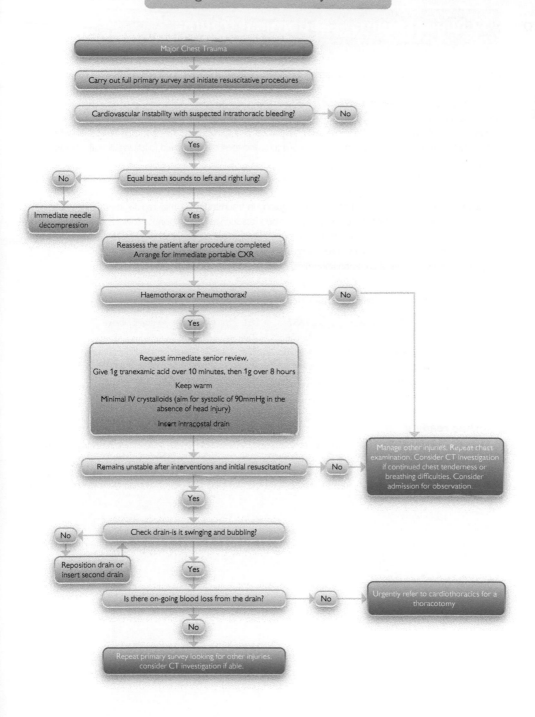

Major Chest Trauma

Carry out full primary survey and initiate resuscitative procedures

Cardiovascular instability with suspected intrathoracic bleeding? — No

Yes

Equal breath sounds to left and right lung? — No → Immediate needle decompression

Yes

Reassess the patient after procedure completed
Arrange for immediate portable CXR

Haemothorax or Pneumothorax? — No

Yes

Request immediate senior review.
Give 1g tranexamic acid over 10 minutes, then 1g over 8 hours
Keep warm
Minimal IV crystalloids (aim for systolic of 90mmHg in the absence of head injury)
Insert intracostal drain

Manage other injuries. Repeat chest examination. Consider CT investigation if continued chest tenderness or breathing difficulties. Consider admission for observation.

Remains unstable after interventions and initial resuscitation? — No

Yes

Check drain-is it swinging and bubbling? — No → Reposition drain or insert second drain

Yes

Is there on-going blood loss from the drain? — No → Urgently refer to cardiothoracics for a thoracotomy

No

Repeat primary survey looking for other injuries. consider CT investigation if able.

5. Major trauma—abdominal trauma

Abdominal injury often co-exists with other significant injuries: as always, a thorough primary survey must be undertaken.

Intravenous access is essential and blood should be taken for urgent FBC, U&E, LFT, amylase, coagulation, lactate, and cross-match.

Pelvic injury should be regarded in the same way as cervical spine injury: a sling should be applied whenever a pelvic fracture is possible from the mechanism of injury, and then only removed following clinical +/− radiological assessment.

Note that in cases of spinal cord injury there may be no abnormal examination features and there should be a low threshold for abdominal imaging.

Note: the use of focused assessment with sonography in trauma (FAST) may rapidly identify free fluid within the abdomen, or other potential sources of major blood loss such as haemothorax. However, it does not exclude significant intra-abdominal injury and will also not identify retroperitoneal injury.

Intra-abdominal bleeding requires urgent surgical or interventional radiological management.

The relative sensitivities of common abdominal investigations are shown in Table 6.3.

Table 6.3 Relative sensitivities of common abdominal investigations

	FAST	CT	Diagnostic peritoneal lavage
Sensitivity	46–85%	97%	87–100%
Specificity	48–95%	98%	52–89%
Negative predictive value	60–98%	98%	78–100%

Early CT is advantageous if the patient is stable enough; it may identify the bleeding site and also inform if radiological embolisation is possible.

Further reading

Bickell WH, Wall MJ, Pepe PE, et al. Immediate versus delayed fluid resuscitation for hypotensive patients with penetrating torso. *New Engl J Med* 1994;331(17):1105–1109.

CRASH-2 trial collaborators, Shakur H, Roberts I, et al. Effects of tranexamic acid on death, vascular occlusive events, and blood transfusion in trauma patients with significant haemorrhage (CRASH-2): a randomised, placebo-controlled trial. *Lancet* 2010;376(9734):23–32.

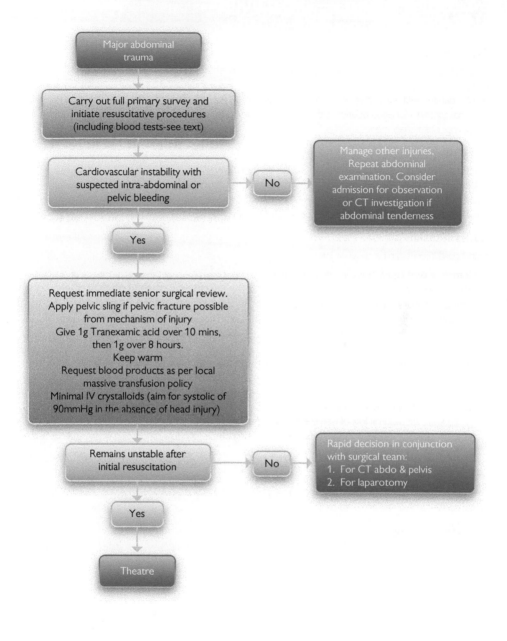

Algorithm for abdominal trauma

Major abdominal trauma

↓

Carry out full primary survey and initiate resuscitative procedures (including blood tests-see text)

↓

Cardiovascular instability with suspected intra-abdominal or pelvic bleeding

→ **No** → Manage other injuries, Repeat abdominal examination. Consider admission for observation or CT investigation if abdominal tenderness

↓ **Yes**

Request immediate senior surgical review.
Apply pelvic sling if pelvic fracture possible from mechanism of injury
Give 1g Tranexamic acid over 10 mins, then 1g over 8 hours.
Keep warm
Request blood products as per local massive transfusion policy
Minimal IV crystalloids (aim for systolic of 90mmHg in the absence of head injury)

↓

Remains unstable after initial resuscitation

→ **No** → Rapid decision in conjunction with surgical team:
1. For CT abdo & pelvis
2. For laparotomy

↓ **Yes**

Theatre

6. Major trauma—spinal injuries

Epidemiology

- Spinal column injury(s) with or without neurological deficit should be considered in patients with multiple injuries
- 1:10 patients with cervical spine facture have a second non-contagious vertebral column fracture
- Spinal column injuries association with spinal cord injury underscores the importance of early recognition and appropriate management

Mechanism of injury

Injury to the vertebral column often occurs secondary to blunt or penetrating trauma.

Injury to the spinal cord might occur due to transection (complete or incomplete), compression (by, for example, bony fragment), or contusion, or by vascular compromise (this should be suspected when there is a discrepancy between a clinically apparent neurologic deficit and the known level of spinal column injury).

Classification

Spinal cord injuries can be classified into:

- **Complete cord injury**: there will be complete sensory and motor loss at the level of the spinal cord injury with no sacral sensation
- **Incomplete injury**: there are various degrees of motor function in muscles controlled by levels of the spinal cord below the injury. Sensation is also partially preserved in dermatomes below the area of injury. Usually, sensation is preserved to a greater extent than motor. The bulbocavernosus reflex and anal sensation are often present
- **Central cord syndrome**: characterised by disproportionately greater motor impairment in the upper than the lower extremities, with variable degree of sensory loss. Often described after relatively mild trauma in the setting of pre-existing cervical spondylosis, e.g. in the elderly
- **Anterior cord syndrome**: characterised by loss of function of the anterior two-thirds of the spinal cord (paraplegia with bilateral loss of pain and temperature sensation with preservation of proprioception and fine touch). Caused by ischaemia of the anterior spinal artery, resulting in loss of function of the anterior two-thirds of the spinal cord

ASIA chart

The American Spinal Injury Association (ASIA) has produced a useful chart that can be used to aid in documenting spinal injuries and can be accessed on line.

Further reading

Spinal column injuries in adults: definitions, mechanisms, and radiographs. https://www.uptodate.com/contents/spinal-col umn-injuries-in-adults-definitions-mechanisms-and-radiographs.
Acute traumatic spinal cord injury. https://www.uptodate.com/contents/acute-traumatic-spinal-cord-injury.

Algorithm for spinal injuries

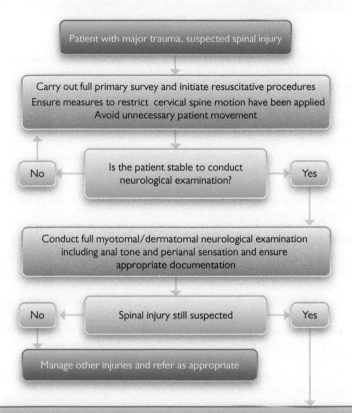

Patient with major trauma, suspected spinal injury

Carry out full primary survey and initiate resuscitative procedures
Ensure measures to restrict cervical spine motion have been applied
Avoid unnecessary patient movement

No ← Is the patient stable to conduct neurological examination? → Yes

Conduct full myotomal/dermatomal neurological examination including anal tone and perianal sensation and ensure appropriate documentation

No ← Spinal injury still suspected → Yes

Manage other injuries and refer as appropriate

- Request radiological imaging as appropriate
- Don't clear cervical spine unless negative clinical and radiological finding
- Avoid hypoxia and hypotension to prevent secondary injury
- Offer appropriate analgesia
- Refer to spinal services

7. Major trauma—maxillofacial

Introduction

As with all cases of major trauma, a primary survey must be carried out in order to identify immediately life-threatening injuries.

Significant maxillofacial trauma may be associated with catastrophic haemorrhage, airway obstruction, serious head injury, and cervical spine injury, all of which must be addressed.

Airway management

Any maxillofacial injury may be associated with airway compromise. This may be due to obstruction, bleeding, distorted anatomy, or swelling. Standard airway management techniques should be used initially.

In cases of bilateral mandibular fracture, the tongue loses its anterior anchor and as such will be pulled back, obstructing the airway. This requires anterior traction in order to clear the airway. This may involve simply holding the tongue or lower incisors and chin with gauze in a gloved hand, or inserting a large silk horizontal mattress suture through the tongue and applying traction to this.

Haemorrhage management

Torrential haemorrhage may occur in maxillofacial injuries from injury to branches of the maxillary artery or ethmoidal arteries. Prompt haemostasis may be necessary for both airway and circulation reasons. In cases of unstable maxilla fractures, inflating unopposed nasal packs may further displace the fracture; as such, nasal packs should only be minimally inflated initially: if bleeding remains uncontrolled the inferior border of the maxilla should be splinted against the mandible using bite blocks, which in turn are splinted by applying a cervical collar to effectively fix the mandible to the sternum. The correct order of application is essential: first collar, then bite blocks, then nasal packs, then inflate. In practice, these patients almost always require intubation prior to these steps.

In cases of posterior impaction of a fractured maxilla, manual disimpaction may be necessary in order to both maintain the airway and reduce bleeding. This is achieved by inserting a gloved index and middle finger into the oropharynx and pulling back from behind the soft palate.

Further reading

Anson J, Nagori SA, Agarwal B, Bhutia O, Roychoudhury A. Management of maxillofacial trauma in emergency: An update of challenges and controversies. *J Emerg Trauma Shock* 2016; 9(2):73–80.

Algorithm for maxillofacial trauma

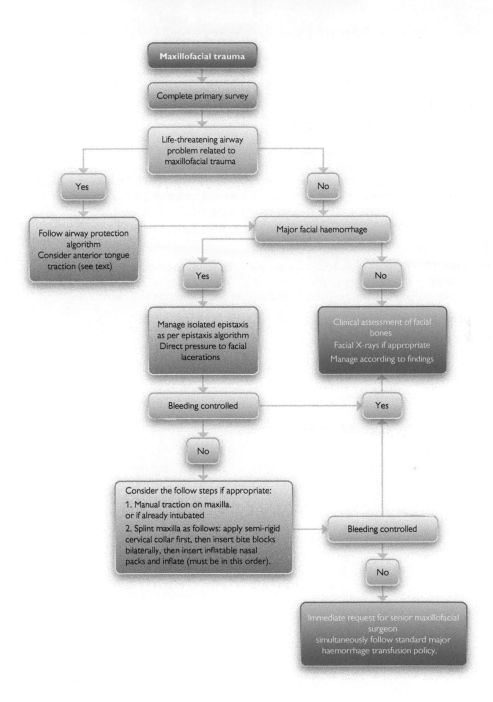

Maxillofacial trauma

Complete primary survey

Life-threatening airway problem related to maxillofacial trauma

Yes → No

Yes: Follow airway protection algorithm
Consider anterior tongue traction (see text)

Major facial haemorrhage

Yes → No

Yes: Manage isolated epistaxis as per epistaxis algorithm
Direct pressure to facial lacerations

No: Clinical assessment of facial bones
Facial X-rays if appropriate
Manage according to findings

Bleeding controlled → Yes

No: Consider the follow steps if appropriate:
1. Manual traction on maxilla.
or if already intubated
2. Splint maxilla as follows: apply semi-rigid cervical collar first, then insert bite blocks bilaterally, then insert inflatable nasal packs and inflate (must be in this order).

Bleeding controlled

No

Immediate request for senior maxillofacial surgeon
simultaneously follow standard major haemorrhage transfusion policy.

8. Major trauma—burns

Epidemiology

- In the UK 130,000 people each year visit the Emergency Department with burns injuries

Types of burns

- Thermal: the most common. Caused by hot liquids (scalds), hot objects (contact), and flames
- Chemical: can be caused by acids or alkalis. These continue to burn skin until completely removed. Thus thorough irrigation is essential
- Electrical: tissue burnt along path of electrical current from 'entry' to 'exit' point. Domestic (low-voltage) exposure is usually less severe. However, because it is alternating current (AC) this can cause arrhythmias
- Cold: ice crystals form intra- and extracellularly, causing cell death
- Radiation: ionizing radiation causes tissue damage. Most common is sunburn

Size of burn

- Burns >15% of body surface area (BSA) in adults and >10% in children can cause circulatory shock due to fluid losses
- Use Lund–Browder chart or the 'Rule of 9s' to assess size of burns. This can be accessed on line

Depth of burn

- Superficial
  - Erythema only (like sunburn)
  - Does **not** count in % BSA
  - Partial thickness
  - Blistering but blanches. Painful
- Full thickness
- Dry and white or black in colour. Painless

Further reading

https://cks.nice.org.uk/burns-and-scalds

Algorithm for burns

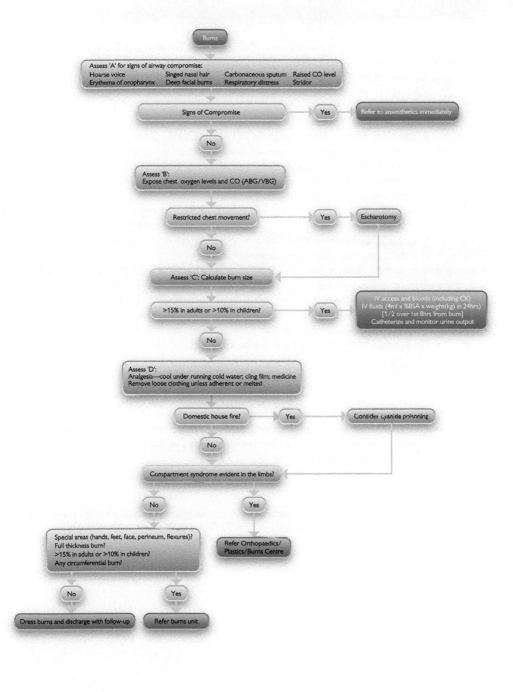

Burns

Assess 'A' for signs of airway compromise:
Hoarse voice   Singed nasal hair   Carbonaceous sputum   Raised CO level
Erythema of oropharynx Deep facial burns   Respiratory distress   Stridor

Signs of Compromise — Yes → Refer to anaesthetics immediately

No

Assess 'B':
Expose chest oxygen levels and CO (ABG/VBG)

Restricted chest movement? — Yes → Escharotomy

No

Assess 'C': Calculate burn size

>15% in adults or >10% in children? — Yes → IV access and bloods (including CK)
IV fluids (4ml x %BSA x weight(kg) in 24hrs)
[1/2 over 1st 8hrs from burn]
Catheterize and monitor urine output

No

Assess 'D':
Analgesia—cool under running cold water; cling film; medicine
Remove loose clothing unless adherent or melted

Domestic house fire? — Yes → Consider cyanide poisoning

No

Compartment syndrome evident in the limbs?

No   Yes

Special areas (hands, feet, face, perineum, flexures)?   Refer Orthopaedics/
Full thickness burn?   Plastics/Burns Centre
>15% in adults or >10% in children?
Any circumferential burn?

No   Yes

Dress burns and discharge with follow-up   Refer burns unit

9. Traumatic limb and joint injuries

Musculoskeletal injuries presenting to the Emergency Department are common and vary from mild injuries into more severe limb threatening ones. However a mild injury might cause serious life long consequences and the treating physician needs to be vigilant when assessing these injuries.

Principles in management

The acute management of bone and/or joint injuries involves the following steps:

- Initial clinical assessment: details of the mechanism of injury and an understanding of the injury patterns associated with particular mechanisms are important. Evaluation should include neurovascular function (NV) and looking for signs of soft tissue damage. Avoid testing passive range of motion or manipulating the affected area or limb until radiologic assessment is completed if required in order to prevent exacerbating fracture displacement, soft tissue damage, or neurovascular compromise
- Pain management: adequate analgesia is key in managing these patients and regularly assess the need for analgesia
- Immobilisation: initially "splint it where it lies." Unless neurovascular compromise is present where urgent manipulation under appropriate analgesia and sedation is needed.
- Radiographic assessment: obtain at least 2 plain x-ray views at 90 degrees to each other. Bear in mind if you don't see a fracture, it does not mean one is not there. E.g. a fractured scaphoid is often not seen on initial x-rays and negative hip x-ray does not rule our neck of femur fracture. Computed tomography (CT) and magnetic resonance imaging (MRI) reveal such occult fractures
- Manipulation and reduction: once imaging has been obtained, manipulate fractures to obtain best anatomical reduction. Dislocated joints need to be reduced as soon as feasible.

Pit falls to avoid

- Always assess and document appropriately the NV status. Both before and after fracture manipulation or joint reduction
- Give early antibiotics in open fractures and consider tetanus status.
- Try to obtain appropriate photos for open fractures before applying a dressing to aid management planning
- Don't use excessive force when manipulating a fracture or reducing a joint. A good understanding of the mechanism of injury and anatomy is key
- Refer to speciality when needed and arrange follow up.

Further reading

Up to date, General principles of acute fracture management. https://www.uptodate.com/contents/general-principles-of-acute-fracture-management?csi=99aee55a-4655-46d7-b733-f743e6a9c640&source=contentShare

Algorithm for traumatic limb and joint injuries

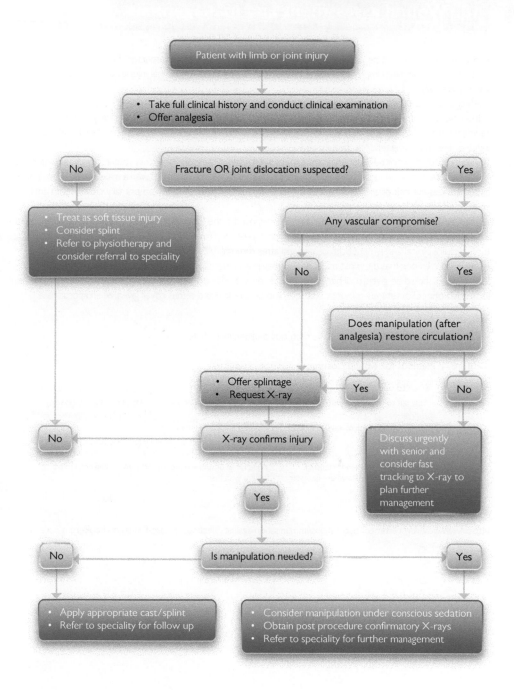

Patient with limb or joint injury

- Take full clinical history and conduct clinical examination
- Offer analgesia

Fracture OR joint dislocation suspected?

No →
- Treat as soft tissue injury
- Consider splint
- Refer to physiotherapy and consider referral to speciality

Yes →

Any vascular compromise?

No →
- Offer splintage
- Request X-ray

Yes →

Does manipulation (after analgesia) restore circulation?

Yes →

No → Discuss urgently with senior and consider fast tracking to X-ray to plan further management

X-ray confirms injury

No

Yes →

Is manipulation needed?

No →
- Apply appropriate cast/splint
- Refer to speciality for follow up

Yes →
- Consider manipulation under conscious sedation
- Obtain post procedure confirmatory X-rays
- Refer to speciality for further management

10. Wound assessment and management

A primary survey should be carried out whenever a significant wound is suspected: beware especially wounds inflicted by narrow sharp implements, which may cause life-threatening internal injuries with only a small skin cut visible externally.

Always take penetrating injuries to the neck, trunk, abdomen, and groin very seriously.

It is essential to be familiar with the relevant anatomy when assessing a wound: if necessary look this up before seeing the patient. This is especially true in the case of hand injuries, where assessment is impossible without knowledge of the underlying tendons, nerves, and vessels.

Wounds that may not be suitable for primary closure include bites, obvious gross contamination, and significant skin loss. *Note*: if these wounds are present on the face they should be discussed with a maxillofacial team: in some circumstances the risk of a disfiguring scar if the wound is not closed may mean primary closure with antibiotic cover is attempted with careful follow-up.

The vast majority of foreign bodies can be safely removed in the Emergency Department following appropriate assessment +/– imaging. **Any** wound caused by broken glass requires a soft-tissue radiograph. All underlying structures require clinical assessment both before and after removal.

Always remember that the most trivial of cuts may leave a significant scar if managed inappropriately.

Antibiotics should be given in all bite wounds and considered in other deep or contaminated wounds. See your local antibiotic policy tetanus immunity status should be checked and tetnus cover given when appropriate.

Wound closure

Wound closure can be achieved using the methods outlined in Table 6.4.

Table 6.4 Methods for wound closure

Material	When to use	Considerations
Steristrips	Minor cut to skin, edges easily opposed	Not suitable where skin under tension (e.g. extensor surfaces). Don't adhere to hair, palms, or soles of feet
Glue	Minor cut to skin, edges easily opposed	Glue must not enter the wound
Staples	Scalp lacerations	Rapid and effective. Poor cosmetic result (suitable for within hair line). Remove in 10–14 days
Sutures	Deep wounds/areas under tension. Allows closure in layers where necessary	Wide range of suture materials are available and need to be familiar with them

Further reading

https://www.gov.uk/government/publications/immunisation-against-infectious-disease-the-green-book-front-cover-and-contents-page

Algorithm for wound assessment and management

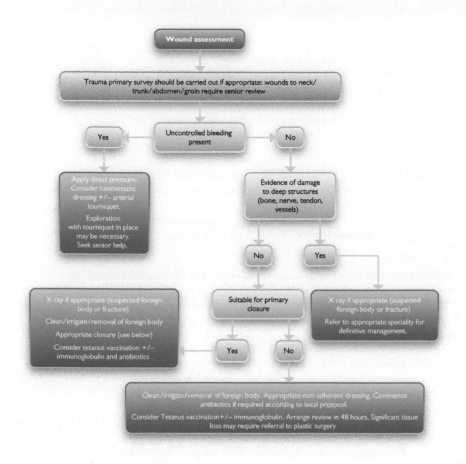

Wound assessment

Trauma primary survey should be carried out if appropriate: wounds to neck/ trunk/abdomen/groin require senior review

Uncontrolled bleeding present

Yes

No

Apply direct pressure. Consider haemostatic dressing +/– arterial tourniquet.
Exploration with tourniquet in place may be necessary. Seek senior help.

Evidence of damage to deep structures (bone, nerve, tendon, vessels)

No

Yes

X-ray if appropriate (suspected foreign body or fracture)
Clean/irrigate/removal of foreign body
Appropriate closure (see below)
Consider tetanus vaccination +/– immunoglobulin and antibiotics

Suitable for primary closure

X-ray if appropriate (suspected foreign body or fracture)
Refer to appropriate speciality for definitive management.

Yes

No

Clean/irrigate/removal of foreign body. Appropriate non-adherent dressing. Commence antibiotics if required according to local protocol.
Consider Tetanus vaccination+/– immunoglobulin. Arrange review in 48 hours. Significant tissue loss may require referral to plastic surgery

11. Shoulder examination

Joint movement

- Flexion (deltoid, pectoralis major, coracobrachialis, biceps)
- Extension (deltoid, latissimus dorsi, teres major and minor, triceps)
- Abduction (deltoid, supraspinatus, infraspinatus, subscapularis, teres minor)
- Adduction (pectoralis major, latissimus dorsi, teres major, subscapularis)
- Internal rotation (subscapularis, pectoralis major, deltoid, latissimus dorsi, teres major)
- External rotation (infraspinatus, deltoid and teres minor)

Other muscle tests

- **Pectoralis major** = shoulder flexion to 90°, push down (lower) and then up (upper)
- **Latissimus dorsi** = shoulder abduction and external rotation to 90° and elbow flexion at 90°, push elbows down
  - Scapula stabilisers = shrug shoulders (**trapezius**)
  - Push against wall (**serratus anterior**), if weak = 'winged scapula'

Special tests

- Lifetime prevalence of 20% for shoulder pain (new incidence of 1% in adults >45 years)
- **Neer's test** for rotator cuff impingement
  - Patient seated, elbow extended, and scapula stabilised by examiner. Passively internally rotate shoulder and then flexion. Pain on passive flexion = +ve test
- **Instability apprehension test**
  - Patient supine. Passively abduct shoulder to 90° and externally rotate
  - Look for apprehension and resistance from patient = +ve test
  - Apply pressure on humeral head. Improvement = +ve test (**relocation sign**)
  - Immediate internal rotation on release = +ve test (**release sign**)
- **Cross-arm/Scarf test** (acromioclavicular joint (ACJ))
  - Place hand on other shoulder. Push so reaching further back (forced adduction). Pain in ACJ = +ve test
- **Drop-arm test** (rotator cuff tear—70% of shoulder disorders)
  - Passively abduct arm to 90°. Actively hold arm at 90° and gently lower to side
  - Inability to hold arm up = +ve test
- Rotator cuff tests
  - **Apley's scratch test** (supraspinatus)
    - ○ Reach between shoulder blades (trying to scratch back)
  - **Empty can test** (supraspinatus)
    - ○ Abduct shoulder 90° with 30° flexion and full internal rotation (thumb pointing down). Abduct shoulder further (+/− resistance). Pain and weakness = +ve test
  - **External rotation lag sign** (infraspinatus and teres minor)
    - ○ Passive flex elbow to 90° and externally rotate shoulder to 90°
    - ○ If patient cannot maintain position (swings back forwards) = +ve test
  - **Gerber's lift-off test** (subscapularis)
    - ○ Hand in small of back and lift hand away from back. Pain or limited movement = +ve test

Further reading

Knott L. Shoulder examination. http://www.patient.co.uk/doctor/shoulder-examination.htm, 2015.
Rothaermel BJ. Shoulder examination. http://emedicine.medscape.com/article/1909254-overview, 2022.
Simons SM, Dixon JB. Physical examination of the shoulder. http://www.uptodate.com/contents/physical-examination-of-the-shoulder, 2021.

Algorithm for shoulder examination

Indication to perform examination of the shoulder

Consent patient, sit patient at 90°, expose both shoulders, offer analgesia

Inspect patient from front, side, and back whilst pushing against a wall
Inspect: skin for erythema, abrasions, contusions, scars, skin colour change,
obvious effusions or deformity (compare sides), winging of scapula

Palpate: temperature, swelling, tenderness, crepitus
Palpate: sternoclavicular joint, clavicle, ACJ, acromion, subacromial space, greater
tuberosity, bicepital groove, coracoid, spine, and inferior pole of scapula

Movement: Screen - hands behind head & reach up back
Movement: Active (flexion (165°), extension (60°), abduction (170°), adduction,
internal rotation (70°), external rotation (70°))
Movement: Passive (same ranges)

Movement: resisted (to grade power)

Test pectoralis major, latissimus dorsi, and scapula stabilizers

Scarf test for ACJ injury

Instability tests

Screen for rotator cuff injury with drop-arm test

Rotator cuff tests

Axillary and distal nerve sensation and pulse check

Check cervical spine

Request x-ray or MRI or orthopaedic opinion if indicated

12. Elbow examination

Analgesia

Options include distraction, entonox, oral analgesia (ibuprofen, paracetamol, codeine, oramorph), IV analgesia (commonly IV morphine), immobilisation (classically a broad arm sling or an above-elbow back slab; these can be used before X-ray for analgesia).

It is important to assess the mechanism of injury, to exclude any other injuries, and to examine the joints above and below (in this case, the shoulder and wrist).

Neurovascular assessment

- Vascular assessment: look for pallor and cyanosis of the limb. Feel for radial, ulnar, and brachial pulses, check warmth of the limb, and compare capillary refill with the other arm.
- Nerve assessment: see Table 6.5.

Table 6.5 Nerve assessment

	MOTOR		SENSORY	
	Innervation	Examination	Innervation	Examination
Radial	Triceps Brachioradialis Hand and wrist extensors	Wrist extension	Dorsum of hand	Check sensation in webspace between thumb and index finger
Median	Most of the forearm flexors. Thenar muscles (LOAF): Lateral two lumbricals Opponens pollicis Abductor pollicis brevis Flexor pollicis brevis	Thumb abduction	Dorsum—index, middle, and ring fingers Palmar—thumb, index, middle, and lateral half of ring finger	Check sensation of index finger
Ulnar	Most intrinsic muscles of the hand (except LOAF)	Little finger abduction (check patient is able to spread fingers)	Little finger Medial half of ring finger and corresponding part of palm	Check sensation of little finger

Examination

- **LOOK**: scars, any obvious deformity, periarticular swellings
- **FEEL**: bony contours (medial and lateral epicondyles, olecranon), feel for local tenderness or heat
- **MOVE**: active and passive:
  - Flexion, extension (0–150°)
  - Pronation (0–90°), supination (0–90°)—best done with elbow at 90° flexion and held by patient's side

Lack of pronation/supination and lack of full extension highly suggests a fracture, commonly the radial head.

Discharge of patients

The following is a general guide; it is important to follow local hospital guidelines and orthopaedic advice.

- Non-displaced radial head fractures: collar and cuff and next available fracture clinic
- Supracondylar fractures: above elbow back slab and admit under orthopaedics
- Proximal radial and ulnar fractures: need full ulnar and radius X-rays, an above-elbow back slab, and admission under orthopaedics
- If no fracture, consider collar and cuff for analgesia, discharge, and follow-up with GP, physio, or soft tissue injury clinic as appropriate
- Elbow dislocations:
  - If relocated, no fracture and neurovascularly intact, above-elbow back slab and fracture clinic
  - If relocated and fracture present (with or without neurovascular compromise), above-elbow back slab and discuss with orthopaedics
  - If unable to relocate, discuss with orthopaedics

Further reading

Mark Dutton. Dutton's Orthopaedic Examination, Evaluation and Intervention. Chapter 17. Fourth Edition 2017.

Algorithm for elbow examination

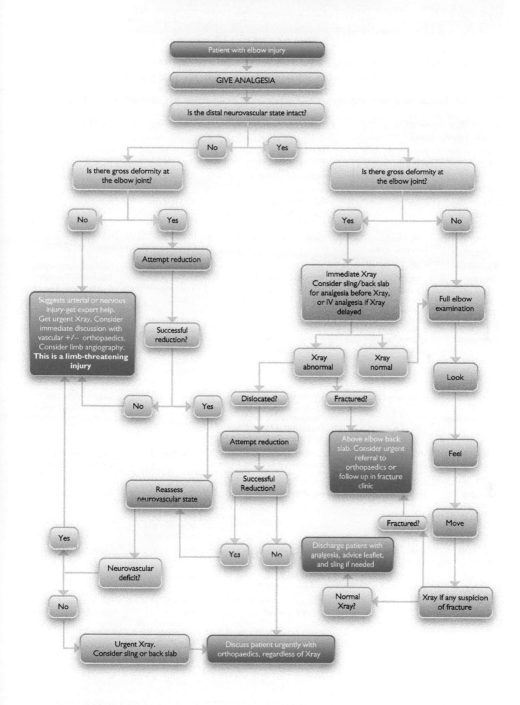

Patient with elbow injury

GIVE ANALGESIA

Is the distal neurovascular state intact?

No — Yes

No branch (left):

Is there gross deformity at the elbow joint?

No — Yes

Attempt reduction

Successful reduction?

Suggests arterial or nervous injury-get expert help. Get urgent Xray. Consider immediate discussion with vascular +/− orthopaedics. Consider limb angiography. **This is a limb-threatening injury**

No — Yes

Reassess neurovascular state

Yes — No

Neurovascular deficit?

Yes — No

Urgent Xray. Consider sling or back slab

Discuss patient urgently with orthopaedics, regardless of Xray

Yes branch (right):

Is there gross deformity at the elbow joint?

Yes — No

Immediate Xray Consider sling/back slab for analgesia before Xray, or IV analgesia if Xray delayed

Full elbow examination

Xray abnormal — Xray normal

Dislocated? — Fractured?

Attempt reduction

Successful Reduction?

Yes — No

Above elbow back slab. Consider urgent referral to orthopaedics or follow up in fracture clinic

Discharge patient with analgesia, advice leaflet, and sling if needed

Normal Xray?

Look

Feel

Move

Fractured?

Xray if any suspicion of fracture

13. Hand examination

The hand should be examined following the general principle of look, feel and move.

Special condition and injuries and principles of examination and management are listed below.

Table 6.6 Special conditions and injuries and principles of examination and management are listed below

Condition	Cause	How to recognise it	Treatment	Follow-up
Tendon/ligament injuries				
Flexor tendon injury	Wounds to palmar aspect of finger	FDP injury—inability to flex at DIPJ FDS injury—inability to flex at PIPJ	Simple dressings	Hand clinic or plastics
Extensor tendon injury	Trauma to dorsum of hand/finger	Inability to extend finger	Splint in extension	Hand clinic or plastics
Ulnar collateral ligament of thumb	Forced thumb abduction	Pain and tenderness around thumb MCPJ Look for laxity of UCL	Scaphoid cast	Fracture clinic or hand clinic Consider US or MRI
Mallet finger Mallet thumb	Forced flexion of extended digit	Inability to extend at DIPJ	Mallet splint—splint finger in extension	Fracture clinic or hand clinic
Boutonniere deformity	Traumatic—a central slip tendon injury, classically a wound on dorsum of finger Non-traumatic—in RA	Flexed PIPJ Hyperextended DIPJ	Non-traumatic— none needed Traumatic—finger splint	Non-traumatic—none Traumatic—fracture clinic, hand clinic, or plastics
Infections				
Paronychia	Infection between base of nail and cuticle	Erythema, tenderness, and swelling around nailbed	Ring block Incise abscess with scalpel Swab pus Oral antibiotics	GP if needed
Tendon sheath infections, classically finger flexors	Penetrating wounds	Erythema Fusiform swelling Tenderness over tendon Finger held in partial flexion Painful to passively extend finger	IV antibiotics	Urgent referral to orthopaedics/plastics
Webspace infections	Wounds or infection around webspace	Swelling, erythema, and tenderness over dorsal webspace	IV antibiotics	Urgent referral to plastics
Other				
Subungual haematoma	Trauma to fingernail	Blood collection under nailbed	Trephine with green needle if haematoma >50% of nailbed and <24 hours old	None
Swan neck deformity	None caused by injury, common in RA	Flexed DIPJ Hyperextended PIPJ	None	None
Z-shaped deformity	None caused by injury, common in RA	Flexed MCPJ Hyperextended IPJ	None	None
Trigger finger/ thumb	Thickening of flexor tendon sheath	Affected finger lags behind others during finger extension	NSAIDS Consider corticosteroid injection	GP to consider corticosteroid injection
Heberden's nodes Bouchard's nodes	Not caused by injury	Nodes on dorsal surface of DIPJs Nodes on dorsal surface of PIPJs	Signs of osteoarthritis. No follow-up needed	None
Fractures				

Fractures and dislocations of carpel bones can be subtle to detect on examination and on X-rays. If in any doubt, discuss with colleagues in orthopaedics/plastics and consider further imaging, e.g. CT. Always refer suspected scaphoid fractures to fracture clinic even if initial X-rays are normal.

FDP, flexor digitorum profundus; FDS, flexor digitorum superficialis.

Further reading

Mark Dutton. Dutton's Orthopaedic Examination, Evaluation and Intervention. Chapter 18. Fourth Edition 2017.

Algorithm for hand examination

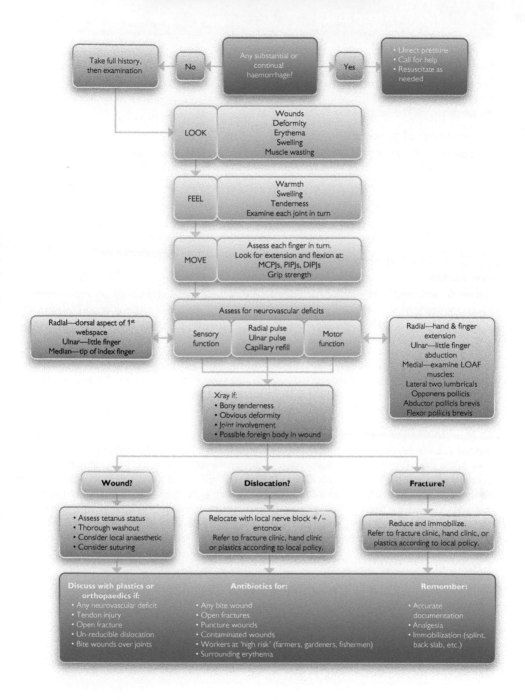

Any substantial or continual haemorrhage?

No → Take full history, then examination

Yes → • Direct pressure
• Call for help
• Resuscitate as needed

LOOK
Wounds
Deformity
Erythema
Swelling
Muscle wasting

FEEL
Warmth
Swelling
Tenderness
Examine each joint in turn

MOVE
Assess each finger in turn.
Look for extension and flexion at:
MCPJs, PIPJs, DIPJs
Grip strength

Assess for neurovascular deficits

Sensory function
Radial pulse
Ulnar pulse
Capillary refill
Motor function

Radial—dorsal aspect of 1st webspace
Ulnar—little finger
Median—tip of index finger

Radial—hand & finger extension
Ulnar—little finger abduction
Medial—examine LOAF muscles:
Lateral two lumbricals
Opponens pollicis
Abductor pollicis brevis
Flexor pollicis brevis

Xray if:
• Bony tenderness
• Obvious deformity
• Joint involvement
• Possible foreign body in wound

Wound?
• Assess tetanus status
• Thorough washout
• Consider local anaesthetic
• Consider suturing

Dislocation?
Relocate with local nerve block +/– entonox
Refer to fracture clinic, hand clinic or plastics according to local policy.

Fracture?
Reduce and immobilize.
Refer to fracture clinic, hand clinic, or plastics according to local policy.

Discuss with plastics or orthopaedics if:
• Any neurovascular deficit
• Tendon injury
• Open fracture
• Un-reducible dislocation
• Bite wounds over joints

Antibiotics for:
• Any bite wound
• Open fractures
• Puncture wounds
• Contaminated wounds
• Workers at 'high risk' (farmers, gardeners, fishermen)
• Surrounding erythema

Remember:
• Accurate documentation
• Analgesia
• Immobilization (splint, back slab, etc.)

14. Hip examination

Introduction

The hip joint is commonly painful following trauma or due to conditions such as arthritis and bursitis. Pain in the hip can be referred from the lumbar spine or the knee, so if no obvious cause is found locally at the hip, to explain the symptoms, the knee and spine should be examined.

Assessment of posture and gait

If the patient is able to stand and walk, the hip examination should begin with an assessment of gait and posture. This enables muscle bulk, symmetry, and gait to be assessed. An antalgic gait, Trendelenburg gait, or other pattern may be seen.

Trendelenburg test

This test is performed by asking the patient to stand on one leg. The examiner stands behind the patient and observes the pelvis. In a normal test the pelvis should remain level. In an abnormal test the pelvis drops markedly on the side of the raised leg. This indicates weakness of the hip abductors of the supporting leg.

Inspection

This can be performed with the patient standing or lying. Care should be taken to look for any scars, deformity, or muscle wasting. Erythema may indicate bursitis, cellulitis, or a septic arthritis. The leg may be obviously shortened or rotated, e.g. if there is a fractured neck of femur.

Palpation

The greater trochanters can be easily palpated and tenderness here can indicate trochanteric bursitis. The head of the femur can be palpated in slim patients and lies below the inguinal ligament, lateral to the femoral artery. The temperature of the hip joints and surrounding tissues should be assessed and compared.

Movements

Range of movement of the hip should be assessed and recorded, and can be compared with the patient's unaffected side. Hip flexion is assessed in a supine patient by flexing the knee to 90° and passively flexing the hip towards the chest. Extension can be examined by positioning the patient prone and lifting each straight leg away from the bed, whilst stabilizing the pelvis. This may not be possible if the hip is very painful, or in elderly patients. An alternative is to put a hand beneath the patient's ankle whilst they lie supine, with straight legs, and ask them to push your hand into the bed. Internal and external rotation can be assessed in the supine position with the knee flexed at 90°, or with the knee extended, by rolling the straight leg medially and laterally. Abduction and adduction are assessed with the leg straight and the examiner's hand positioned over the anterior superior iliac spines to stabilize the pelvis.

Thomas' test

This is a test of hip extension. The patient lies supine and the examiner's hand is placed under the patient's lumbar spine. One of the hips is then fully flexed. The contralateral hip is observed—if it rises from the bed it suggests a fixed flexion deformity of that hip (i.e. the one that lifts off the bed).

X-rays

If required, an AP view of the pelvis and hip and a lateral hip view should be requested in the first instance. Oblique or Judet views can be useful to assess the acetabulum, if fracture here is suspected.

Further reading

Mark Dutton. Dutton's Orthopaedic Examination, Evaluation and Intervention. Chapter 19. Fourth Edition 2017.

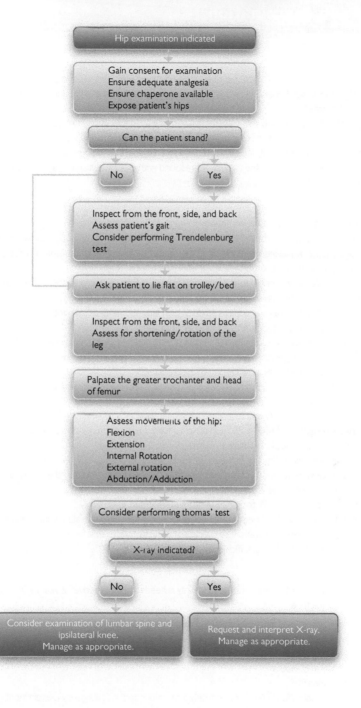

Algorithm for hip examination

Hip examination indicated

Gain consent for examination
Ensure adequate analgesia
Ensure chaperone available
Expose patient's hips

Can the patient stand?

No   Yes

Inspect from the front, side, and back
Assess patient's gait
Consider performing Trendelenburg test

Ask patient to lie flat on trolley/bed

Inspect from the front, side, and back
Assess for shortening/rotation of the leg

Palpate the greater trochanter and head of femur

Assess movements of the hip:
Flexion
Extension
Internal Rotation
External rotation
Abduction/Adduction

Consider performing thomas' test

X-ray indicated?

No   Yes

Consider examination of lumbar spine and ipsilateral knee.
Manage as appropriate.

Request and interpret X-ray.
Manage as appropriate.

15. Knee examination

Patella

- **Patella tap test** (ballottement): positive when >10–15 mL of intra-articular fluid
  - With slight downward pressure, milk the suprapatellar pouch into the knee joint. Use the other hand to push on the patella
- **Bulge sign**: milk fluid proximally from the medial patella into the suprapatellar pouch and then distally along the lateral patella. Apply pressure to the lateral dimple—the fluid will reappear medially
- **Patella apprehension test**: apply lateral pressure on the patella with knee extended and slowly flex knee. When subluxation is imminent, the patient will respond with quadriceps spasm as a guarding reflex (sensitivity is reported to be 39%)

Joint stability

- Patient may report acute pain, swelling, hearing a 'pop', and instability
- Collaterals (in 30° (and full extension if +ve))
  - Stabilise the joint by placing one hand along the medial joint line. With the other hand, hold the ankle and apply a valgus force to the knee
  - If medcial collateral ligament is torn, the joint 'opens up' along the medial aspect (this may also elicit pain)
    - Sensitivity of 86–96% is reported for this test
  - Repeat with opposite hands and varus stress to test lateral collateral ligamant
- Cruciates (anterior and posterior draw tests in 90° flexion)
  - **Anterior drawer test**: flex knee to 90° and sit on the patient's foot. Pull forward on tibia just distal to the knee—movement suggests ACL damage
    - Sensitivity and specificity are 62% and 67% respectively
  - **Lachman test**: flex the knee only 20–30°, then pull tibia anterior relative to femur. A deficient anterior cruciate ligament demonstrates increased movement forward
    - Sensitivity and specificity are 87% and 93% respectively
  - **Posterior sag sign**: flex knee to 90° and observe from the side for any posterior lag of the joint; this suggests posterior cruciate ligament damage
    - Sensitivity and specificity are 79% and 100% respectively
  - **Posterior drawer test**: sit on foot of patient and apply a posterior force to the proximal tibia. Increased posterior tibial displacement suggests posterior cruciate ligament tear
    - Sensitivity ranges from 51 to 90%. Specificity is reported to be 99%.
- Menisci: **McMurray's test**: flex knee to 90°. Slowly extend knee while palpating joint line in external (medial meniscus) + internal (lateral) rotation. Pain or click confirms torn menisci
  - Sensitivity around 52%, but specificity varies ranging from 59 to 97%

Ottawa knee rule

This rule can be used to determine whether an X-ray is needed in people over 2 years with suspected knee fractures to exclude a fracture.

Any one of the following indications is sufficient to order an X-ray:

- Age ≥55 years
- Isolated patella tenderness
- Tenderness at head of fibula
- Inability to flex knee 90°
- Inability to weight bear (four steps) immediately after injury and in Emergency Department

Further reading

Beutler A, Alexander A. Physical examination of the knee. http://www.uptodate.com/contents/physical-examination-of-the-knee, 2020.

Bert Boonen, MD, PhD Orthopaedic Surgeon. https://emedicine.medscape.com/article/1909230-overview.

Stiell IG, Wells GA, Hoag RH, et al. Implementation of the Ottawa knee rule for the use of radiography in acute knee injuries. J Am Med Assoc1997; 278:2075–2079.

Algorithm for knee examination

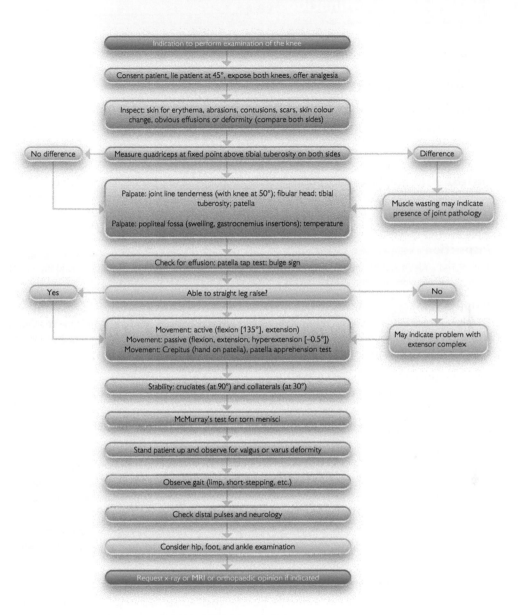

Indication to perform examination of the knee

Consent patient, lie patient at 45°, expose both knees, offer analgesia

Inspect: skin for erythema, abrasions, contusions, scars, skin colour change, obvious effusions or deformity (compare both sides)

No difference ← Measure quadriceps at fixed point above tibial tuberosity on both sides → Difference

Palpate: joint line tenderness (with knee at 50°); fibular head; tibial tuberosity; patella

Palpate: popliteal fossa (swelling, gastrocnemius insertions); temperature

Muscle wasting may indicate presence of joint pathology

Check for effusion: patella tap test; bulge sign

Yes ← Able to straight leg raise? → No

Movement: active (flexion [135°], extension)
Movement: passive (flexion, extension, hyperextension [–0.5°])
Movement: Crepitus (hand on patella), patella apprehension test

May indicate problem with extensor complex

Stability: cruciates (at 90°) and collaterals (at 30°)

McMurray's test for torn menisci

Stand patient up and observe for valgus or varus deformity

Observe gait (limp, short-stepping, etc.)

Check distal pulses and neurology

Consider hip, foot, and ankle examination

Request x-ray or MRI or orthopaedic opinion if indicated

16. Ankle examination

Introduction

Ankle injuries are a common presentation. Examination of the ankle is important to determine the nature of the injury and decide if X-ray or emergent treatment is required.

Ankle joint

The true ankle joint (tibiotalar joint) is the articulation of the distal tibia, medial and lateral malleoli, and the body of the talus. The subtalar joint is the articulation of the talus and calcaneus.

Ankle dislocation

This requires prompt reduction and immobilisation to prevent neurovascular complications. Dislocation is usually but not always associated with fracture of the ankle. A frankly dislocated ankle should be reduced prior to X-ray. It is important to photograph and document any wounds in the case of an open injury, prior to application of plaster of Paris.

Inspection

The injured ankle should be checked carefully for swelling, bruising, and any wounds over or around the site of injury. A joint effusion can sometimes be seen as a fullness either side of the Achilles tendon.

Palpation

Bony, ligamentous, and soft tissue structures of the ankle should all be palpated. The distal 6 cm of the tibia should be carefully palpated, along with the entire fibula. The knee and foot may also need to be examined depending on the nature and mechanism of injury.

Ankle ligaments

Ankle sprains are common. The anterior and posterior talofibula, calcaneofibular, and deltoid ligaments should all be carefully palpated.

Ottawa Ankle Rules

The Ottawa Ankle Rules are a set of guidelines to assist in deciding which patients should be offered X-ray of their ankle injury. Ankle X-ray is indicated if there is pain in the malleolar zone and any one of the following:

- Bone tenderness along the distal 6 cm of the posterior edge of the tibia or tip of the medial malleolus, **or**
- Bone tenderness along the distal 6 cm of the posterior edge of the fibula or tip of the lateral malleolus, **or**
- An inability to weight bear both immediately and in the Emergency Department for four steps

Clinical judgement should be used in patients under 18 years old and in patients who are intoxicated, are un-cooperative, have distracting painful injuries, have decreased sensation in legs, or have gross swelling preventing palpation of malleolar bones.

Simmonds calf squeeze test

This test can be performed in patients where there is a suspicion of Achilles tendon injury. The patient kneels or lies face down on the bed, with the feet hanging over the edge of the bed or chair. The calf muscle is then squeezed to elicit plantar flexion of the foot. The test is abnormal when there is decreased or no plantar flexion of the foot of the injured leg, indicating likely rupture/partial rupture of the Achilles tendon.

Further reading

Mark Dutton. Dutton's Orthopaedic Examination, Evaluation and Intervention. Chapter 21. Fourth Edition 2017.

Algorithm for ankle examination

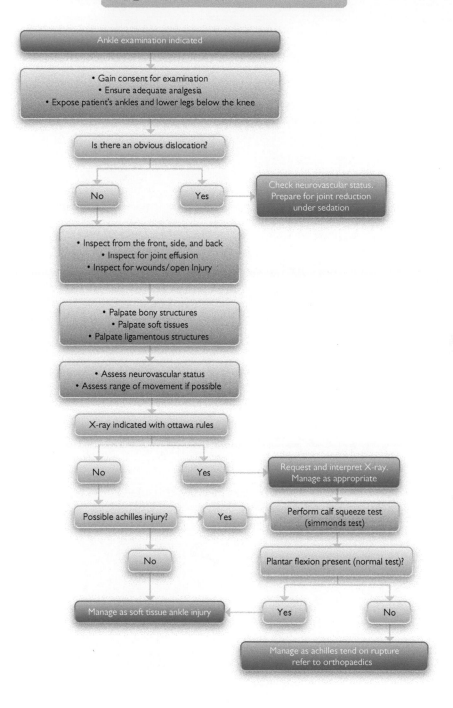

Ankle examination indicated

- Gain consent for examination
- Ensure adequate analgesia
- Expose patient's ankles and lower legs below the knee

Is there an obvious dislocation?

No   Yes → Check neurovascular status. Prepare for joint reduction under sedation

- Inspect from the front, side, and back
- Inspect for joint effusion
- Inspect for wounds/open Injury

- Palpate bony structures
- Palpate soft tissues
- Palpate ligamentous structures

- Assess neurovascular status
- Assess range of movement if possible

X-ray indicated with ottawa rules

No   Yes → Request and interpret X-ray. Manage as appropriate

Possible achilles injury? ← Yes ← Perform calf squeeze test (simmonds test)

No

Plantar flexion present (normal test)?

Manage as soft tissue ankle injury ← Yes   No

Manage as achilles tend on rupture refer to orthopaedics

SECTION 7

Environmental emergencies

1. Heat stroke and heat exhaustion

There is a spectrum of heat-related disease, from rashes and cramps through to heat stroke. Heat exhaustion is characterized by non-specific symptoms such as malaise, headache, and nausea and may progress to heat stroke which involves the central nervous system (CNS) and results in altered conscious state.

Heat stroke is defined as a core temperature of >40.6°C due to environmental exposure and lack of thermoregulation. This differentiates it from fever and has a significant mortality associated with it. It can be classified as exertional or non-exertional.

Exertional heat stroke (EHS) results from strenuous activity in hot conditions. Non-exertional heat stroke (NEHS) describes loss of thermoregulation resulting in overheating and particularly affects infants, children, and the elderly. CNS disorder, medications, and endocrine abnormalities (e.g. thyrotoxicosis) may all contribute to NEHS.

Clinical presentation

- Patients may present with a hyperdynamic state, cramps, tachycardia, CNS disturbance including seizures and coma, and coagulopathy sometimes with GI bleeding
- Blood investigations should include FBC, U&E, liver function, Mg, Ca, phosphate, lactate, creatine kinase (CK), arterial gas, coagulation screen, thyroid function, and glucose
- A CT head scan may be required to exclude intracerebral bleeding
- Sinus tachycardia and non-specific ST and T wave changes may be seen on ECG
- Aggressive reduction of temperature to 39°C can be life-saving
- Benzodiazepines may be required for fits or shivering, but antipyretics have no role in the management of heat stroke

Cooling methods

- Immersion in a bath of iced water is rapidly effective but largely impractical
- Evaporative cooling involves removing the patient's clothes and spraying with a fine mist of water at 15°C, followed by fanning
- Ice packing involves placing ice packs in the groin and axillae, and even covering the whole trunk
- Gastric lavage requires intubation with a cuffed ET tube prior to instilling 10 mL/kg iced water via an NG tube, and suctioning out after 1 minute
- Cardiac bypass or haemodialysis may be considered in refractory cases
- Care should be taken with IV fluids to avoid pulmonary oedema

Further reading

McDermott BP, Casa DJ, Ganio MS, et al. Acute whole-body cooling for exercise-induced hyperthermia: a systematic review. *J Athl Train* 2009;44(1):84–93.

McGugan EA. Hyperpyrexia in the emergency department. *Emerg Med (Fremantle)* 2001;13(1):116–120.

Moran DS, Gaffin SL. Clinical management of heat-related illness. In: Auerbach PS. Wilderness Medicine, 4th edn. St Louis, MO: Mosby, 2001, pp. 290–316.

Schraga E. Cooling techniques for hyperthermia. https://emedicine.medscape.com/article/149546-overview, 2020.

Algorithm for heat stroke and heat exhaustion

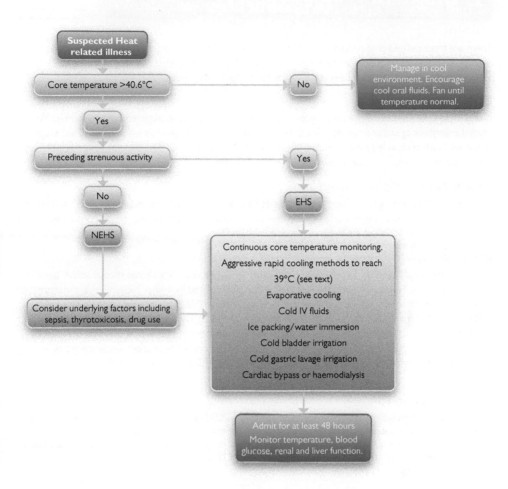

Suspected Heat related illness

Core temperature >40.6°C — No → Manage in cool environment. Encourage cool oral fluids. Fan until temperature normal.

Yes

Preceding strenuous activity — Yes → EHS

No

NEHS

Consider underlying factors including sepsis, thyrotoxicosis, drug use →

Continuous core temperature monitoring.
Aggressive rapid cooling methods to reach 39°C (see text)
Evaporative cooling
Cold IV fluids
Ice packing/water immersion
Cold bladder irrigation
Cold gastric lavage irrigation
Cardiac bypass or haemodialysis

Admit for at least 48 hours
Monitor temperature, blood glucose, renal and liver function.

2. Drug-related hyperthermias

There are three defined drug-related conditions that include hyperthermia as a feature: malignant hyperthermia, neuroleptic malignant syndrome, and serotonin syndrome. Hyperpyrexia related to stimulant drug use including amphetamines is also increasingly seen and is similar to serotonin syndrome.

Malignant hyperthermia

This is an inherited disorder resulting in hypermetabolism in skeletal muscle triggered by certain drugs (typically inhaled anaesthetic agents or suxamethonium). Acidosis, rigidity, and hyperkalaemia will be present, and a rapid rise in end tidal carbon dioxide in anaesthetized patients is often the first sign of development. Anaesthetic management guidelines should be followed (see Further reading) and dantrolene may be life-saving.

Neuroleptic malignant syndrome

This refers to the combination of hyperthermia, rigidity, and autonomic dysfunction associated with antipsychotic mediation. Bradykinesia or akinesia is typical and delirium is common. The onset may be over a number of days. Raised CK and/or WBC count is also commonly found.

Serotonin syndrome

This has some similar features to neuroleptic malignant syndrome, including altered mental status, autonomic dysfunction, and neuromuscular abnormalities, but may be distinguished by tremor, hyperreflexia, and more rapid onset over a period of hours. Selective serotonin reuptake inhibitor (SSRI) medications are the typical cause.

Blood investigations should include FBC, U&E, liver function, Mg, Ca, lactate, CK, arterial gas, coagulation screen, and glucose. Rhabdomyolysis may be seen with all causes and monitoring of CK and renal function is essential.

The role of pharmacological agents such as dantrolene or bromocriptine is unproven; however, as with any toxicological presentation, advice can be sought from the NPIS. If indicated, the initial dose of dantrolene is 1 mg/kg given intravenously.

Further reading

Association of Anaesthetists. Malignant Hyperthermia Crisis. AAGBI Safety Guideline 2011. https://anaesthetists.org/home/resources-publications/guidelines/archived-guidelines/malignant-hyperthermia-crisis.

Gurrera RJ, Caroff SN, Cohen A, et al. An international consensus study of neuroleptic malignant syndrome diagnostic criteria using the Delphi method. *J Clin Psychiatry* 2011;72(9):1222–1228.

Algorithm for drug-related hyperthermias

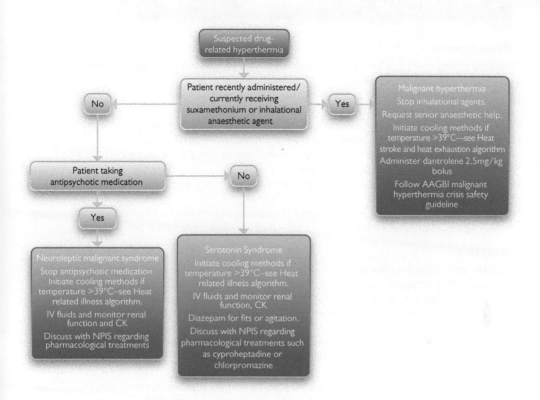

Suspected drug-related hyperthermia

↓

Patient recently administered/currently receiving suxamethonium or inhalational anaesthetic agent

No ← → Yes

Yes → Malignant hyperthermia
Stop inhalational agents.
Request senior anaesthetic help.
Initiate cooling methods if temperature >39°C—see Heat stroke and heat exhaustion algorithm
Administer dantrolene 2.5mg/kg bolus
Follow AAGBI malignant hyperthermia crisis safety guideline

No ↓

Patient taking antipsychotic medication — No

No ↓ → Serotonin Syndrome

Yes ↓

Neuroleptic malignant syndrome
Stop antipsychotic medication
Initiate cooling methods if temperature >39°C–see Heat related illness algorithm.
IV fluids and monitor renal function and CK
Discuss with NPIS regarding pharmacological treatments

Serotonin Syndrome
Initiate cooling methods if temperature >39°C–see Heat related illness algorithm.
IV fluids and monitor renal function, CK
Diazepam for fits or agitation.
Discuss with NPIS regarding pharmacological treatments such as cyproheptadine or chlorpromazine

3. Hypothermia and frostbite

Hypothermia

Hypothermia describes a core body temperature of <35°C. Conventionally it is classified as follows: mild 32–35°, moderate 28–32°, and severe <28°C.

Along with environmental exposure, other causes include impaired thermoregulation (e.g. drug use, Parkinson's disease), sepsis, endocrine dysfunction, and alcohol use.

Symptoms range from mild confusion to ataxia, agitation, and coma. *Note*: below 31° the shivering response ceases. Arrhythmias are common below 30°, and the pupils may become fixed and dilated.

When suspected, a core temperature should be obtained urgently (rectal or oesophageal).

Always check blood glucose, and correct if low.

ECG may demonstrate prolonged PR, QRS, and QT intervals, and J or Osborn waves (Figure 7.1) may be present when temperature falls below 30°.

Aggressive rewarming may be necessary: bladder irrigation can be performed using a three-way catheter, peritoneal irrigation via a diagnostic peritoneal lavage set, and pleural irrigation via chest drains.

Frostbite

Frostbite refers to tissue damage as a result of freezing. Although commonly associated with mountaineering or polar exploration, it is seen in urban populations, particularly in people who work outdoors or are homeless. Risk factors include peripheral vascular disease, diabetes, Raynaud's disease, and use of beta-blockers.

Typically it is caused when temperatures are below −10°C and affects exposed areas including ears, nose, fingers, and toes.

Symptoms include pain, paraesthesia or anaesthesia of the affected part, and loss of movement or coordination. Skin may feel cold and, depending on the depth of the damage, the underlying tissues may feel soft (favourable prognosis) or hard (poor prognosis).

When suspected in the Emergency Department, rapid rewarming is appropriate using immersion in water at 37–39°C. *Note*: this may precipitate extreme pain and appropriate analgesia should be given. This should continue until the distal parts are pink/red, then they should be gently dried and padded or splinted for protection. Reperfusion injury, characterized by oedema and sloughing of devitalized tissue, occurs over the following 2–3 days. Consultation should be made with a vascular or burns service, as occasionally thrombolysis or prostaglandin analogues may be considered. Amputation is rarely needed acutely, and a period of observation of up to 3 months may be appropriate before the decision is made.

Figure 7.1 Osborn (J) wave.

Further reading

Brown DJA, Brugger H, Boyd J, Paal P. Accidental hypothermia. *N Engl J Med* 2012;367(20):1930–1938.
Epstein E, Anna K. Accidental hypothermia. *BMJ* 2006;332(7543):706–709.

Algorithm for hypothermia and frostbite

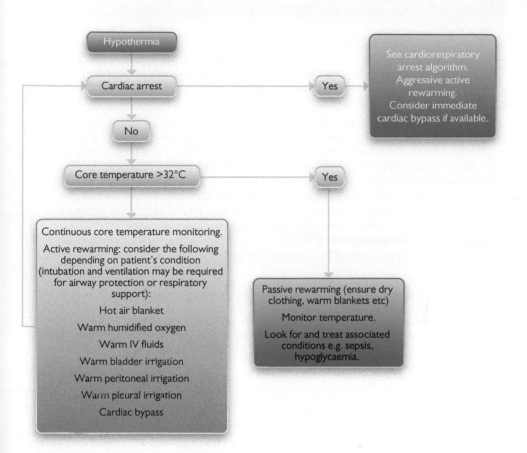

Hypothermia

Cardiac arrest

Yes → See cardiorespiratory arrest algorithm. Aggressive active rewarming. Consider immediate cardiac bypass if available.

No

Core temperature >32°C

Yes → Passive rewarming (ensure dry clothing, warm blankets etc)

Monitor temperature.

Look for and treat associated conditions e.g. sepsis, hypoglycaemia.

Continuous core temperature monitoring.

Active rewarming: consider the following depending on patient's condition (intubation and ventilation may be required for airway protection or respiratory support):

Hot air blanket

Warm humidified oxygen

Warm IV fluids

Warm bladder irrigation

Warm peritoneal irrigation

Warm pleural irrigation

Cardiac bypass

4. Electrical burns/electrocution

There are four described mechanisms of electrical injury:
- True electrical injury: electricity passes through the person as part of a circuit
- Flash injuries: superficial burns from electrical arcing—current does not pass through the person
- Flame injuries: clothing ignited by an electrical arc
- Lightning injuries: extremely high voltage for short duration

When current passes through the body, aside from thermal injury there may also be tetanic muscle contractions prohibiting the person from releasing their grip on the source, and if the current passes through the thorax or head there may be respiratory arrest, cardiac dysrhythmias, seizures, and brain injury. Electrothermal damage includes burns and muscle oedema which may result in compartment syndrome and rhabdomyolysis.

High-voltage injuries may cause considerable internal burns but minimal skin damage.

Care should be taken not to miss associated injuries resulting from falls or severe muscle contraction.

Note that cases of high voltage (including lightning strike) may result in fixed, dilated pupils, but this should not be seen as a marker of futility when considering prolonged resuscitative efforts.

Studies have shown that patients receiving a transthoracic shock with voltage <1000 V, a normal ECG on presentation, and no loss of consciousness (LOC) can safely be discharged without a period of cardiac monitoring.

Further reading

Bailey B, Gaudreault P, Thivierge RL. Cardiac monitoring of high-risk patients after an electrical injury: a prospective multicenter study. *Emerg Med J* 2007;24(8):605.

Cooper MA. Electrical and lightning injuries. *Emerg Med Clin North Am* 1984;2(3):489–501.

Daley BJ. Electrical injuries treatment & management. https://emedicine.medscape.com/article/433682-treatment, 2021.

Algorithm for electrical burns/electrocution

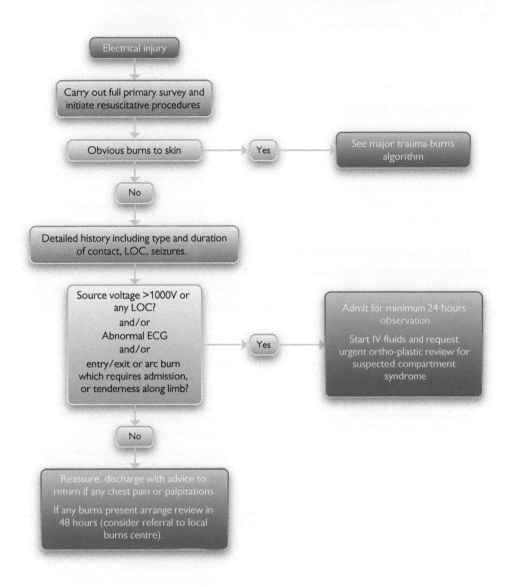

Electrical injury

Carry out full primary survey and initiate resuscitative procedures

Obvious burns to skin — Yes → See major trauma-burns algorithm

No

Detailed history including type and duration of contact, LOC, seizures.

Source voltage >1000V or any LOC?
and/or
Abnormal ECG
and/or
entry/exit or arc burn which requires admission, or tenderness along limb?

Yes → Admit for minimum 24 hours observation

Start IV fluids and request urgent ortho-plastic review for suspected compartment syndrome

No

Reassure. discharge with advice to return if any chest pain or palpitations.

If any burns present arrange review in 48 hours (consider referral to local burns centre).

5. Drowning

The World Health Organization (WHO) has defined drowning as 'the process of experiencing respiratory impairment from submersion/immersion in liquid'. If this causes death, this is a fatal drowning: survival becomes non-fatal drowning. This has replaced previous terms such as 'near-drowning'.

Management of drowning

There are several points to consider when managing cases of drowning:

- Management is the same for salt and fresh water drowning
- Cervical spine injury should be considered in all cases of drowning; however, it is very unlikely in cases where a witness confirms the drowning did not occur immediately following diving/jumping in or, for example, after collision with rocks or a rapidly moving vehicle such as a jet ski
- Consideration should always be given to potential causative medical conditions such as subarachnoid haemorrhage, poisoning, or MI, and these should be investigated accordingly
- There is no role for the routine administration of steroids. Antibiotics should not be routinely given unless the submersion was in heavily contaminated liquid

Management of hypothermia

There is some controversy regarding core temperature targets for resuscitation in drowning. It is generally accepted that resuscitation should continue until at least a temperature of 30°C is achieved, using active rewarming strategies up to and including extracorporeal blood rewarming. However, there have been a number of case reports where it was felt that hypothermia provided a degree of neuro-protection during prolonged resuscitation. The WHO has made the following consensus statement: 'Drowning victims with restoration of adequate spontaneous circulation who remain comatose should not be actively warmed to temperature values above 32–34°C. If core temperature exceeds 34°C, hypothermia should be achieved as soon as possible and sustained for 12 to 24 hours.'

Stopping resuscitation

This is always a difficult decision as there are very few absolute markers of futility.

- A consensus statement from the UK suggests that after 30 minutes' submersion in waters of >6°C, survival is extremely unlikely: in a water temperature of 6°C or less, survival is extremely unlikely if submersion exceeds 90 minutes
- A serum potassium level >10 mmol/L is incompatible with successful resuscitation
- pH of <7.1 is associated with a poor prognosis; however, successful resuscitation and neurological outcome has been reported following drowning with a presenting pH of 6.47

Further reading

Final Recommendations of the World Congress on Drowning, Amsterdam, 26–28 June 2002.
Szpilman D, Bierens JJLM, Handley A, et al. Current Concepts: Drowning. *New Engl J Med* 2012;366:2102–2110.
Tipton MJ, Golden FStC. A proposed decision-making guide for the search, rescue and resuscitation of submersion victims based on expert opinion. *Resuscitation* 2011;82:819–824.

Algorithm for drowning

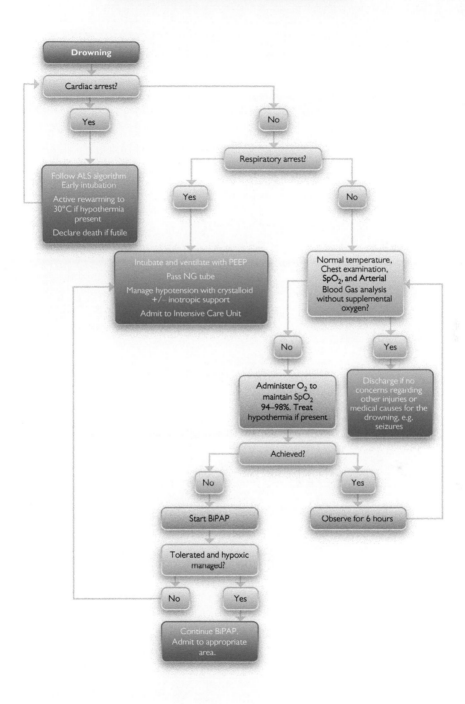

Drowning

Cardiac arrest?

Yes → Follow ALS algorithm
Early intubation

Active rewarming to 30°C if hypothermia present

Declare death if futile

No → Respiratory arrest?

Yes → Intubate and ventilate with PEEP

Pass NG tube

Manage hypotension with crystalloid +/– inotropic support

Admit to Intensive Care Unit

No → Normal temperature, Chest examination, SpO₂, and Arterial Blood Gas analysis without supplemental oxygen?

No → Administer O₂ to maintain SpO₂ 94–98%. Treat hypothermia if present

Yes → Discharge if no concerns regarding other injuries or medical causes for the drowning, e.g. seizures

Achieved?

No → Start BiPAP

Tolerated and hypoxic managed?

No / Yes → Continue BiPAP, Admit to appropriate area.

Yes → Observe for 6 hours

SECTION 8

Other medical

1. The septic patient

Introduction

Sepsis is a complex syndrome presenting with systemic manifestations of infection and can be defined as life-threatening organ dysfunction caused by a dysregulated host response to infection.

Identification

It is identified using a compilation of various signs, symptoms, and investigations, although no definitive diagnostic test currently exists.

There is increasing acknowledgment that previous definitions used in this field, such as systemic inflammatory response syndrome (SIRS) (Table 8.1) and severe sepsis, are unhelpful: SIRS is neither sensitive nor specific for infection for sepsis, and sepsis *itself* carries a high enough mortality and morbidity to be labelled as a 'severe' condition.

The algorithm identifies a place for the SIRS criteria, as this is still used in many hospitals around the world to identify sepsis; however, there is newer evidence suggesting that the Sequential (sepsis-related) Organ Failure Assessment (SOFA) score has a higher accuracy in identifying early those patients with a higher morbidity and mortality and thereby needing more urgent and thorough medical input. The SOFA score examines six areas of physiology (respiratory, coagulation, liver, cardiovascular, CNS, and renal) and the presence of abnormalities. A shorter scoring system—Quick SOFA (qSOFA; Table 8.2)—looks at three aspects of physiology and can be measured rapidly and easily at the bedside.

Septic shock

Septic shock (previously known as 'severe sepsis') is a state of acute circulatory failure associated with a significantly higher mortality. Its definition is not exact; however, two tests point towards this: a lactate >2 despite adequate fluid resuscitation and the need for vasopressor support to maintain a mean arterial pressure (MAP) >65 mmHg.

Including the initial investigations, further investigations may be needed, depending on the clinical picture, including radiological (CXR, abdominal US, CT) and microbiological (urine dip/mid-stream urine (MSU)/catheter specimen urine (CSU), sputum and wound samples, diagnostic pleural or ascetic or joint aspirations).

Table 8.1 SIRS criteria

SIRS criteria	(≥2 = SIRS)	
Temperature >38°C or <36°C	1	point
Respiratory rate >20	1	point
Acutely altered mental state	1	point
Blood glucose >7.7 mmol/L in absence of diabetes	1	point
WBC count >12 × 10⁹/L or <4 × 10⁹/L	1	point
Heart rate >90/minute	1	point

Table 8.2 qSOFA

qSOFA score		
Respiratory rate ≥22/min	1	point
Altered mentation (GCS <15)	1	point
Systolic BP <100 mmHg	1	point

Further reading

NICE guideline (NG51) Sepsis: recognition, diagnosis and early management. https://www.nice.org.uk/guidance/ng51
Seymour et al. Assessment of Clinical Criteria for Sepsis. *JAMA* 2016;315(8):762–774.
Singer et al. The Third International Consensus Definitions for Sepsis and Septic Shock. *JAMA* 2016;315(8):801–810.

Algorithm for the septic patient

INFECTION SUSPECTED OR PROVEN?

1. Full set of observations including BM
2. Calculate qSOFA score
3. Examine for SIRS
4. Call for help.
Consider senior input early

IF qSOFA≥2 or SIRS≥2 PERFORM SEPSIS 6

GIVE OXYGEN	**IV ANTIBIOTICS**	**TAKE BLOODS**	**MEASURE LACTATE**	**IV FLUID**	**FLUID BALANCE**
Target O2 sats: • 96–98% (88–92% if at risk of hypercapnia)	Follow local trust guidelines	Blood cultures, FBC, U&E, CRP, LFT, clotting, glucose, ESR, VBG, or ABG	Aim to repeat after adequate fluid resuscitation	0.9% saline 500ml stat. Then **reassess**. May need up to 2–3 L	Consider catheter OR strict input/ output measurements

FIND SOURCE OF SEPSIS
- ENT/maxillofacial
- CNS
- Abdominal/GI
- Intravascular catheter
- Foreign body/implanted device
- Female reproductive tract/Perineal/Genital
- Recent operation/trauma
- Pneumonia
- Endocarditis
- Urinary tract
- Biliary tract
- Bone or joint infection
- Skin or wound

Consider other investigations

Continual reassessment is vital.
Consider further fluid boluses up to 30ml/kg
Urgent referral needed to senior in the relevant specialty

If despite adequate fluid resuscitation:
Mean arterial pressure <65 AND
Lactate ≥2, the patient is in

SEPTIC SHOCK
Consider discussion with
Critical care, microbiology, senior registrar
May need vasopressor support

2. The shocked patient

Introduction

Shock is a clinical condition characterised by a failure to adequately perfuse vital organs. It is recognised by:

- Hypotension (systolic BP <90 mmHg)
- Tachycardia (HR >100 bpm)
- Altered consciousness
- Poor peripheral perfusion
- Oliguria (urine output (UO) <50 mL/hour)
- Tachypnoea (>20 breaths per minute)

Shock is traditionally classified into five broad groups, although there may be overlap between these.

Anaphylactic shock

This is a generalised immunological condition of sudden onset following exposure to an allergen. Management of anaphylaxis is outlined in the anaphylaxis algorithm in this book (see Section 2, Chapter 1).

Cardiogenic shock

This can have a primary cardiac cause, such as MI, dysrhythmia, or valvular dysfunction. It can be secondary due to cardiac tamponade, pulmonary embolus, or tension pneumothorax. Management depends on the underlying cause. Please refer to the relevant algorithm in this book.

Hypovolaemic shock

This can be due to blood loss, e.g. following trauma or GI haemorrhage. It can be due to fluid losses following burns or as a consequence of pancreatitis or other disease processes. Please refer to the relevant algorithms within this book.

Neurogenic shock

This is caused by disruption of the autonomic pathways within the spinal cord. It can occur after damage to the CNS such as spinal cord injury. Management of spinal cord injury is outlined in the spinal trauma algorithm in this book (see Section 6, Chapter 6).

Septic shock

Septic patients have a suspected or proven infection in combination with SIRS. Patients who are immunocompromised may be neutropaenic and should be managed appropriately as neutropaenic sepsis. Please refer to septic shock algorithm in this book.

Further reading

Wyatt JP, Illingworth RN, Graham CA, Hogg K, Robertson C, Clancy M. Oxford Handbook of Emergency Medicine, 4th edn. Oxford: Oxford University Press, 2012.

Algorithm for the shocked patient

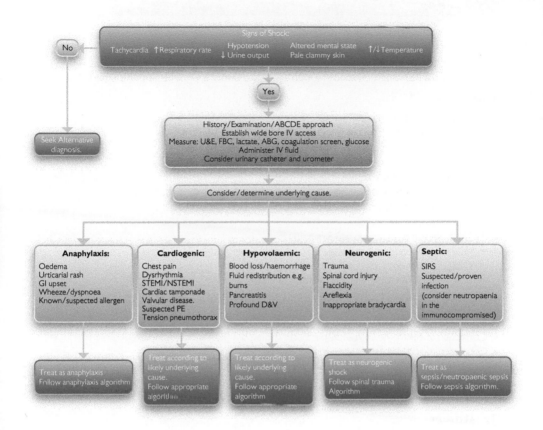

Signs of Shock:

Tachycardia ↑Respiratory rate Hypotension Altered mental state ↑/↓ Temperature
↓ Urine output Pale clammy skin

No

Seek Alternative diagnosis.

Yes

History/Examination/ABCDE approach
Establish wide bore IV access
Measure: U&E, FBC, lactate, ABG, coagulation screen, glucose
Administer IV fluid
Consider urinary catheter and urometer

Consider/determine underlying cause.

Anaphylaxis:

Oedema
Urticarial rash
GI upset
Wheeze/dyspnoea
Known/suspected allergen

Cardiogenic:

Chest pain
Dysrhythmia
STEMI/NSTEMI
Cardiac tamponade
Valvular disease.
Suspected PE
Tension pneumothorax

Hypovolaemic:

Blood loss/haemorrhage
Fluid redistribution e.g.
burns
Pancreatitis
Profound D&V

Neurogenic:

Trauma
Spinal cord injury
Flaccidity
Areflexia
Inappropriate bradycardia

Septic:

SIRS
Suspected/proven
infection
(consider neutropaenia
in the
immunocompromised)

Treat as anaphylaxis
Follow anaphylaxis algorithm

Treat according to
likely underlying
cause.
Follow appropriate
algorithm

Treat according to
likely underlying
cause.
Follow appropriate
algorithm

Treat as neurogenic
shock
Follow spinal trauma
Algorithm

Treat as
sepsis/neutropaenic sepsis
Follow sepsis algorithm.

3. Abnormal blood glucose—diabetic ketoacidosis

Introduction

- More than 10% of type 1 diabetics have an episode of DKA
- This remains a life-threatening condition, with a mortality rate of approximately 2–5% in the UK

Definition

- Insulin deficiency state characterised by:
  - Acidosis: venous pH ≤7.3 and/or venous bicarbonate ≤15 mmol/L
  - Dehydration: typical DKA patient has fluid deficit of 6–8 L
  - Ketonuria: urinalysis +++ on dipstick or ≥3 mmol/L blood ketone level
  - Hyperglycaemia: blood glucose level >11 mmol/L
- Severe DKA characterised by:
  - pH <7.1 and/or bicarbonate <5 mmol/L
  - Blood ketones >6 mmol/L
  - Hypokalaemia on admission (<3.5 mmol/L)
  - GCS <12 or abnormal Alert, Voice, Pain, Unresponsive (AVPU)
  - Oxygen saturations <92% on air
  - Shock (systolic BP <90 mmHg, pulse >100 or <60 bpm)

Management

- Restoration of circulatory volume
- Correction of electrolyte imbalance (particularly potassium (K) loss)
- Correction of acid-base balance (reversal of acidosis)
- Suppression of ketogenesis/clearance of ketones
- Correction of hyperglycaemia
- Identification and treatment of precipitating factors (e.g. insulin omission, infection)

Treatment

- IV fluids
  - Replace total fluid deficit over 24 hours (typically 6–8 L) with 0.9% saline
  - Caution in elderly, pregnant, heart or kidney failure
- IV glucose
  - Start 10% glucose at 50 ml/hour when blood glucose level ≤14 to prevent hypoglycaemia and allow continued IV insulin until acidosis resolved
- Potassium
  - Monitor 2-hourly and replace to maintain normal range
  - Usually required with 2nd or 3rd litre of replacement fluid
- Insulin
  - If delay >30 minutes for IV insulin infusion, give 10 units Actrapid® stat IM or IV
  - Start infusion at 0.1 units/kg/hour and continue until acidosis corrected (bicarbonate >20)

Complications

- Cerebral oedema—risk can be reduced by correcting acidosis and hydration gradually
- Acute respiratory distress syndrome (ARDS)
- Hypoglycaemia
- Hypokalaemia—leading to cardiac dysrhythmias
- Aspiration—frequently associated with ileus, so consider NG tube if vomiting/low GCS

Further reading

Clinical guideline (CG15) Diagnosis and management of type 1 diabetes in children, young people and adults

Savage MW, Dhatariya KK, Klivert A, et al. Joint British Diabetes Societies guideline for the management of diabetic ketoacidosis. *Diabet Med* 2011;28(5):508–515.

Algorithm for diabetic ketoacidosis

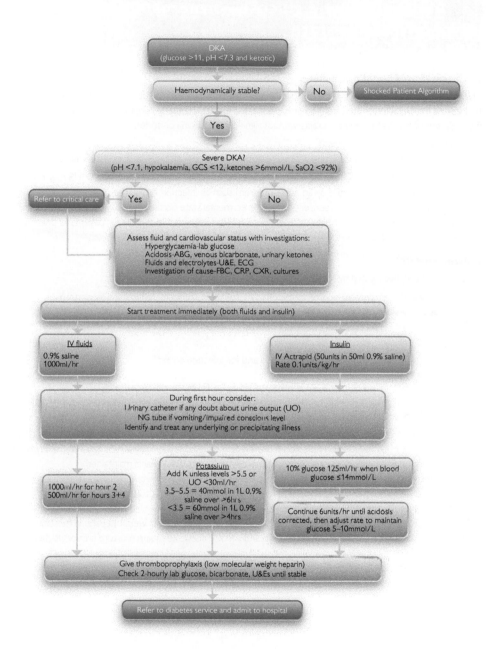

DKA
(glucose >11, pH <7.3 and ketotic)

Haemodynamically stable? → No → Shocked Patient Algorithm

Yes

Severe DKA?
(pH <7.1, hypokalaemia, GCS <12, ketones >6mmol/L, SaO2 <92%)

Refer to critical care — Yes / No

Assess fluid and cardiovascular status with investigations:
Hyperglycaemia-lab glucose
Acidosis-ABG, venous bicarbonate, urinary ketones
Fluids and electrolytes-U&E, ECG
Investigation of cause-FBC, CRP, CXR, cultures

Start treatment immediately (both fluids and insulin)

IV fluids
0.9% saline
1000ml/hr

Insulin
IV Actrapid (50units in 50ml 0.9% saline)
Rate 0.1units/kg/hr

During first hour consider:
Urinary catheter if any doubt about urine output (UO)
NG tube if vomiting/impaired conscious level
Identify and treat any underlying or precipitating illness

1000ml/hr for hour 2
500ml/hr for hours 3+4

Potassium
Add K unless levels >5.5 or
UO <30ml/hr
3.5–5.5 = 40mmol in 1L 0.9%
saline over >6hrs
<3.5 = 60mmol in 1L 0.9%
saline over >4hrs

10% glucose 125ml/hr when blood
glucose ≤14mmol/L

Continue 6units/hr until acidosis
corrected, then adjust rate to maintain
glucose 5–10mmol/L

Give thromboprophylaxis (low molecular weight heparin)
Check 2-hourly lab glucose, bicarbonate, U&Es until stable

Refer to diabetes service and admit to hospital

4. Abnormal blood glucose—hyperosmolar hyperglycaemic state

Definition and typical features

There is no precise definition for hyperosmolar hyperglycaemic state (HHS), but there are characteristic features that enable it to be differentiated from other hyperglycaemic states. These features include hypovolaemia, marked hyperglycaemia, and high plasma osmolality without significant ketonuria or acidosis.

- Serum glucose typically >30 mmol/L
- Serum osmolarity typically >320 mmol/L: can be measured or estimated ($2Na^+$ + glucose + urea)

The unwell patient with HHS may represent the first presentation of type 2 diabetes or HHS may occur in a known type 2 diabetic, precipitated by an acute problem such as infection or MI. Classically, HHS occurs in the elderly, but it is increasingly seen in younger adults. Altered mental state occurs in up to 25% of patients. Mild acidosis may occur in patients with concurrent renal failure (pH >7.30) and it is possible for patients to present with a mixed picture of HHS and DKA.

Management

Patients should be investigated by obtaining the following:

- Bloods—U&E, serum glucose, laboratory osmolality, HbA1c, bicarbonate, lactate, and troponin T
- Urinalysis to assess ketonuria and/or plasma ketones and possible UTI
- ECG
- CXR

Further tests may be necessary as clinically indicated and for infection screening.

Treatment

Once diagnosed, the patient with HHS requires the following treatment (*note: fluid replacement is the priority and often very little insulin is required*):

- Slow and careful rehydration with correction of any identified electrolyte abnormalities (HHS patients typically have fluid deficit of 6–10 L). Take into account pre-existing conditions such as heart or renal failure. Encourage patients to drink as soon as it is safe to do so, with accurate fluid balance charts maintained
- Gradual restoration of normal blood glucose. This minimizes the risk of cerebral oedema. Target blood glucose is 10–15 mmol/L at 48–72 hours and is usually achieved using IV Actrapid at 2 units/hour
- Identify and treat any underlying precipitants (e.g. infection/steroid use)
- Patients are hypercoagulable and should receive prophylactic low molecular weight heparin in most cases
- Patients are at high risk of foot and leg ulceration and should receive adequate pressure area protection and daily foot checks
- Patients may require high-dependency/level 2 care, e.g. if significant impairment of conscious level, electrolyte abnormalities, or there is a need for central venous monitoring

Complications

- Fluid overload
- Cerebral oedema
- Central pontine myelinosis

Further reading

https://www.diabetes.org.uk/professionals/position-statements-reports/specialist-care-for-children-and-adults-and-compli cations/management-of-the-hyperosmolar-hyperglycaemic-state-hhs-in-adults-with-diabetes

Algorithm for hyperosmolar hyperglycaemic state

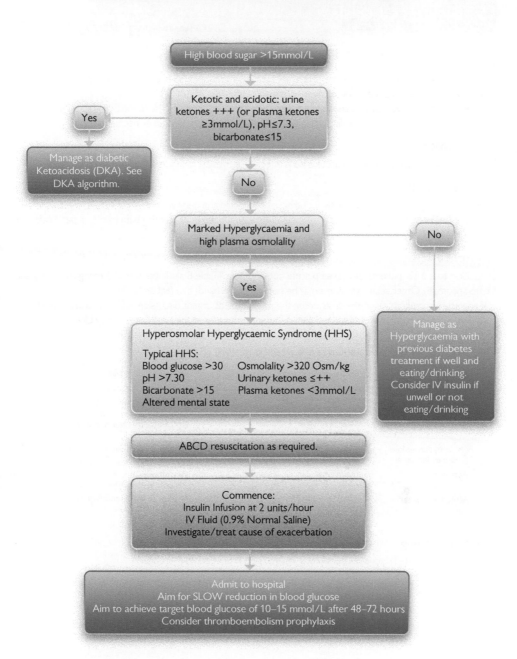

High blood sugar >15mmol/L

Ketotic and acidotic: urine ketones +++ (or plasma ketones ≥3mmol/L), pH≤7.3, bicarbonate≤15

Yes → Manage as diabetic Ketoacidosis (DKA). See DKA algorithm.

No

Marked Hyperglycaemia and high plasma osmolality

No → Manage as Hyperglycaemia with previous diabetes treatment if well and eating/drinking. Consider IV insulin if unwell or not eating/drinking

Yes

Hyperosmolar Hyperglycaemic Syndrome (HHS)

Typical HHS:
Blood glucose >30   Osmolality >320 Osm/kg
pH >7.30   Urinary ketones ≤++
Bicarbonate >15   Plasma ketones <3mmol/L
Altered mental state

ABCD resuscitation as required.

Commence:
Insulin Infusion at 2 units/hour
IV Fluid (0.9% Normal Saline)
Investigate/treat cause of exacerbation

Admit to hospital
Aim for SLOW reduction in blood glucose
Aim to achieve target blood glucose of 10–15 mmol/L after 48–72 hours
Consider thromboembolism prophylaxis

5. Sickle cell crisis

Introduction

Sickle cell disease is a group of inherited conditions caused by a mutation in one of the haemoglobin (Hb) chains. In homozygotes, the sickle red blood cells are hard and fragile.

Patients generally have a chronic anaemia and present in situations of acute crisis to the Emergency Department. An acute crisis occurs when the sickling red blood cells block small blood vessels or haemolyse.

Management

The primary goal in patients with an acute crisis is effective analgesia and to identify any acute complications.

Causes and diagnosis

There are many causes of an acute crisis, including infection, cold and dehydration.

It is also important to recognize any alternative diagnoses in patients presenting with pain (e.g. pancreatitis or pneumothorax).

Complications

In addition to a crisis, patients can develop acute complications (Table 8.3). These must be recognised early and treated promptly. Other acute symptoms may be swelling of the hands and feet and priapism.

If any acute complications of the crisis occur, the patient needs urgent discussion with the haematologist (and consideration for a blood transfusion) and consideration for transfer to the High Dependency Unit.

Table 8.3 Acute complications of sickle cell crisis

Complication	Symptoms/signs	Investigation findings
Chest syndrome	Chest pain, breathlessness, wheeze, fever Oxygen saturation <95% Escalating oxygen requirements	Pulmonary infiltrates on CXR— usually secondary to fat emboli
Splenic sequestration	Hepatoplenomegaly Tender RUQ	Increased prothrombin time (PT) Decreased Hb
Osteomyelitis—often caused by *Salmonella*	High fever Pain that is not characteristic of a usual crisis	Blood cultures. Consider aspiration of joint under orthopaedics
Aplastic crisis	Generally secondary to parvovirus (extreme lethargy and tiredness)	Pancytopaenia Reduced reticulocytes
Acute neurological symptoms	Acute-onset focal neurological signs, psychosis, seizures	Urgent CT scan of head needed

Further reading

Clinical guideline (CG143) Sickle cell disease: managing acute painful episodes in hospital

Algorithm for sickle cell crisis

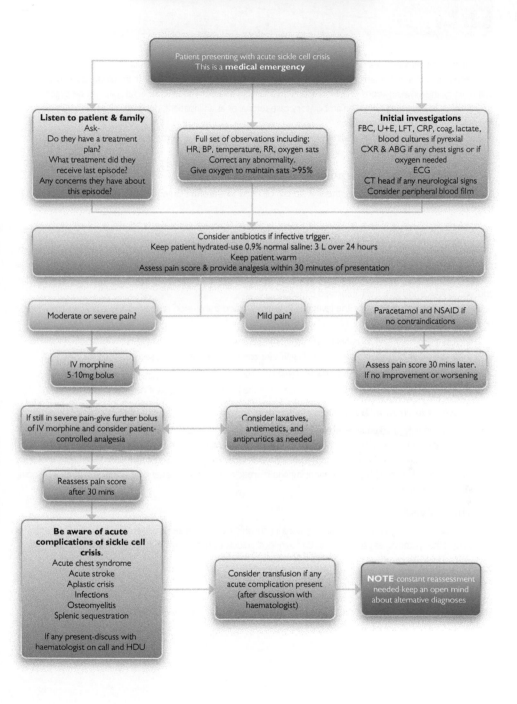

Patient presenting with acute sickle cell crisis
This is a **medical emergency**

Listen to patient & family
Ask-
Do they have a treatment plan?
What treatment did they receive last episode?
Any concerns they have about this episode?

Full set of observations including:
HR, BP, temperature, RR, oxygen sats
Correct any abnormality.
Give oxygen to maintain sats >95%

Initial investigations
FBC, U+E, LFT, CRP, coag, lactate, blood cultures if pyrexial
CXR & ABG if any chest signs or if oxygen needed
ECG
CT head if any neurological signs
Consider peripheral blood film

Consider antibiotics if infective trigger.
Keep patient hydrated-use 0.9% normal saline: 3 L over 24 hours
Keep patient warm
Assess pain score & provide analgesia within 30 minutes of presentation

Moderate or severe pain?

Mild pain?

Paracetamol and NSAID if no contraindications

IV morphine 5-10mg bolus

Assess pain score 30 mins later.
If no improvement or worsening

If still in severe pain-give further bolus of IV morphine and consider patient-controlled analgesia

Consider laxatives, antiemetics, and antipruritics as needed

Reassess pain score after 30 mins

Be aware of acute complications of sickle cell crisis.
Acute chest syndrome
Acute stroke
Aplastic crisis
Infections
Osteomyelitis
Splenic sequestration

If any present-discuss with haematologist on call and HDU

Consider transfusion if any acute complication present (after discussion with haematologist)

NOTE-constant reassessment needed-keep an open mind about alternative diagnoses

6. Anaemia

The most common form of anaemia is one of iron deficiency (iron deficiency anaemia (IDA)). Once this diagnosis has been made, it is important to identify the *cause* of the IDA (most commonly from blood loss). The patient will need further investigations (e.g. endoscopy, colonoscopy) and/or specialist referral. This can be organised either through the patient's GP, via an ambulatory care setting, or as an inpatient, depending on the patient's current medical status and local protocols.

Coeliac disease is a common autoimmune condition that can present with malabsorption of iron, or B12/folate, so it may present with a microcytic or a macrocytic anaemia.

To transfuse or not to transfuse?

If patients are not bleeding acutely, there is no clinical need to transfuse urgently; blood transfusions come with the risk of severe reactions.

Transfusions in IDA

Transfusions are rarely needed in stable patients with IDA and oral/IV iron is usually the preferred treatment option. Transfusions should only be considered if an immediate increase in Hb is essential to improve the clinical situation acutely (e.g. in ACS, severe sepsis, congestive cardiac failure (CCF)). The patient should receive written and verbal advice and give their informed consent.

General recommendations for the level of Hb when a blood transfusion is needed are as follows (however, if possible, treat with oral/IV iron):

- Transfuse if Hb is <70 g/L in patients who are otherwise well
- Transfuse if Hb is <80 g/L in patients with significant comorbidities (e.g. ACS, severe sepsis, CCF)

This recommendation is a guide only. Review the symptoms and signs of the patient, discuss with a senior colleague, refer to local guidelines, and obtain advice from the local haematologists if necessary.

Transfusions in vitamin B12/folate deficiency

This can present with marked anaemia and the temptation is to transfuse. However, the vast majority of patients improve rapidly with vitamin B12 injections and folate replacement. If a blood transfusion is essential due to critical illness (e.g. heart failure or ACS being caused or exacerbated by the anaemia), a single unit of red cells should be transfused over 4 hours, with close monitoring and diuretic cover—these patients are at high risk of developing heart failure from transfusions.

Further advise

Further advice with regard to treatment options in chronic kidney disease, preoperative anaemia, and anaemia caused by other pathologies can be found through local guidelines or through the Further reading below.

Further reading

NICE guideline (NG24) Blood transfusion
British Committee for Standards in Haematology.
The Joint United Kingdom Blood Transfusion and Tissue Transplantation Services Professional Advisory Committee.

Algorithm for anaemia

Anaemia
Male <130g/l
Female <120g/l
If acute blood loss, pulmonary oedema, or haemodynamically unstable,
admit patient under appropriate inpatient team
and resuscitate as needed.
Consider major haemorrhage protocol

Initial Investigations
FBC, U+E, calcium+phosphate, LFT, coag screen, TSH, B12, ferritin, folate, CRP, ESR.
Peripheral Blood Film (PBF) & Group & Save

Further Investigations to consider:
Reticulocyte and haptoglobins
Myeloma screen
Transferrin saturations and Iron stores
Intrinsic factor antibodies if B12 deficiency
Direct coombs test if haemolysis is a possibility
Autoantibodies
Urgent inpatient referral to haematology
Tissue transglutaminase if coeliac disease is a possibility

Transfusion criteria:
- Acute blood loss
- Hb<70 OR Hb<80 if significant comorbidities
BUT follow local guidelines and discuss with haematology

LOOK AT MCV

Microcytic		Normocytic		Macrocytic	
Common causes	Rare causes	Common causes	Rare causes	Common causes	Rare causes
Iron deficiency- ? malignancy ? chronic GI loss ? menstruation	- Thalassaemia - Chronic disease - Lead poisoning - Congenital sideroblastic anaemia	- Chronic disease - Acute blood loss - Renal failure	- Myeloma - Marrow failure - Haemolysis	- Alcohol - Chronic liver disease - Pregnancy	- B12/folate deficiency - Hypothyroid - Marrow infiltration - Haemolysis - Drugs

Treatment-treat the cause
If iron deficient-investigate to find a cause, either as inpatient or outpatient, depending on patient's symptoms and
signs, e.g. endoscopy, cystoscopy, gynaecology referral etc
If B12/folate deficient do not transfuse even with profound anaemia unless patient's clinical status is unstable. Treat
with B12 injections, then folate supplements.
Use clinical judgement to decide about admission or not.
If discharging patient, ensure has appropriate follow up and safety net advice

7. Purpura and bruising in children

Purpura

Bleeding under the skin or into mucosal membranes is called purpura. Purpura can be subdivided according to size into small petechiae (<2 mm) or larger confluent areas, called ecchymoses.

Causes

- Meningococcal disease
- Henoch–Schönlein purpura
- Thrombocytopaenia
  - Idiopathic thrombocytopaenic purpura
  - Leukaemia
  - Aplastic anaemia
  - Septic shock
- Viral illness
- Trauma
- Forceful coughing or vomiting (usually superior vena cava (SVC) distribution)

Meningococcal disease

Rash may be a late feature of meningococcal disease. Children presenting with petechial rash and fever who are objectively or subjectively unwell should be treated urgently, as possible meningococcal sepsis. Failure to treat aggressively is associated with a high mortality.

Treatment involves administration of third-generation cephalosporin, such as ceftriaxone or cefotaxime, according to local guidelines. Fluid resuscitation should be commenced and urgent referral to paediatrics should be arranged. Referral to the PICU team should be considered if signs of sepsis are displayed or if there is any ongoing concern.

Non-accidental injury

Purpura or unexplained bruising can be a presenting feature of a non-accidental injury (NAI). NAI should be considered for the following:

- Bruising in a non-mobile child
- Bruising at unusual sites
- Linear bruising/petechiae
- History incompatible with injury
- Delayed presentation of significant injury
- Petechiae co-existing with bruising, which should prompt suspicion of NAI

Any lesions suspicious of NAI should be discussed promptly with a senior colleague and referred to paediatrics for further assessment.

Further reading

UpToDate. Evaluation of Purpura in Children. https://www.uptodate.com/contents/evaluation-of-purpura-in-children

UpToDate. Differential Diagnosis of suspected child abuse. https://www.uptodate.com/contents/differential-diagnosis-of-suspected-child-physical-abuse

Wyatt JP, Illingworth RN, Graham CA, Hogg K, Robertson C, Clancy M. Oxford Handbook of Emergency Medicine, 4th edn. Oxford: Oxford University Press, 2012.

Algorithm for purpura and bruising in children

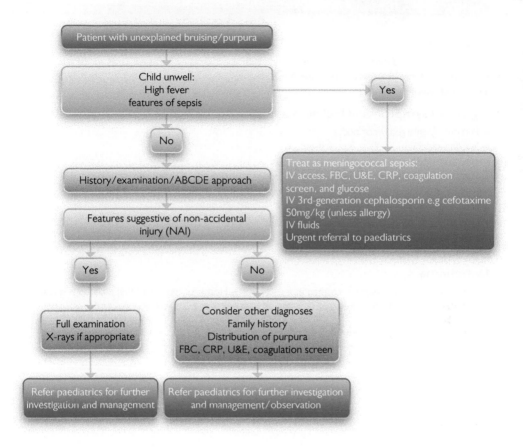

Patient with unexplained bruising/purpura

Child unwell:
High fever
features of sepsis

→ Yes

No

History/examination/ABCDE approach

Features suggestive of non-accidental injury (NAI)

Treat as meningococcal sepsis:
IV access, FBC, U&E, CRP, coagulation screen, and glucose
IV 3rd-generation cephalosporin e.g cefotaxime 50mg/kg (unless allergy)
IV fluids
Urgent referral to paediatrics

Yes

No

Full examination
X-rays if appropriate

Consider other diagnoses
Family history
Distribution of purpura
FBC, CRP, U&E, coagulation screen

Refer paediatrics for further investigation and management

Refer paediatrics for further investigation and management/observation

8. Leukaemia/lymphoma in children

Leukaemia

One-third of all childhood cancers are leukaemia, with approximately 400 new cases in the UK each year. Approximately three-quarters of these cases are acute lymphoblastic leukaemia (ALL). ALL can affect children of any age but is more common in children aged 1–4. It is more common in boys than girls.

Signs and symptoms of leukaemia

- Persistently enlarged lymph nodes
- Swollen abdomen
- Abdominal pain
- Hepatomegaly/splenomegaly
- Shortness of breath
- Frequent infections
- Bone and joint pain
- Weight loss
- Anaemia

Lymphoma

The most common lymphoma in children in the UK is non-Hodgkin lymphoma (NHL), although it is still rare. About 80 children of all ages develop NHL in the UK each year. It is more common in boys than girls.

Signs and symptoms of lymphoma

- Persistent enlarged lymph nodes
- Swollen abdomen
- Early fullness when eating
- Shortness of breath
- Persistent cough
- Fever
- Weight loss
- Night sweats
- Fatigue
- Bleeding or bruising easily

Management

Patients presenting with signs or symptoms suggestive of leukaemia or lymphoma should have bloods taken, along with a CXR if indicated. They should then be referred to the paediatric team for further investigation and to ensure appropriate follow-up is arranged.

Further reading

UpToDate. Evaluation of Purpura in Children. https://www.uptodate.com/contents/evaluation-of-purpura-in-children
Wyatt JP, Illingworth RN, Graham CA, Hogg K, Robertson C, Clancy M. Oxford Handbook of Emergency Medicine, 4th edn. Oxford: Oxford University Press, 2012.

Algorithm for leukaemia/lymphoma in children

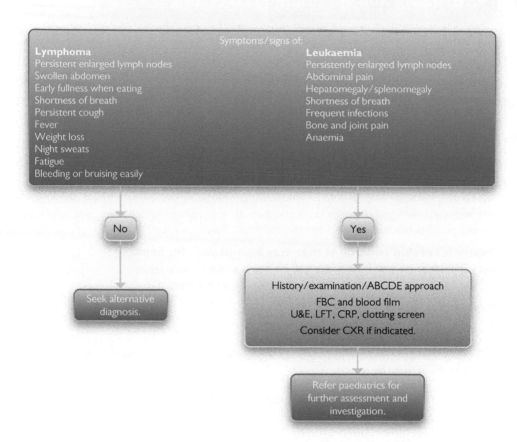

Symptoms/signs of:

Lymphoma
Persistent enlarged lymph nodes
Swollen abdomen
Early fullness when eating
Shortness of breath
Persistent cough
Fever
Weight loss
Night sweats
Fatigue
Bleeding or bruising easily

Leukaemia
Persistently enlarged lymph nodes
Abdominal pain
Hepatomegaly/splenomegaly
Shortness of breath
Frequent infections
Bone and joint pain
Anaemia

No

Yes

Seek alternative diagnosis.

History/examination/ABCDE approach
FBC and blood film
U&E, LFT, CRP, clotting screen
Consider CXR if indicated.

Refer paediatrics for further assessment and investigation.

9. Bruising and spontaneous bleeding

Introduction and definition

This chapter deals solely with adults.

A bruise is a haematoma or diffuse extravasation of blood without rupture of the skin, resulting from injury. The discoloration of a bruise (usually initially red but can be purple or brownish/yellow) does not blanch on pressure.

Excessive bruising or bruising occurring due to very minor trauma may be associated with:

- Abnormalities of the blood vessels or dermis
- Abnormalities of platelet function or number
- Abnormalities of coagulation   • Abnormalities caused by drugs   • Non-accidental injury

Drugs known to cause problems with bruising

The following are known to cause problems with bruising: corticosteroids, amitriptyline, NSAIDs, cephalosporins, chloramphenicol (systemically), cisplatin, clopidogrel, doxorubicin, glycoprotein IIb/IIIa inhibitors, gold, heparin, propranolol, penicillins, quinidine, quinine, sulphonamides, thiazide diuretics, warfarin.

Examples of skin conditions that may be mistaken for bruising

- Allergic contact dermatitis   • Stretch marks   • Phytophotodermatitis
- Mongolian spots   • Urticarial pigmentosa • Bullous impetigo

Salient points in the history

- Symptoms suggesting platelet or coagulation disorder, e.g. nosebleeds, bleeding gums, blood per urine, per rectum or menorrhagia
- Excessive bruising or exessive or prolonged bleeding especially if only after minor trauma or occurring after a delay or only of recent onset
- Previous radio- or chemotherapy
- Past medical history of autoimmune disorders, kidney disease, liver disease, or thyroid dysfunction
- Appetite, weight loss, and general nutrition
- Tiredness, night sweats, and joint pains
- Alcohol consumption
- Medications including over-the-counter
- Family history of bleeding disorders, easy bruising, menorrhagia, or Ehlers–Danlos syndrome

Examination

- Pattern of bruising   • More general examination of skin   • Assess hair and nails
- Examine joints
- Examine abdomen: look especially for hepatomegaly, splenomegaly, and ascites
- Examine gums and eyes including fundoscopy   • Assess for lymphadenopathy   • Perform urinalysis

Patterns of bruising

- Dependent areas—suggests thrombocytopenia or stasis factors
- Atypical areas—suggests underlying bleeding diathesis or NAI
- Only on limbs—suggests trauma or changes in the skin or subcutaneous tissues
- Around the eyes—suggests connective tissue disorder
- Extensor surfaces of hands, forearms, and shins—suggests senile purpura in the elderly

Further reading

NICE Clinical Knowledge Summaries. Bruising. March 2021

Algorithm for bruising and spontaneous bleeding

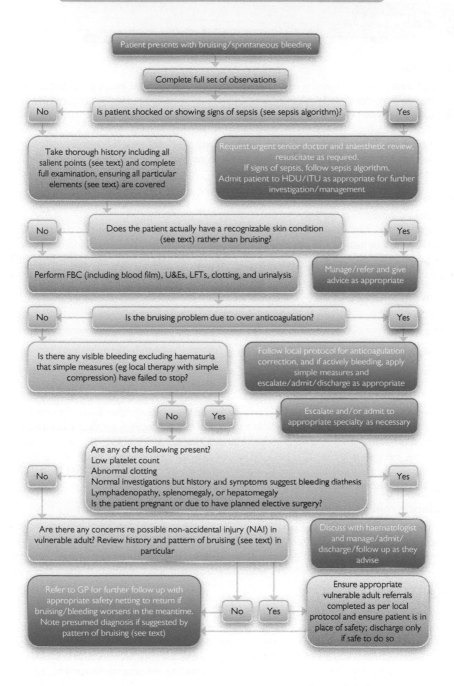

Patient presents with bruising/spontaneous bleeding

Complete full set of observations

Is patient shocked or showing signs of sepsis (see sepsis algorithm)?
No — Yes

No: Take thorough history including all salient points (see text) and complete full examination, ensuring all particular elements (see text) are covered

Yes: Request urgent senior doctor and anaesthetic review, resuscitate as required. If signs of sepsis, follow sepsis algorithm. Admit patient to HDU/ITU as appropriate for further investigation/management

Does the patient actually have a recognizable skin condition (see text) rather than bruising?
No — Yes

No: Perform FBC (including blood film), U&Es, LFTs, clotting, and urinalysis

Yes: Manage/refer and give advice as appropriate

Is the bruising problem due to over anticoagulation?
No — Yes

No: Is there any visible bleeding excluding haematuria that simple measures (eg local therapy with simple compression) have failed to stop?

Yes: Follow local protocol for anticoagulation correction, and if actively bleeding, apply simple measures and escalate/admit/discharge as appropriate

No / Yes

Yes: Escalate and/or admit to appropriate specialty as necessary

Are any of the following present?
Low platelet count
Abnormal clotting
Normal investigations but history and symptoms suggest bleeding diathesis
Lymphadenopathy, splenomegaly, or hepatomegaly
Is the patient pregnant or due to have planned elective surgery?
No — Yes

No: Are there any concerns re possible non-accidental injury (NAI) in vulnerable adult? Review history and pattern of bruising (see text) in particular

Yes: Discuss with haematologist and manage/admit/discharge/follow up as they advise

No: Refer to GP for further follow up with appropriate safety netting to return if bruising/bleeding worsens in the meantime. Note presumed diagnosis if suggested by pattern of bruising (see text)

No / Yes

Yes: Ensure appropriate vulnerable adult referrals completed as per local protocol and ensure patient is in place of safety; discharge only if safe to do so

10. Fever

Introduction

There are different definitions regarding fever (pyrexia) and hyperthermia. These involve the distinction between increased temperature due to the body's thermoregulatory centre increasing the set level required (for a variety of reasons) and increased temperature due to the body's thermoregulatory centre losing control (again due to a number of possible causes).

For the purposes of this algorithm we will ignore these distinctions and consider patients presenting with a markedly increased temperature as one group. Body temperature ≥40°C is generally considered to be dangerous and is the cut-off used for the purposes of this algorithm.

Signs and symptoms

Possible signs and symptoms of markedly elevated temperature include:

Weakness or fatigue, headache and/or impaired judgement, thirst, nausea and/or vomiting, dizziness/stumbling gait, anxiety/agitation or hysteria, tachypnoea and tachycardia, paraesthesia, myalgia, cramps, or tetany, diarrhea, excessive salivation and swallowing dysfunction, collapse, seizures, or coma Any of these can occur at any time and in any combination.

Elements suggestive of a thyroid storm

History of thyroid dysfunction or symptoms of hyperthyroidism, tachycardia and palpitations, chest pain or shortness of breath, anxiety and irritability or disorientation, heart failure, increased sweating or high temperature, weakness.

Evaporative cooling

Strip patient to underwear, sponge or spray the patient with cool water, and apply fans to encourage evaporation.

Malignant hyperthermia

This is a particular presentation with markedly increased temperature (among other signs). Here patients with the genetic predisposition when exposed to suitable triggers, e.g. volatile anaesthetic agents or succinylcholine, can develop an uncontrolled and extreme increase in skeletal muscle oxidative metabolism. This usually occurs when patients receive anaesthetics for surgical procedures within the theatre area; however, there is a possibility that it may occur in the Emergency Department if a patient receives an RSI for the first time. The AAGBI has produced a safety guideline for use when malignant hyperthermia occurs.

Neuroleptic malignant syndrome

This is another particular type of presentation where, along with increased temperature, muscle rigidity and autonomic hyperactivity predominate. This is caused by various antipsychotics (including haloperidol, olanzapine, and risperidone) and some antiemetics (including droperidol, metoclopramide, and prochlorperazine). These lists are by no means exhaustive; it is vital that any history of the patient having taken antipsychotics or antiemetics is sought.

Serotonin syndrome

A very similar picture is seen with serotonin syndrome; this is due to an accumulation of serotonin, which can be caused by a wide variety of drugs including SSRIs, serotonin-norepinephine reuptake inhibitors, tricyclic antidepressants, monoamine oxidase inhibitors, some migraine medications, antiemetics and analgesics, illegal substances (lysergic acid diethylamide (LSD), 3,4-methylenedioxy-methamphetamine (MDMA, commonly known as ecstasy), cocaine, amphetamines), and even some herbal remedies. Again this list is not exhaustive but emphasizes the need for a very careful and thorough drug history.

Further reading

Association of Anaesthetists of Great Britain and Ireland Safety Guideline Malignant Hyperthermia Crisis August 2011.
Ministry of Defence Joint Service Publication 539 Climatic Illness and Injury in the Armed Forces. Force Protection and Initial Medical Treatment Version 2 August 2014.
Nickson C. Hyperthermia. Life in the Fast Lane. https://litfl.com/hyperthermia/

Algorithm for fever

Patient presents with temperature ≥40°C

Full set of observations including Glasgow Coma Scale & core temperature

Does patient fulfil two or more Systemic Inflammatory Response Syndrome criteria with suspicion of infection?

No

Yes → Follow sepsis algorithm

Give antipyretics (paracetamol or ibuprofen (if not contraindicated)) and if core temperature >40°C institute evaporative cooling (see notes), & apply ice packs
Take thorough history and perform full examination, paying particular attention to signs and symptoms listed in the text and prescribed, over-the-counter and illegal drug history (see notes)

Has patient just received anaesthetic drugs (volatile agents or succinylcholine)?

No

Yes

Ensure appropriate investigations completed including Full Blood Count, clotting, Urea & electrolytes, Magnesium, bone profile, lactate, Liver function tests Creatinine kinase, glucose, cross match, Arterial blood gases and urinalysis

Activate Association of Anaesthetists of Great Britain and Ireland (AAGBI) malignant hyperthermia safety guideline

Are there signs/symptoms/history to suggest a thyroid storm (see notes)?

Yes

Discuss with endocrinologist/senior medic regarding further management and admit. Management will depend on cause of thyroid toxicity but beta-blockers may be useful in symptomatic control

No

Is patient Glasgow Coma Scale ≥13?

Yes

No

Is Glasgow Coma Scale ≤8, i.e. airway protection required?

If safe to do so supply patient with cold fluids to drink; if any problems with hypersalivation or swallowing problems provide cooled intravenous fluids (eg Normal saline). If patient requires sedation use benzodiazepines

No

Organize immediate intubation & ventilation of patient

Yes

Treat with cooled intravenous fluids and request urgent anaesthetic review. Consider alkalization of urine. Discuss with senior emergency physicians & anaesthetic colleagues regarding use of drugs such as Dantrolene

Has temperature reduced and patient's condition improved?

No

Yes → Continue to monitor and provide cold intravenous fluids, being wary of fluid overload

Discuss with anaesthetic colleagues regarding need for intubation and ventilation and further drug treatment including Dantrolene

11. The oliguric patient

Definition

- In infants: <1 mL/kg/hour urine output
- In children and adults: <0.5 mL/kg/hour urine output for 6 consecutive hours
- Anuria—defined in adults as <50 mL of urine/day
- Oliguria is important as it is associated with acute kidney injury (AKI), and in particular AKI is associated with fluid overload if oliguria is present.

Types

- **Pre-renal**: functional response of structurally normal kidneys to hypoperfusion. Associated with high-output GI losses, haemorrhage, sepsis, congestive heart failure, or decreased oral intake
- **Intrinsic renal problem**: associated with structural renal damage. Includes acute tubular necrosis (ATN) (from prolonged ischaemia, drugs, or toxins), primary glomerular disease, or vascular lesions
- **Post-renal**: consequence of mechanical or functional obstruction of flow of urine. This form of oliguria and renal insufficiency usually responds to release of the obstruction
- **Fictitious**: if all other causes above are ruled out. Patients may report oliguria in order to avoid supplying a urine sample (e.g. due to fear of exposure of recent illicit drug use)

Salient points in the history

- Duration of oliguria and if any associated suprapubic pain or discomfort
- Recent urinary symptoms, e.g. dysuria, haematuria, poor flow, hesitancy, urgency, post micturition dribbling
- Recent fevers
- Recent back injury or pain or neurological deficit in lower limbs
- Lethargy or itching
- Peripheral oedema
- Drug history, especially any potentially nephrotoxic drugs, e.g. NSAIDs, ACE inhibitors, diuretics
- Recent renal tract instrumentation
- Previous renal problems
- Systemic review including past medical history (PMH), diabetes mellitus (DM), hypertension, ischaemic heart disease (IHD), stroke, peripheral vascular disease (PVD), and any recent respiratory symptoms
- Any testicular pain or swelling

Examination

- Any evidence of anaemia
- Excoriation or rashes
- Volume status
- Palpable bladder
- Loin/flank tenderness
- Peripheral oedema
- Prostate examination in males

Further reading

NICE guideline (NG148) Acute kidney injury: prevention, detection and management.

Algorithm for the oliguric patient

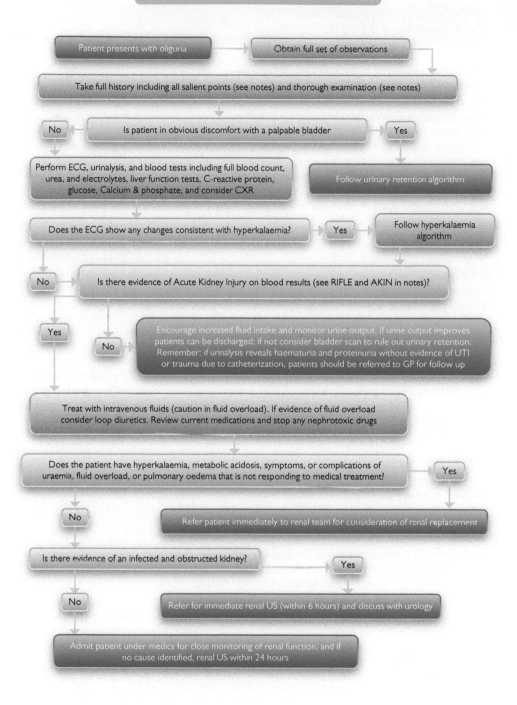

Patient presents with oliguria → Obtain full set of observations

Take full history including all salient points (see notes) and thorough examination (see notes)

No ← Is patient in obvious discomfort with a palpable bladder → Yes

Perform ECG, urinalysis, and blood tests including full blood count, urea, and electrolytes, liver function tests, C-reactive protein, glucose, Calcium & phosphate, and consider CXR

Follow urinary retention algorithm

Does the ECG show any changes consistent with hyperkalaemia? → Yes → Follow hyperkalaemia algorithm

No → Is there evidence of Acute Kidney Injury on blood results (see RIFLE and AKIN in notes)?

Yes

No → Encourage increased fluid intake and monitor urine output. If urine output improves patients can be discharged; if not consider bladder scan to rule out urinary retention. Remember: if urinalysis reveals haematuria and proteinuria without evidence of UTI or trauma due to catheterization, patients should be referred to GP for follow up

Treat with intravenous fluids (caution in fluid overload). If evidence of fluid overload consider loop diuretics. Review current medications and stop any nephrotoxic drugs

Does the patient have hyperkalaemia, metabolic acidosis, symptoms, or complications of uraemia, fluid overload, or pulmonary oedema that is not responding to medical treatment? → Yes

No

Refer patient immediately to renal team for consideration of renal replacement

Is there evidence of an infected and obstructed kidney? → Yes

No

Refer for immediate renal US (within 6 hours) and discuss with urology

Admit patient under medics for close monitoring of renal function, and if no cause identified, renal US within 24 hours

12. Oncology emergencies

Malignant superior vena cava obstruction

There are several 'oncology emergencies', including symptoms due to a cancer as yet undiagnosed, complications of a known cancer, or complications caused by a cancer treatment. Some of these are covered in other algorithms within this book, e.g. spinal cord compression and neutropaenic sepsis. This chapter deals solely with malignant SVC obstruction.

The majority of cases of SVC obstruction are due to the presence of a malignant tumour in the mediastinum preventing venous drainage from the head, arms, and upper trunk. Lung cancer is the commonest cancer associated with SVC obstruction, but it can occur with lymphoma or cancers that metastasize to the mediastinal lymph nodes.

SVC obstruction usually develops over weeks or even months (chronic presentation is best managed with a phone call to an oncologist for advice), but occasionally it can develop over days and present acutely (patients in this situation may present to the Emergency Department).

Signs and symptoms

- Facial swelling, redness, headache (worse with stooping), periorbital oedema, engorged conjunctivae, papilloedema (late sign)
- Swelling of the arms, prominent distended veins on neck and upper chest wall
- Breathlessness, increased RR, cough, chest pain, stridor, cyanosis
- Other symptoms, e.g. dysphagia, visual disturbance, dizziness

Treatment

This depends on the cause of the obstruction, the severity of the symptoms, and the patient's prognosis. This makes obtaining a thorough history, performing a comprehensive examination, and relevant investigations key to decisions regarding management. The acute oncology team will make the decision regarding which treatments will be recommended for each individual patient; options include radiotherapy, chemotherapy, and minimally invasive stent placement.

History

This should include (if known):

- Cancer diagnosis
- Disease stage
- Treatment intent
- Drugs and timings of most recent treatment
- Has patient received treatment within last 6 weeks?
- Is patient for further treatment including resuscitation?
- What is the DNACPR (do not attempt cardiopulmonary resuscitation) status?
- Where is preferred place of care and death?

Note: it may be possible to obtain more detailed information via the cancer treatment centre's triage line or via direct access to oncology case notes.

Further reading

Acute care toolkit 7 Acute oncology on the acute medical unit October 2013
Scottish Palliative Care Guidelines Superior Vena Cava Obstruction May 2014

Algorithm for oncology emergencies

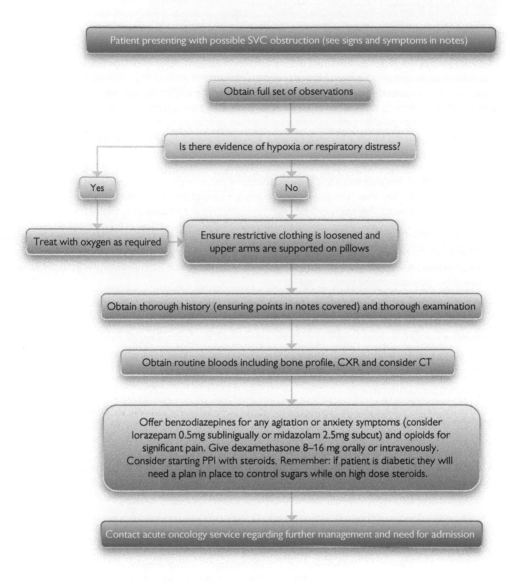

Patient presenting with possible SVC obstruction (see signs and symptoms in notes)

Obtain full set of observations

Is there evidence of hypoxia or respiratory distress?

Yes

No

Treat with oxygen as required

Ensure restrictive clothing is loosened and upper arms are supported on pillows

Obtain thorough history (ensuring points in notes covered) and thorough examination

Obtain routine bloods including bone profile, CXR and consider CT

Offer benzodiazepines for any agitation or anxiety symptoms (consider lorazepam 0.5mg sublingually or midazolam 2.5mg subcut) and opioids for significant pain. Give dexamethasone 8–16 mg orally or intravenously. Consider starting PPI with steroids. Remember: if patient is diabetic they will need a plan in place to control sugars while on high dose steroids.

Contact acute oncology service regarding further management and need for admission

13. Poisoning/self-harm

Introduction

There are two obvious aspects to assessment and management of patients who present with overdoses or self-harm. The medical assessment including resuscitation and emergency management must take precedence, but the psychosocial assessment is equally important and should not be delayed until after medical management is complete unless life-saving treatment is required, the patient has reduced conscious level, or there is another reason precluding assessment.

All staff dealing with patients presenting with poisoning must have access to TOXBASE and the NPIS telephone number. It is vital that TOXBASE is consulted for all patients presenting with poisoning at triage so that staff can be alerted early if any urgent treatment or monitoring is required.

All staff dealing with poisoning and self-harm patients should have a good working knowledge of the Mental Capacity Act (MCA), the steps required to assess capacity, the principles underlying the Act, and treating patients under Common Law. They should also be aware of the relevant parts of the Mental Health Act (MHA) that can be invoked in the area in which they work, and understand the limitations and responsibilities involved.

Australian Mental Health Triage Tool

This clinical tool can be used at point of entry to the ED to provide a systematic way of categorising the urgency of clinical presentations, and determining an appropriate service response and an optimal timeframe for intervention.

Table 8.4 … Australian Mental Health Triage Tool

Medical and traumatic management

This chapter covers a wide variety of presentations; therefore it is extremely important that TOXBASE advice is followed for specific overdoses. Where a patient has self-harmed, advanced trauma life support (ATLS) principles and/or usual wound management (see wound assessment and management in Section 6, Chapter 10) should be employed and surgical advice (where appropriate) should be followed.

Psychosocial assessment

Psychosocial assessment should include identification of the main clinical and demographic features known to be associated with risk of further self-harm and/or suicide, and identification of the key psychological characteristics associated with risk, in particular depression, hopelessness, and continuing suicidal intent. This assessment should be documented in the patient's notes and communicated to the patient's GP.

Psychosocial assessments done by ED staff will not be as comprehensive as those done by a mental health team; with this in mind it is best if ED staff have a locally agreed proforma to follow, and if there is any doubt as to the level of risk posed by the patient, the mental health team should be contacted.

Table 8.4 Australian Mental Health Triage Tool

Category	When to be seen	Situation
Red	Immediate	Definite danger to life (self or others)
Orange	Within 10 minutes	Probable risk of danger (self or others) Severe behavioural disturbance Patient physically restrained in department
Yellow	Within 30 minutes	Possible danger to self or others Moderate behavioural disturbance Severe distress
Green	Within 60 minutes	Moderate distress
Blue	Within 120 minutes	No danger to self or others No acute distress No behavioural disturbance

Further reading

NICE guideline (CG16) Self-harm: The short-term physical and psychological management and secondary prevention of self-harm in primary and secondary care. July 2004

NICE Clinical Knowledge Summaries, Poisoning or Overdose. May 2012

Algorithm for poisoning/self-harm

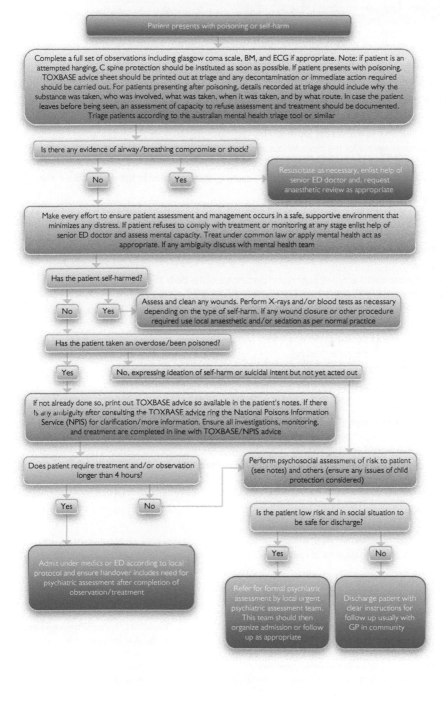

Patient presents with poisoning or self-harm

Complete a full set of observations including glasgow coma scale, BM, and ECG if appropriate. Note: if patient is an attempted hanging, C spine protection should be instituted as soon as possible. If patient presents with poisoning, TOXBASE advice sheet should be printed out at triage and any decontamination or immediate action required should be carried out. For patients presenting after poisoning, details recorded at triage should include why the substance was taken, who was involved, what was taken, when it was taken, and by what route. In case the patient leaves before being seen, an assessment of capacity to refuse assessment and treatment should be documented. Triage patients according to the australian mental health triage tool or similar

Is there any evidence of airway/breathing compromise or shock?

No

Yes

Resuscitate as necessary, enlist help of senior ED doctor and, request anaesthetic review as appropriate

Make every effort to ensure patient assessment and management occurs in a safe, supportive environment that minimizes any distress. If patient refuses to comply with treatment or monitoring at any stage enlist help of senior ED doctor and assess mental capacity. Treat under common law or apply mental health act as appropriate. If any ambiguity discuss with mental health team

Has the patient self-harmed?

No

Yes

Assess and clean any wounds. Perform X-rays and/or blood tests as necessary depending on the type of self-harm. If any wound closure or other procedure required use local anaesthetic and/or sedation as per normal practice

Has the patient taken an overdose/been poisoned?

Yes

No, expressing ideation of self-harm or suicidal intent but not yet acted out

If not already done so, print out TOXBASE advice so available in the patient's notes. If there is any ambiguity after consulting the TOXBASE advice ring the National Poisons Information Service (NPIS) for clarification/more information. Ensure all investigations, monitoring, and treatment are completed in line with TOXBASE/NPIS advice

Does patient require treatment and/or observation longer than 4 hours?

Perform psychosocial assessment of risk to patient (see notes) and others (ensure any issues of child protection considered)

Yes

No

Is the patient low risk and in social situation to be safe for discharge?

Yes

No

Admit under medics or ED according to local protocol and ensure handover includes need for psychiatric assessment after completion of observation/treatment

Refer for formal psychiatric assessment by local urgent psychiatric assessment team. This team should then organize admission or follow up as appropriate

Discharge patient with clear instructions for follow up usually with GP in community

14. Rashes

Introduction

This chapter covers rashes occurring in adults, which fall into four basic categories:

- Petechial/purpuric
- Erythematous
- Maculopapular
- Vesiculobullous

For petechial/purpuric rashes see the algorithm for bruising and spontaneous bleeding in this book (Section 8, Chapter 9). Remember, it is not the job of any ED doctor to diagnose every rash, but we should recognize or at least ask for senior review for the more serious and certainly life-threatening rashes, and there may be some more typical rashes that can be easily diagnosed in the Emergency Department.

Nikolsky's sign—With an erythematous rash, try applying lateral pressure to the skin and see if it sloughs

History and examination

Important questions to answer within the history and examination include:

- When did the rash appear and how quickly did it progress?
- What is the overall morphology (remember, there can be secondary changes) and did the rash change over time?
- What is the overall pattern, distribution, and percentage of the body affected and where did it start?
- Is the patient sick or not sick?
- Is the rash pruritic?
- Is there any past medical history and any history of recent travel?
- What is the patient's occupation/what are their hobbies?
- What medications is the patient taking?
- Have there been any recent changes in medication or products used?

Red flags for toxic rash

- Extremes of age
- Adenopathy or arthralgia
- Toxic appearance, hypotension, or high fever
- Severe pain or rapidly progressive rash
- Extensive skin involvement (anything >10% BSA should be concerning)
- Mucosal involvement (never good)
- Immunocompromised
- Positive Nikolsky's sign
- Petechial or purpuric morphology
- Specific lab abnormalities
- Common recognisable patterns of rash

Table 8.5 Common recognisable patterns of rash

Some common recognisable patterns	Diagnosis to consider
Preceded by pain, then blistering rash in dermatomal distribution	Shingles
Viral infection with bright red rash on cheeks usually seen in children	Parvovirus B19, slapped cheek syndrome
Hypersensitivity reaction usually to infection or various drugs, presents with typical target lesion	Erythema multiforme
Red rounded lumps beneath the skin usually on shins	Erythema nodosum
Fine, itchy, scaly rash. Starts with herald patch on chest, abdomen, or back, then spreads as patches to back, chest, and neck	Pityriasis rosea

Further reading

EM Practice.NET an evidence based approach to Emergency Medicine. Dermatology Emergencies: diagnosing and managing life threatening rashes

EmDOCs.NET Don't be rash: Emergency physician' approach to the undifferentiated lesion, Genine Sicilano MD

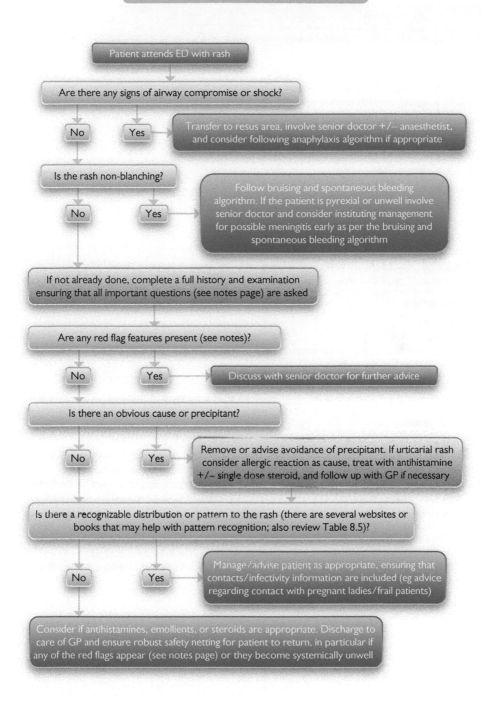

Algorithm for rashes

Patient attends ED with rash

↓

Are there any signs of airway compromise or shock?

No ↓   Yes → Transfer to resus area, involve senior doctor +/– anaesthetist, and consider following anaphylaxis algorithm if appropriate

↓

Is the rash non-blanching?

No ↓   Yes → Follow bruising and spontaneous bleeding algorithm. If the patient is pyrexial or unwell involve senior doctor and consider instituting management for possible meningitis early as per the bruising and spontaneous bleeding algorithm

↓

If not already done, complete a full history and examination ensuring that all important questions (see notes page) are asked

↓

Are any red flag features present (see notes)?

No ↓   Yes → Discuss with senior doctor for further advice

↓

Is there an obvious cause or precipitant?

No ↓   Yes → Remove or advise avoidance of precipitant. If urticarial rash consider allergic reaction as cause, treat with antihistamine +/– single dose steroid, and follow up with GP if necessary

↓

Is there a recognizable distribution or pattern to the rash (there are several websites or books that may help with pattern recognition; also review Table 8.5)?

No ↓   Yes → Manage/advise patient as appropriate, ensuring that contacts/infectivity information are included (eg advice regarding contact with pregnant ladies/frail patients)

↓

Consider if antihistamines, emollients, or steroids are appropriate. Discharge to care of GP and ensure robust safety netting for patient to return, in particular if any of the red flags appear (see notes page) or they become systemically unwell

15. Acute red eye

Definition

The differential diagnosis of acute red eye ranges from benign conditions that can be managed by the emergency physician to serious vision-threatening ones that require emergent ophthalmologic evaluation. Emergency physicians should be adept at recognizing high-risk features from the history and examination that would require urgent ophthalmologic referral and treatment.

History

The history should address the following essential components:

- Time of onset
- Photophobia
- Any visual disturbances
- Recent illnesses and trauma
- Ophthalmologic history
- Presence or absence of pain, foreign body sensation, and itching
- Presence and type of discharge

Examination

- Visual acuity
- Extraocular muscle function
- Gross appearance of sclera and conjunctiva
- Palpation for preauricular nodes
- Pupil shape and reactivity and comparison between pupils

Often, evaluation of the affected eye requires fluorescein staining and a cobalt blue light using a slit lamp.

Management

- Urgent referral means within 12 hours, emergency referral is within 1–2 days
- Treatment of acute angle-closure glaucoma mandates prompt and rapid transfer to an eye specialist. In the Emergency Department, IV acetazolamide 500 mg and topical pilocarpine 2% should be given
- Patients with allergic conjunctivitis almost always present with itching and may or may not have associated watery eyes and rhinorrhea
- Keratitis must be suspected in any patient presenting with painful red eye who uses contact lenses

Further reading

Ahmed R. Diagnosis and management of the acute red eye. *Emerg Med Clin N Am* 2008;26:35–55.
Carney S, Weisenthal RW. The red eye. In: Mushlin SB, Greene HL. Decision Making in Medicine: An Algorithmic Approach. Philadelphia: Mosby Elsevier, 2010, pp. 26–31.

Algorithm for acute red eye

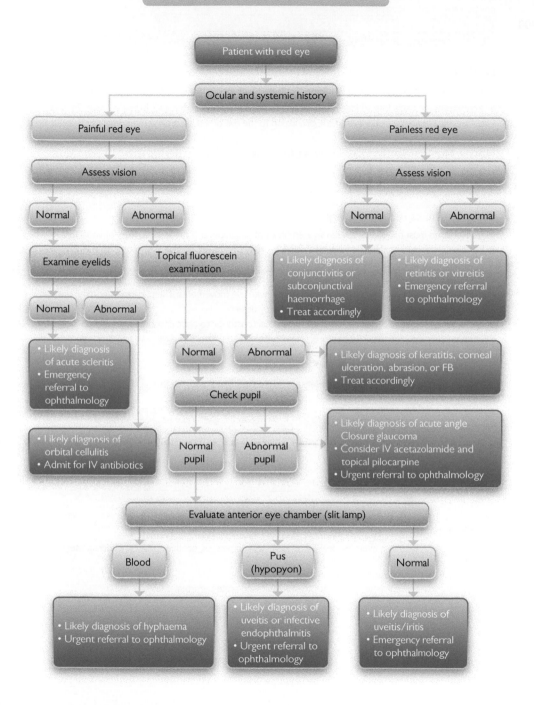

16. Acute visual loss

Definition

Loss of vision is considered acute if it develops within a few minutes to a couple of days and is classified as follows:

- Acute transient visual loss: sudden deficit in visual function in one or both eyes lasting less than 24 hours. It is caused by a temporary occlusion in the circulation to the eye or visual cortex, or by neuronal depression after a seizure or migraine
- Acute persistent visual loss: visual loss lasting more than 24 hours

Causes

Presence or absence of pain helps categorize acute loss of vision (Table 8.6).

Salient points in the history

- A distinction must be made between sudden onset of visual loss and sudden discovery of visual loss
- Keratitis produces a sharp superficial pain, while acute glaucoma produces a deep brow ache with **nausea and vomiting**
- Patients with keratitis, acute glaucoma, and uveitis usually present with conjunctival hyperaemia (red eye)
- Optic neuritis typically causes eye pain, particularly with eye movements. The pupil looks normal, but pupil reaction is abnormal with a relative afferent pupillary defect
- Bilateral loss of vision often suggests a retro-chiasmal (posterior to optic chiasm) visual pathway disorder
- Urgent referral means within 12 hours; emergency referral is within 1–2 days

Table 8.6 Causes of acute visual loss

Acute loss of vision without pain	Acute loss of vision with pain
• TIA (amaurosis fugax) or stroke • Retinal vein occlusion • Retinal artery occlusion • Retinal detachment • Optic neuropathies, e.g. non-arteritic ischaemic optic neuropathy • Vitreous haemorrhage • Macular degeneration • Ocular migraine • Functional loss of vision	• Acute angle-closure glaucoma • Painful optic neuropathies, e.g. arteritic ischaemic optic neuropathy (giant cell arteritis, GCA), or optic neuritis (usually painful but not always) • Corneal ulcer • Endophthalmitis • Ocular trauma

Further reading

http://www.merckmanuals.com/professional/eye_disorders/symptoms_of_ophthalmologic_disorders/acute_vision_loss.html
Approach to the adult with acute persistent visual loss
http://www.uptodate.com/contents/approach-to-the-adult-with-acute-persistent-visual-loss

Algorithm for acute visual loss

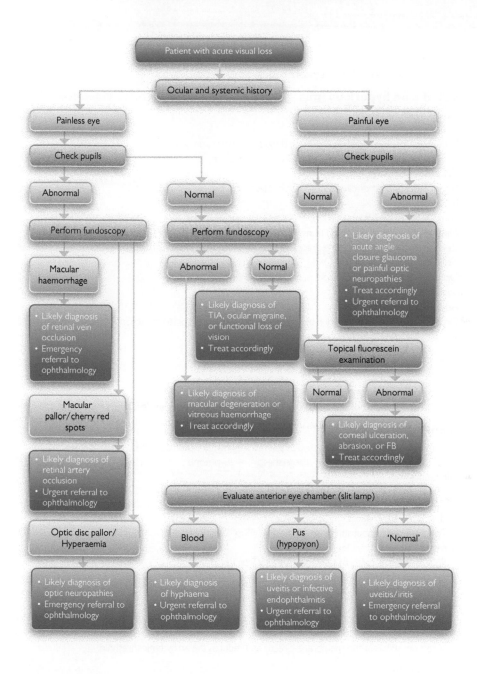

Patient with acute visual loss

Ocular and systemic history

Painless eye

Check pupils

- Abnormal

  Perform fundoscopy

  Macular haemorrhage
  - Likely diagnosis of retinal vein occlusion
  - Emergency referral to ophthalmology

  Macular pallor/cherry red spots
  - Likely diagnosis of retinal artery occlusion
  - Urgent referral to ophthalmology

  Optic disc pallor/ Hyperaemia
  - Likely diagnosis of optic neuropathies
  - Emergency referral to ophthalmology

- Normal

  Perform fundoscopy

  Abnormal
  - Likely diagnosis of macular degeneration or vitreous haemorrhage
  - Treat accordingly

  Normal
  - Likely diagnosis of TIA, ocular migraine, or functional loss of vision
  - Treat accordingly

Painful eye

Check pupils

- Normal
- Abnormal
  - Likely diagnosis of acute angle closure glaucoma or painful optic neuropathies
  - Treat accordingly
  - Urgent referral to ophthalmology

Topical fluorescein examination

- Normal
- Abnormal
  - Likely diagnosis of corneal ulceration, abrasion, or FB
  - Treat accordingly

Evaluate anterior eye chamber (slit lamp)

- Blood
  - Likely diagnosis of hyphaema
  - Urgent referral to ophthalmology

- Pus (hypopyon)
  - Likely diagnosis of uveitis or infective endophthalmitis
  - Urgent referral to ophthalmology

- 'Normal'
  - Likely diagnosis of uveitis/iritis
  - Emergency referral to ophthalmology

17. Hyperkalaemia

Introduction

True hyperkalaemia is rare in the presence of normal renal function.

Causes of true hyperkalaemia

- Decreased renal excretion
  - Acute renal failure
  - Patients with chronic renal failure or on dialysis with potassium load
  - Potassium-sparing diuretics (e.g. spironolactone, amiloride)
- Cell injury
  - Crush injury and other causes of rhabdomyolysis
  - Burns
  - Tumour lysis syndrome
  - Massive or incompatible blood transfusions
- K+ cellular shifts (intracellular to extracellular)
  - Acidosis from any cause (e.g. DKA)
  - Drugs (suxamethonium, β-blockers, digoxin poisoning)
- Hypoaldosterone
  - Addison's disease
  - Drug induced (NSAIDs, ACE inhibitors, angiotensin II receptor blockers, heparin)
- Renal tubular acidosis type IV

Degree of hyperkalaemia

- Mild: K+ 5.5–5.9 mmol/L
- Moderate: K+ 6.0–6.4 mmol/L
- Severe: K+ ≥6.5 mmol/L, or if ECG changes or symptoms occurring at any level ≥5.5 mmol/L

Signs and symptoms

Even extremely severe, life-threatening hyperkalaemia may be asymptomatic There may, however, be

- Muscle weakness and cramps
- Paraesthesia
- Hypotonia
- Focal neurological deficit
- Palpitations

ECG changes

- Peaked, tall, 'tented' T waves
- Small/flattened, broad or absent P waves
- Widening of the QRS complex
- Sinusoidal ('sine wave' pattern) QRST leading to VT or VF
- Atrioventricular block or dissociation

Treatment

Both insulin/glucose combination and salbutamol work by shifting K+ from the extracellular compartment to the intracellular compartment, which in turn should minimize the effects of K+ on the electrical stability of the membranes. IV calcium stabilizes the membrane directly and reduces the arrhythmic threshold.

Further reading

Clinical Practice Guidelines. Treatment of Acute Hyperkalaemia in Adults. UK Renal Association. July 2012

Guidelines for the Treatment of Hyperkalaemia in Adults, Clinical Resource Efficiency Support Team (CREST). http://www.crestni.org.uk/publications/hyperkalaemia-booklet.pdf

Algorithm for hyperkalaemia

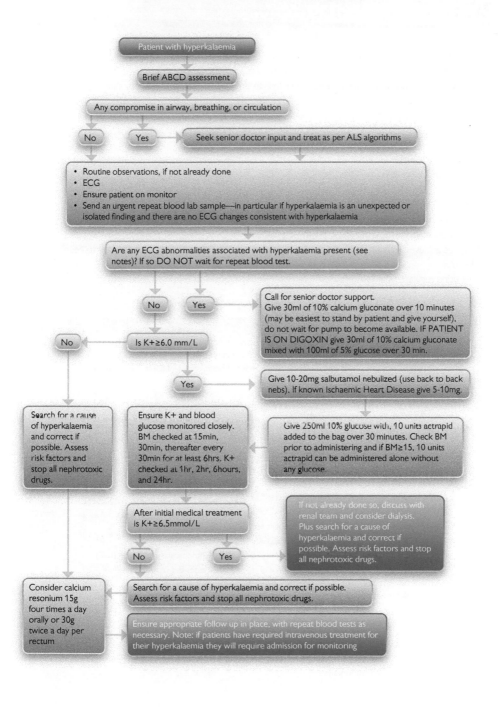

Patient with hyperkalaemia

Brief ABCD assessment

Any compromise in airway, breathing, or circulation

No   Yes → Seek senior doctor input and treat as per ALS algorithms

- Routine observations, if not already done
- ECG
- Ensure patient on monitor
- Send an urgent repeat blood lab sample—in particular if hyperkalaemia is an unexpected or isolated finding and there are no ECG changes consistent with hyperkalaemia

Are any ECG abnormalities associated with hyperkalaemia present (see notes)? If so DO NOT wait for repeat blood test.

No   Yes →

Call for senior doctor support.
Give 30ml of 10% calcium gluconate over 10 minutes (may be easiest to stand by patient and give yourself), do not wait for pump to become available. IF PATIENT IS ON DIGOXIN give 30ml of 10% calcium gluconate mixed with 100ml of 5% glucose over 30 min.

No ←   Is K+≥6.0 mm/L

Yes → Give 10-20mg salbutamol nebulized (use back to back nebs). If known Ischaemic Heart Disease give 5-10mg.

Search for a cause of hyperkalaemia and correct if possible. Assess risk factors and stop all nephrotoxic drugs.

Ensure K+ and blood glucose monitored closely. BM checked at 15min, 30min, thereafter every 30min for at least 6hrs. K+ checked at 1hr, 2hr, 6hours, and 24hr.

Give 250ml 10% glucose with, 10 units actrapid added to the bag over 30 minutes. Check BM prior to administering and if BM≥15, 10 units actrapid can be administered alone without any glucose.

After initial medical treatment is K+≥6.5mmol/L

No   Yes → If not already done so, discuss with renal team and consider dialysis. Plus search for a cause of hyperkalaemia and correct if possible. Assess risk factors and stop all nephrotoxic drugs.

Consider calcium resonium 15g four times a day orally or 30g twice a day per rectum ←

Search for a cause of hyperkalaemia and correct if possible. Assess risk factors and stop all nephrotoxic drugs.

Ensure appropriate follow up in place, with repeat blood tests as necessary. Note: if patients have required intravenous treatment for their hyperkalaemia they will require admission for monitoring

18. Rhabdomyolysis

Rhabdomyolysis is a syndrome characterised by muscle necrosis and release of intracellular muscle constituents into the circulation. Typically, CK levels are markedly elevated. Disease severity ranges from isolated CK rise to life-threatening disease with enzyme release, electrolyte disturbance, and acute kidney injury.

Causes

Common causes of rhabdomyolysis can be summarised in table 8.7

Diagnostic tests

See table 8.8.

Alkalinisation of urine

- This is said to enhance the solubility of myoglobin
- Usually effective in first 8 hours
- It can be achieved by 1 L 1.26% sodium bicarbonate over 2 hours and repeat as necessary to keep urinary pH >7.5
- Test urine regularly with pH strips to monitor

Table 8.7 Common causes of rhabdomyolysis can be summarised

Causes	Examples
Crush injury	Trauma, long lie
Exertional	Extreme physical exercise, seizures
Drugs	Statins, SSRIs, antipsychotics, heroin, cocaine, MDMA, ketamine, LSD
Toxins	Snake/insect bite, mushroom poisoning
Body temperature	Hyperthermia
Metabolic	HHS, DKA
Infection	Coxsackie virus, influenza A and B viruses, HIV, Epstein–Barr, bacterial infection, malaria (*Falciparum*)

Table 8.8 Diagnostic tests

Test	Important findings
U&E	Elevated K+ and AKI
ABG	Metabolic acidosis
CK	Elevated CK indicates rhabdomyolysis
Coagulation profile	Deranged in disseminated intravascular coagulation (DIC)
Urine	Presence of myoglobin—causes dirty red-brown colour (looks like cola)
Calcium and phosphate	High phosphate Calcium initially low, then rebounds and rises

Further reading

UpToDate, Clinical manifestations and diagnosis of rhabdomyolysis, https://www.uptodate.com/contents/clinical-manifestations-and-diagnosis-of-rhabdomyolysis

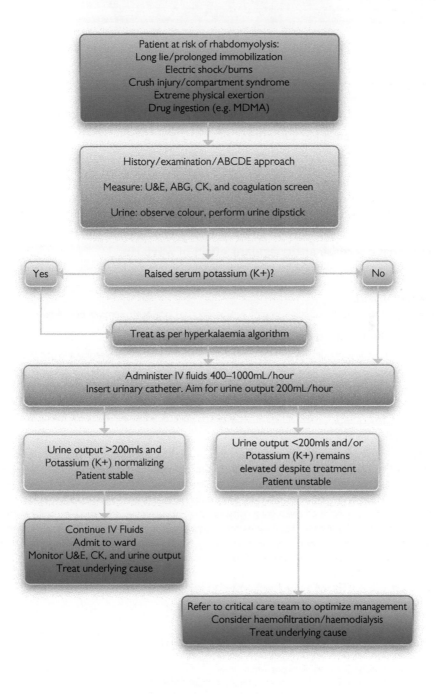

Algorithm for rhabdomyolysis

Patient at risk of rhabdomyolysis:
Long lie/prolonged immobilization
Electric shock/burns
Crush injury/compartment syndrome
Extreme physical exertion
Drug ingestion (e.g. MDMA)

History/examination/ABCDE approach

Measure: U&E, ABG, CK, and coagulation screen

Urine: observe colour, perform urine dipstick

Raised serum potassium (K+)?

Yes

No

Treat as per hyperkalaemia algorithm

Administer IV fluids 400–1000mL/hour
Insert urinary catheter. Aim for urine output 200mL/hour

Urine output >200mls and
Potassium (K+) normalizing
Patient stable

Urine output <200mls and/or
Potassium (K+) remains
elevated despite treatment
Patient unstable

Continue IV Fluids
Admit to ward
Monitor U&E, CK, and urine output
Treat underlying cause

Refer to critical care team to optimize management
Consider haemofiltration/haemodialysis
Treat underlying cause

19. High INR

Warfarin

Warfarin is an oral anticoagulant that antagonizes the effect of vitamin K. It takes at least 48–72 hours for the anticoagulant effect to fully develop and anticoagulation can last for 4–5 days. Careful monitoring of PT, expressed as the INR, especially in the early stages of anticoagulation, is essential. Warfarin therapy is complicated by the delayed effect of dose alteration and because various medical conditions and other drugs modify warfarin activity.

Factors that increase anticoagulant effect of warfarin

- Liver disease
- Infection/sepsis
- Thyrotoxicosis
- Alcohol/major dietary changes (consumption of cranberry and grapefruit juices)
- Drugs, e.g. ciprofloxacin, NSAIDs, salicylates, metronidazole, chloramphenicol, cephalosporins, amiodarone, antifungals (azoles)

Factors that decrease anticoagulant effect of warfarin

- Pregnancy
- Anaemia
- Nephrotic syndrome
- Drugs, e.g. rifampicin, carbamazepine, griseofulvin, barbiturates, oral contraceptives, penicillins

Life-/sight-/limb-threatening bleeding

Life-threatening bleeding includes intracranial, retroperitoneal, and significant GI bleeding and pericardial bleeding. Sight-threatening bleeding refers to intraocular and not conjunctival bleeding. Limb-threatening bleeding would include muscle bleeding leading to or threatening the development of compartment syndrome. A **strong** clinical suspicion of intracranial bleed following head injury should trigger administration of Beriplex® prior to the results of investigations.

Warfarin reversal

The anticoagulant effect of warfarin can be antagonized by administering vitamin K. This can be given orally or intravenously. Oral vitamin K is safe and adequate treatment for the majority of patients, but it can be given IV in life-, limb-, or sight-threatening bleed or in patients with significant bleeding or at high risk of bleeding or falls. IV vitamin K should be given as a slow bolus as it can cause anaphylaxis.

Full warfarin reversal can be achieved using human prothrombin complex (Beriplex) in combination with IV vitamin K. Depending on local guidelines, Beriplex often requires authorization for use by a consultant haematologist. Human prothrombin complex is prepared from human plasma and contains Factor IX together with Factors II, VII, and X. The standard dose is 30 units/kg rounded up to the nearest 500 units and is given over 10 minutes as a slow IV bolus injection.

Fresh frozen plasma (FFP) use is now largely limited to areas/situations where human prothrombin complex is not available.

Further reading

Biss T et al. Northern Region Haematologists Group Guide to Warfarin Reversal.
BNF
NICE Clinical Knowledge Summary: Anticoagulation—oral.
Huyen A, Tran SD, Chunilal PL, et al., on behalf of the Australasian Society of Thrombosis and Haemostasis. An update of consensus guidelines for warfarin reversal. Med J Aust 2013;198(4):198–199.

Algorithm for high INR

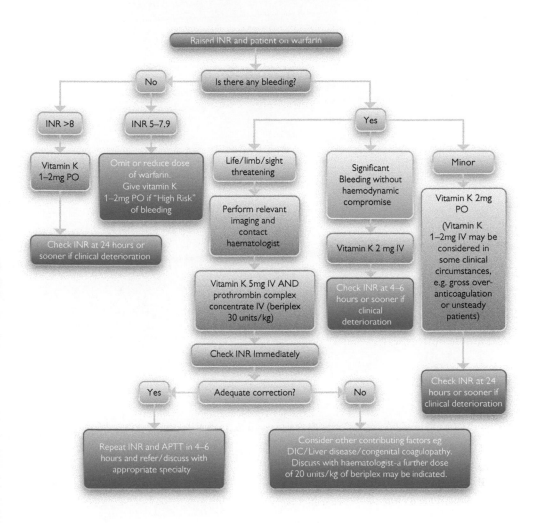

SECTION 9

Other surgical

1. Acute back pain

Definition

Most people will experience at least one episode of low back pain during their adult lifetime. Most of these are of short duration, lasting from days to a few weeks, and resolve with little if any therapeutic intervention. The challenge to the emergency physician is to identify those patients who may benefit from diagnostic interventions to further evaluate their pain.

Red flags

For red flags in back pain see Table 9.1.

Table 9.1 Back pain red flags

Features	Age 16< or >50 with **new-onset** pain History of malignancy Unexplained weight loss Previous longstanding steroid use Recent serious illness Recent significant infection
Signs	Saddle paraesthesia Reduced anal tone Hip or knee weakness Generalised neurological deficit Progressive spinal deformity Urinary retention
Symptoms	Non-mechanical pain (worse at rest) Thoracic pain Fevers/rigors General malaise Urinary retention

Cauda equina syndrome

Cauda equina syndrome is rare but catastrophic and requires urgent surgical consultation. All patients with back pain should be asked about urinary retention. Those reporting this symptom should be examined for bilateral leg weakness, depressed leg deep tendon reflexes, and perineal numbness. These patients may report bowel, bladder, and sexual dysfunction, and severe pain.

Malignancy

Recurrent metastatic cancer must be considered in all cases of back pain in cancer survivors. Cancers frequently metastatic to the spine include breast, lung, gut, prostate, renal, and thyroid. Clues to the diagnosis include a gradual onset of symptoms and a history of cancer.

Non-spine causes

AAA dissection or rupture should be suspected in any patients with lumbar pain who are known to have AAA or in those at risk of AAA.

When to obtain plain radiography

Clinicians should not routinely obtain plain imaging in patients with low back pain; exposure to unnecessary ionizing radiation should be avoided. The amount of gonadal radiation from obtaining a single plain radiograph (two views) of the lumbar spine is equivalent to being exposed to a daily chest radiograph for more than 1 year.

Plain imaging is recommended in:

- Suspected fracture (trauma, prolonged steroid use, osteoporosis, etc.)
- Suspected cancer (new onset of low back pain with history of cancer, multiple risk factors for cancer, or strong clinical suspicion for cancer)
- Low back pain >6 weeks duration

Further reading

Chou R, Qaseem A, Snow V, et al. Diagnosis and treatment of low back pain: a joint clinical practice guideline from the American College of Physicians and the American Pain Society. *Ann Intern Med* 2007;147(7):478–491.

Goertz M, Thorson D, Bonsell J, Bonte B, Campbell R, Haake B. Adult acute and subacute low back pain; institute for clinical systems improvement. Bloomington, MN, USA, 2012; pp. 1–91.

Algorithm for acute back pain

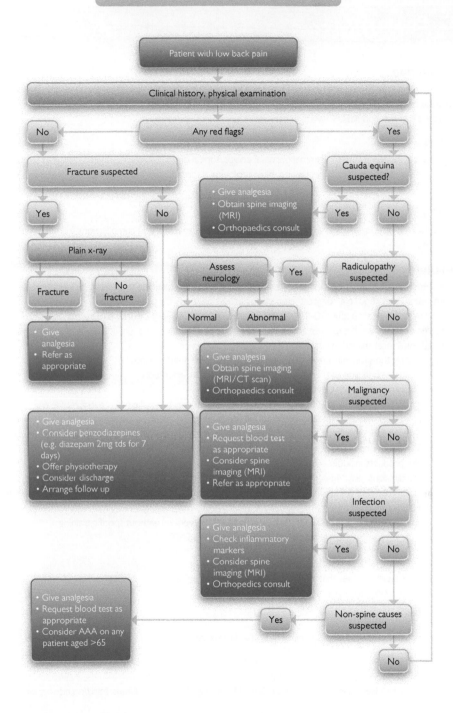

Patient with low back pain

Clinical history, physical examination

Any red flags? — No / Yes

No:
Fracture suspected

Yes / No

Yes (Fracture suspected):
Plain x-ray

Fracture / No fracture

Fracture:
- Give analgesia
- Refer as appropriate

- Give analgesia
- Consider benzodiazepines (e.g. diazepam 2mg tds for 7 days)
- Offer physiotherapy
- Consider discharge
- Arrange follow up

Yes (Any red flags):
Cauda equina suspected?

Yes:
- Give analgesia
- Obtain spine imaging (MRI)
- Orthopaedics consult

No:
Radiculopathy suspected

Yes:
Assess neurology — Normal / Abnormal

Abnormal:
- Give analgesia
- Obtain spine imaging (MRI/CT scan)
- Orthopaedics consult

No:
Malignancy suspected

Yes:
- Give analgesia
- Request blood test as appropriate
- Consider spine imaging (MRI)
- Refer as appropriate

No:
Infection suspected

Yes:
- Give analgesia
- Check inflammatory markers
- Consider spine imaging (MRI)
- Orthopedics consult

No:
Non-spine causes suspected

Yes:
- Give analgesia
- Request blood test as appropriate
- Consider AAA on any patient aged >65

No

2. Epistaxis

Introduction

- Most epistaxis is self-limiting and harmless; often a cause is not identified
- 80–90% of cases originate from Little's area on the anterior nasal septum
- Up to 60% of the population have experienced an episode of epistaxis

Causes

- Local causes include trauma, inflammation, nasal polyps, topical drugs, surgery, vascular causes, and tumours
- More general causes include hypertension, haematological disorders, environmental factors, systemic drugs, and excessive alcohol consumption

Complications

- Complications of epistaxis are rare and include hypovolaemia, anaemia, and complications from nasal packing treatment

Management

- A posterior bleed (bleeding is profuse, from both nostrils, and the bleeding site cannot be identified on examination) may require a Foley catheter and/or admission to ENT
- If bleeding does not stop after 10–15 minutes of pressure, nasal cautery or nasal packing may be used
- Consider nasal cautery if expertise and facilities are available:
  - Use topical local anaesthetic spray
  - Lightly apply the silver nitrate stick to the bleeding point for 3–10 seconds
  - Only cauterize one side of the septum to avoid nasal septal perforation
  - Avoid touching areas that do not need treatment
- If bleeding stops, a topical antiseptic such as Naseptin® cream may be applied to prevent rebleeding (qds for 10 days), particularly in children for whom cautery is not an option (beware peanut allergy)
- Consider nasal packing:
  - Anaesthetize the nasal cavity with topical local anaesthetic spray
  - Available products include:
    - Nasal tampons (e.g. Merocel®)— effective and easy to use
    - Inflatable packs (e.g. Rapid-Rhino®)— effective and more comfortable to insert and remove than nasal tampons
    - Ribbon gauze impregnated with Vaseline®— not recommended without specific training
  - Admit the person to hospital for observation, preferably to ENT

Discharge self-care advice

- For 24 hours avoid activities that may increase the risk of rebleeding:
  - Blowing or picking the nose
  - Heavy lifting or strenuous exercise
  - Drinking alcohol or hot drinks
- If bleeding restarts and does not respond to first-aid measures, the person should seek medical advice

Further reading

Kucik CJ, Clenney T. Management of epistaxis. *Am Fam Phys* 2005;71(2):305–311.

National Institute for Health and Care Excellence. Clinical Knowledge Summary: Epistaxis. http://cks.nice.org.uk/epistaxis.

Algorithm for epistaxis

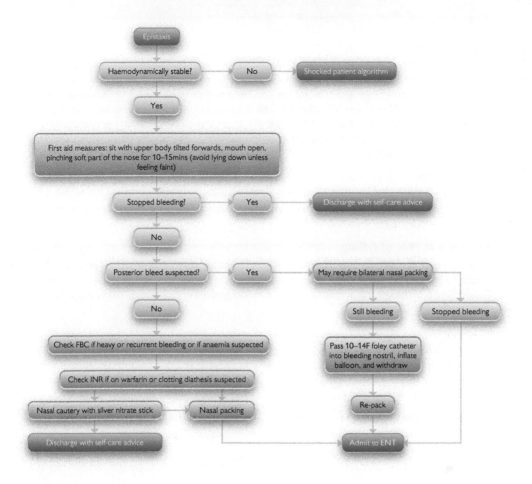

Introduction

Falls are increasingly common with advancing age, with 30% of over 65-year-olds and 50% of over 80-year-olds having at least one fall per year.

This algorithm should be applied to all patients presenting to Emergency Departments who are 65 years or over and any patient 50–64 years old if deemed to be at increased risk of falling due to an underlying condition. As part of the NICE guidance for prevention of falls, all such patients during any contact with health professionals should now routinely be asked if they have fallen in the past year and asked about the frequency, context, and characteristics of such fall(s).

Assessment

A multifactorial falls assessment may occur as an inpatient or in the setting of a falls clinic service. The focus of these may be slightly different, but in both cases the assessment should be carried out by a healthcare professional with appropriate skills and experience.

Patients at risk of falling

It is important to identify patients at risk of falling as early as possible, and appropriate equipment and staffing levels should be provided during the patient's time in the Emergency Department. Ideally, an area of the Emergency Department could be designated for such patients with appropriate flooring, lighting, furniture, and fittings.

Awareness

All ED staff should undergo regular training in basic falls assessment and prevention and be aware of local pathways to refer to falls services. ED staff should have access to patient information leaflets regarding falls.

It is vitally important that ED staff are aware of the services available to them with regard to access to physiotherapy and occupational therapy (OT) assessment, access to short-term increase in social services, and referral pathways to falls services in their locality.

Further reading

NICE guideline (CG161) Falls Assessment and prevention of falls in older people June2013

Algorithm for falls

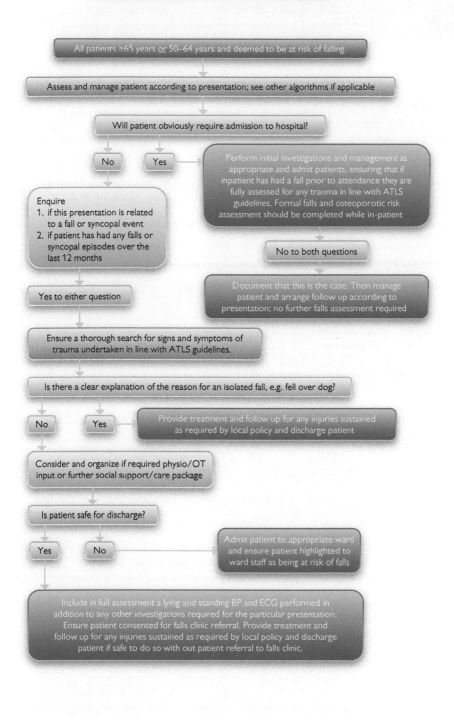

All patients >65 years or 50–64 years and deemed to be at risk of falling

Assess and manage patient according to presentation; see other algorithms if applicable

Will patient obviously require admission to hospital?

No

Yes

Perform initial investigations and management as appropriate and admit patients, ensuring that if inpatient has had a fall prior to attendance they are fully assessed for any trauma in line with ATLS guidelines. Formal falls and osteoporotic risk assessment should be completed while in-patient

Enquire
1. if this presentation is related to a fall or syncopal event
2. if patient has had any falls or syncopal episodes over the last 12 months

No to both questions

Document that this is the case. Then manage patient and arrange follow up according to presentation; no further falls assessment required

Yes to either question

Ensure a thorough search for signs and symptoms of trauma undertaken in line with ATLS guidelines.

Is there a clear explanation of the reason for an isolated fall, e.g. fell over dog?

No

Yes

Provide treatment and follow up for any injuries sustained as required by local policy and discharge patient

Consider and organize if required physio/OT input or further social support/care package

Is patient safe for discharge?

Yes

No

Admit patient to appropriate ward and ensure patient highlighted to ward staff as being at risk of falls

Include in full assessment a lying and standing BP and ECG performed in addition to any other investigations required for the particular presentation. Ensure patient consented for falls clinic referral. Provide treatment and follow up for any injuries sustained as required by local policy and discharge patient if safe to do so with out patient referral to falls clinic.

4. Non-traumatic limb pain and swelling

Introduction

This chapter focuses on acute pain/swelling (<3 months).

D-dimer

D-dimer is a fibrin degradation product. It is detectable at levels >500 ng/mL of fibrinogen equivalent units in nearly all patients with venous thromboembolism. It is a sensitive test but lacks specificity for the diagnosis of DVT and is therefore only useful when negative (value <500 ng/mL).

If DVT is not a diagnostic possibility, a D-dimer test should not be done, because a positive result may redirect a clinician away from investigating the true cause of the leg symptoms towards unnecessarily investigating for DVT

Revised Wells score

A variety of clinical decision rules can be used to assess the clinical probability of having DVT. The Revised Wells score (RWS) is the most commonly used (Table 9.2).

Table 9.2 The Revised Wells Score—a commonly used clinical decision tool

Symptom and risk factors	Points
Active cancer, or cancer that's been treated within last 6 months	1
Paralysed leg	1
Recently bedridden for more than 3 days or had major surgery within last four weeks	1
Tenderness near a deep vein	1
Swollen leg	1
Swollen calf with diameter that's more than 3 cm larger than the other calf's	1
Pitting edema in one leg	1
Large veins in your legs that aren't varicose veins	1
Previously diagnosed with DVT	1
Other diagnosis more likely	−2
Score	Result
2 or higher	DVT is likely
1 or lower	DVT is not likely

Data from Wells et al. Evaluation of D-Dimer in the Diagnosis of Suspected Deep-Vein Thrombosis, N Engl J Med 2003; 349:1227–1235.
DOI: 10.1056/NEJMoa023153.

It is important to bear in mind that the RWS for DVT is not validated for use in patients with suspected DVT at sites other than the lower limb, in hospitalised patients, or in pregnant women.

Acute limb ischaemia should be thought of in patients presenting with acute non-traumatic limb pain and distal pulses should be assessed with or without the assistance of hand-held Doppler.

Ankle-brachial pressure index

The resting systolic blood pressure at the ankle is compared with the systolic brachial pressure and the ratio of the two pressures defines the ankle-brachial pressure index (ABPI).

- Claudication: 0.4 and 0.9 • Rest pain: 0.2–0.4 • Tissue loss (ulcer, gangrene): 0–0.4

Notes

- Stress fractures most frequently occur in weight-bearing bones, such as tibia. Initial plain imaging might look normal
- Be aware of compartment syndrome after heavy exercise like running. A high index of suspicion is crucial

Further reading

Scarvelis D, Wells PS. Diagnosis and treatment of deep-vein thrombosis. *CMAJ* 2006;175(9):1087–1092.
Scottish Intercollegiate Guidelines Network (SIGN) 2010. Prevention and Management of Venous Thromboembolism.

Algorithm for non-traumatic limb pain and swelling

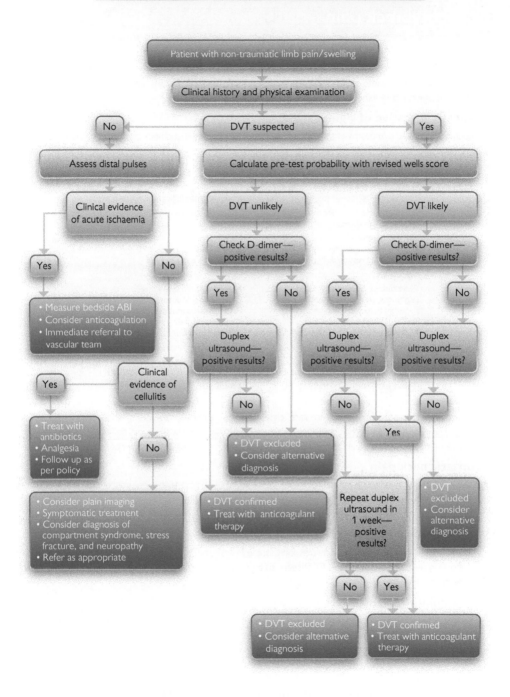

5. Acute neck pain

Background

Neck pain can be classified into acute (< 6 weeks), sub-acute (6 weeks-6 months) and chronic (>6 months). Acute neck pain can be further classified into traumatic and non-traumatic.

Features suggestive of significant disease

The following signs and symptoms in patients presenting with non-traumatic neck pain suggest the potential for significant disease (see Table 9.3).

Table 9.3 Neck pain red flags

Red flag	Potential pathological process
Concurrent chest pain, shortness of breath, autonomic symptoms	Myocardial ischaemia
Infective symptoms: (e.g. fever, meningism, history of immunosuppression or IV drug use)	Meningitis Discitis Epidural abscess
Headache, vomiting, altered mental status	Subarachnoid haemorrhage
Constitutional symptoms: (e.g. fevers, weight loss, anorexia, past or current history of malignancy)	Malignancy/infiltrative process Rheumatological disease: Polymyalgia rheumatica Giant cell arteritis
Neurology: (e.g. signs or symptoms of upper motor neuron pathology)	Cervical cord compression Demyelinating process
Ripping/tearing neck sensation	Arterial dissection (carotid/vertebral)
History of rheumatoid arthritis	Atlanto-axial disruption

Although sinister causes of neck pain are rare, clinicians must be mindful of red flags that may indicate serious pathology. The clinical history, rather than the physical examination, remains the most critical step in determining the likely cause of cervical spine pain, whereas biochemical tests and imaging are not part of routine assessment.

Traumatic neck pain

Patients with trauma presenting to the Emergency Departments with neck pain is not uncommon and fortunately most are soft tissue related however, very few of them have a cervical-spine fracture and must be managed appropriately to prevent spinal cord injuries and long term sequelae

Which patient needs imaging?

There are 2 widely used clinical decision rules for C spine imaging, NEXUS rules and the Canadian C spine Rule (CCR). For the alert stable patient, the CCR seem to be superior to NEXUS rule with respect to sensitivity and specificity for cervical spine injuries.

Salient points

- A dangerous mechanism is considered to be a fall from an elevation ≥3 ft or 5 stairs; an axial load to the head (e.g., diving); a motor vehicle collision at high speed (>100 km/hr) or with rollover or ejection; a collision involving a motorized recreational vehicle; or a bicycle collision.
- No force should be used when assessing neck movements and the patient should be asked to actively movement their neck.
- To be able to assess neck movement, you would need a fully cooperative alert patient
- Adequate lateral spine X ray should show the entire 7 cervical spine vertebras and the top of the first thoracic vertebrae.

Further reading

Teichtahl AJ, McColl G. An approach to neck pain for the family physician. *Aust Fam Physician*. 2013 Nov;42(11):774–777.
Stiell IG, Clement CM, McKnight RD et al. The Canadian C-Spine Rule versus the NEXUS low-risk criteria in patients with trauma. *N Engl J Med*. 2003;349:2510–2518.

Algorithm for acute neck pain

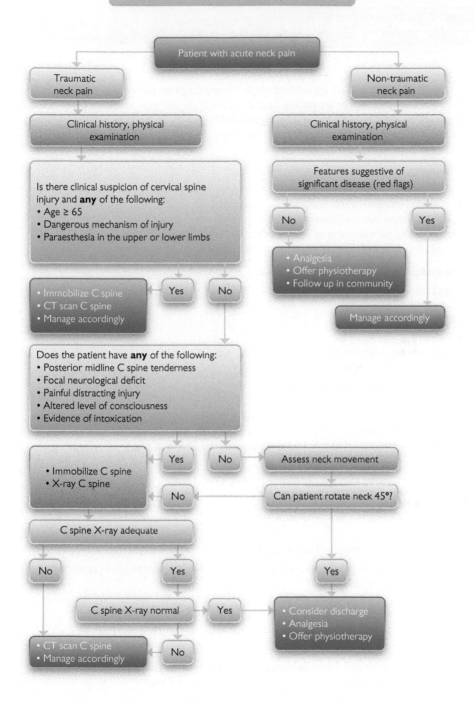

Patient with acute neck pain

Traumatic neck pain

Clinical history, physical examination

Is there clinical suspicion of cervical spine injury and **any** of the following:
• Age ≥ 65
• Dangerous mechanism of injury
• Paraesthesia in the upper or lower limbs

Yes   No

• Immobilize C spine
• CT scan C spine
• Manage accordingly

Does the patient have **any** of the following:
• Posterior midline C spine tenderness
• Focal neurological deficit
• Painful distracting injury
• Altered level of consciousness
• Evidence of intoxication

Yes   No   Assess neck movement

• Immobilize C spine
• X-ray C spine

No   Can patient rotate neck 45°?

C spine X-ray adequate

No   Yes   Yes

C spine X-ray normal   Yes   • Consider discharge
• Analgesia
• Offer physiotherapy

• CT scan C spine
• Manage accordingly   No

Non-traumatic neck pain

Clinical history, physical examination

Features suggestive of significant disease (red flags)

No   Yes

• Analgesia
• Offer physiotherapy
• Follow up in community

Manage accordingly

6. Painful ear (otalgia)

Definitions

Otalgia can be divided into primary and referred otalgia. Primary otalgia can be caused by disease in the external, middle, or inner ear, but the three are indistinguishable in terms of the pain experienced.

The general ear region has a sensory innervation provided by four cranial nerves (V, VII, IX, X) and two spinal segments (C2, C3). Hence, pathology in other 'non-ear' parts of the body innervated by these neural pathways may cause referred otalgia.

Assessment

- The history should be complete and specifically encompass a review of otologic symptomatology, swallowing disorders, sinus problems, and cervicofacial pain syndromes
- Physical examination should include otologic, head, and neck examination
- In primary otalgia, ear examination is usually abnormal, and vice versa
- The initial aim is to differentiate primary from referred otalgia

Causes of primary otalgia

- Foreign body
- Otitis media
- Otitis externa
- Trauma

Less common causes, which should not be overlooked, include:

- Necrotizing otitis externa (suspect in refractory otitis externa in patients with diabetes, older patients, and immunocompromised patients, and pain disproportionate to examination findings)
- Ramsay–Hunt syndrome (herpes zoster oticus)
- Mstoiditis (recent or concurrent otitis media, retroauricular pain, protrusion of auricle, and tender edematous mastoid on examination)
- Acute cholesteatoma (epidermal cysts composed of desquamating epithelium)

Causes of referred otalgia

- Dental causes
- Pharyngitis or tonsillitis
- Temporomandibular joint (TMJ) syndrome
- Abscess

Less common causes, which should not be overlooked, include:

- Temporal arteritis (age >50, jaw claudication, diplopia, temporal arteries may be tender, prominent, or beaded, and ESR usually >50)
- Neuralgias (e.g. trigeminal, glossopharyngeal)
- Thoracic aneurysms (more common in older men and may have risk factors for atherosclerosis)
- Referred pain from angina pectoris or MI

Further reading

Otalgia, Author John C Li. https://emedicine.medscape.com/article/845173-overview

John W. Ely, Marlan R. Hansen, Elizabeth C. Clark. University of Iowa Carver College of Medicine, Iowa City, Iowa. *Am Fam Physician.* 2008 Mar 1;77(5):621–628.

Algorithm for painful ear (otalgia)

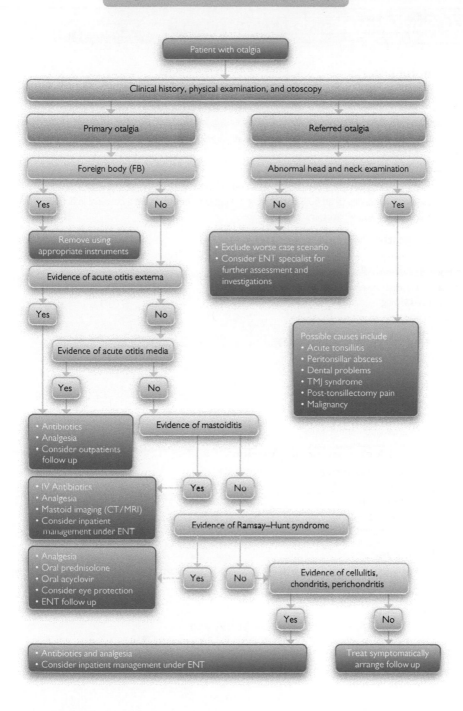

7. Sore throat

The Centor criteria

The Centor criteria were developed to predict bacterial infection (group A beta-haemolytic streptococcus, GABHS) in people with acute sore throat.

- Presence of tonsillar exudate
- Presence of tender anterior cervical lymphadenopathy or lymphadenitis
- History of fever
- Absence of cough

>= of these criteria equates to a 40–60% chance of GABHS and therefore the patient may benefit from antibiotics. <3 of these criteria equates to an 80% chance that the patient does not have a bacterial infection and therefore antibiotics are unlikely to be necessary.

Signs suggestive of acute epiglottitis

- Respiratory distress
- Drooling
- Systemically very unwell
- Painful swallowing
- Muffled voice

Extra signs suggestive of quinsy

- Drooling
- Trismus
- Hot potato or muffled voice
- Asymmetric tonsillar hypertrophy
- Inferior and medial displacement of the tonsil
- Contralateral deviation of the uvular

Patients at risk of immunosuppression

- Taking disease-modifying antirheumatic drugs (DMARDs)
- Taking carbimazole
- On or recent chemotherapy
- Known or suspected leukaemia, asplenia, aplastic anaemia, HIV/AIDs
- Taking immunosuppressive drugs post transplant

Glandular fever

Glandular fever is likely if the FBC has >20% atypical lymphocytes or >10% atypical lymphocytes and the lymphocyte count is >50% of the total WBC count.

Further reading

NICE Clinical Knowledge Summaries Glandular Fever February 2010
SIGN 117 Management of Sore Throat and Indications for Tonsillectomy April 2010

Algorithm for sore throat

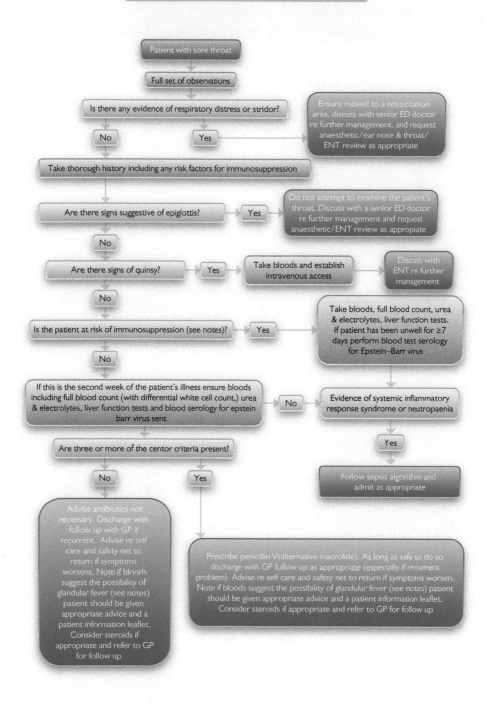

Patient with sore throat

Full set of observations

Is there any evidence of respiratory distress or stridor?

No → Yes → Ensure moved to a resuscitation area, discuss with senior ED doctor re further management, and request anaesthetic/ear nose & throat/ENT review as appropriate

Take thorough history including any risk factors for immunosuppression

Are there signs suggestive of epiglottis? → Yes → Do not attempt to examine the patient's throat. Discuss with a senior ED doctor re further management and request anaesthetic/ENT review as appropiate

No

Are there signs of quinsy? → Yes → Take bloods and establish intravenous access → Discuss with ENT re further management

No

Is the patient at risk of immunosuppression (see notes)? → Yes → Take bloods, full blood count, urea & electrolytes, liver function tests. If patient has been unwell for ≥7 days perform blood test serology for Epstein–Barr virus

No

If this is the second week of the patient's illness ensure bloods including full blood count (with differential white cell count,) urea & electrolytes, liver function tests and blood serology for epstein barr virus sent → No → Evidence of systemic inflammatory response syndrome or neutropaenia

Are three or more of the centor criteria present?

Yes → Follow sepsis algorithm and admit as appropriate

No → Advise antibiotics not necessary. Discharge with follow up with GP if recurrent. Advise re self care and safety net to return if symptoms worsens. Note if bloods suggest the possibility of glandular fever (see notes) patient should be given appropriate advice and a patient information leaflet. Consider steroids if appropriate and refer to GP for follow up

Yes → Prescribe penicillin V (alternative macrolide). As long as safe to do so discharge with GP follow up as appropriate (especially if recurrent problem). Advise re self care and safety net to return if symptoms worsen. Note if bloods suggest the possibility of glandular fever (see notes) patient should be given appropriate advice and a patient information leaflet. Consider steroids if appropriate and refer to GP for follow up

8. Scrotal pain

Definition

The spectrum of conditions that affect the scrotum and its contents ranges from incidental findings that merely require patient reassurance to acute pathologic events that require immediate surgical intervention. Delayed surgical intervention can lead to loss of the testis and infertility.

The mainstay in assessing patients with scrotal pain is to differentiate between acute and chronic (>6 weeks) scrotal pain.

Causes

- Testicular torsion
- Epididymitis and epididymo-orchitis
- Fournier's gangrene (necrotizing fasciitis of the perineum caused by a mixed infection with aerobic/anaerobic bacteria)
- Torsion of the appendix testis
- Testicular cancer
- Trauma/surgery
- Others like inguinal hernia, Henoch–Schönlein purpura (IgA vasculitis), mumps, and referred pain

Management

- The most sensitive physical finding in testicular torsion is absence of the cremasteric reflex (this reflex is elicited by stroking or pinching the medial thigh, causing contraction of the cremaster muscle, which elevates the testis)
- Normal lie testis (longitudinally) with normal cremasteric reflex makes testicular torsion highly unlikely
- False-negative results on Doppler ultrasonography may be caused by intermittent torsion or by early torsion when only venous outflow is occluded
- In epididymitis, the scrotal skin becomes oedematous and its appearance has been likened to an orange peel. This change occurs late in the course of the disease, however. Initially, the only sign may be tenderness of the epididymis and possibly pyuria
- When the appendix testis undergoes torsion, a hard, tender nodule 2–3 mm in diameter may be palpable on the upper pole of the testicle. A blue discoloration may be visible in this area ('blue dot sign')
- Fournier's gangrene, antibiotic therapy alone is usually associated with a 100% mortality rate, highlighting the need for immediate surgical debridement

Further reading

Angela M. Arlen. Children's Healthcare of Atlanta and Emory University, Atlanta, Georgia. *Am Fam Physician*. 2013 Dec 15;88(12):835–840.

Robert C. Eyre. Evaluation of the acute scrotum in adults. http://www.uptodate.com/contents/evaluation-of-the-acute-scrotum-in-adults

Victoria J. Sharp, Kathleen Kieran. Testicular Torsion: Diagnosis, Evaluation, and Management. University of Iowa Carver College of Medicine, Iowa City, Iowa.

Algorithm for scrotal pain

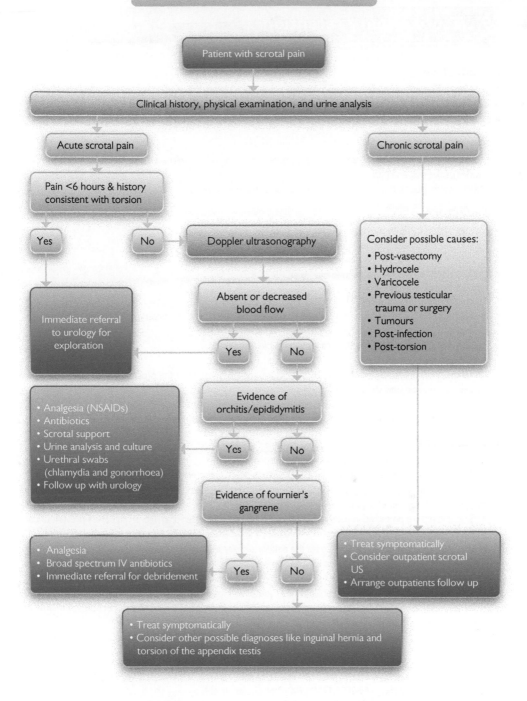

Patient with scrotal pain

Clinical history, physical examination, and urine analysis

Acute scrotal pain

Chronic scrotal pain

Pain <6 hours & history consistent with torsion

Yes

No → Doppler ultrasonography

Consider possible causes:
• Post-vasectomy
• Hydrocele
• Varicocele
• Previous testicular trauma or surgery
• Tumours
• Post-infection
• Post-torsion

Immediate referral to urology for exploration

Absent or decreased blood flow

Yes   No

• Analgesia (NSAIDs)
• Antibiotics
• Scrotal support
• Urine analysis and culture
• Urethral swabs (chlamydia and gonorrhoea)
• Follow up with urology

Evidence of orchitis/epididymitis

Yes   No

Evidence of fournier's gangrene

• Analgesia
• Broad spectrum IV antibiotics
• Immediate referral for debridement

Yes   No

• Treat symptomatically
• Consider outpatient scrotal US
• Arrange outpatients follow up

• Treat symptomatically
• Consider other possible diagnoses like inguinal hernia and torsion of the appendix testis

9. Acute urinary retention

Introduction
- The most frequent aetiology is benign prostatic hyperplasia (BPH)
- Incidence in England is approximately 3/1000 men per annum
- Acute urinary retention (AUR) occurs in approximately 10% of men over the age of 70 in a 5-year period

Causes
- Most commonly secondary to an obstructive process including BPH, malignancy, urethral stricture, urolithiasis (stones), phimosis, and paraphimosis
- Other causes include the use of medications, trauma, neurologic disease, and infection

Risk factors
- Male gender—10 times more likely than in women
- Age >70 years carries a relative risk (RR) of 7.8
- Prostatic volumes >30 mL associated with an RR of 3.0
- Urinary flow rate of <12 mL/second carries an RR of 3.9

History and examination
- Relevant history should include prior episodes of retention, prior urologic surgery, prior radiation, or trauma, haematuria, dysuria, fever, back pain, and a list of medications
- Palpation of the lower abdomen can reveal a palpable bladder
  - May contain over 500 mL
- Rectal examination: rectal masses, impaction of stool, and examination of the prostate gland to evaluate for malignancy or prostatitis should be performed
  - A prostate of normal consistency and size does not rule out obstructive pathology
- Urine should be sent for routine urinalysis and culture (usually after catheter placement)

Management
- Initial management involves prompt bladder decompression
  - This can be accomplished with urethral or suprapubic (SP) catheterisation
- SP catheter may be necessary in patients with urethral stricture, severe BPH, or other anatomic abnormalities that preclude Foley catheter placement per urethra
  - SP catheters are preferred in patients who require long-term bladder drainage. SP catheters prevent urinary incontinence resulting from sphincter dysfunction, and avoid the risk of subsequent urethral stricture
- Partial drainage and clamping may increase the risk for urinary tract infection
- Hospitalisation is indicated for patients who are uroseptic or have obstruction related to malignancy or spinal cord compression
  - The majority of patients can be managed on an outpatient basis
- Prophylactic antibiotics are not routinely indicated unless suspicion exists for a urinary infection at the time of drainage or traumatic catheterisation
- Additional instructions regarding catheter and drainage bag management should be given prior to discharge

Further reading
Cathcart P, van der Meulen J, Armitage J, et al. Incidence of primary and recurrent acute urinary retention between 1998 and 2003 in England. *J Urol* 2006;176(1):200–204; discussion 204.

Curtis LA, Dolan TS, Cespedes RD. Acute urinary retention and urinary incontinence. *Emerg Med Clin North Am* 2001;19(3):591–619.

NICE guideline (97), Lower Urinary Tract Symptoms. The management of lower urinary tract symptoms in men. www.nice.org.uk/cg97, 2010.

Roehrborn KG. Acute urinary retention: risks and management. *Rev Urol* 2005; 7(Suppl 4): S31–S41.

Algorithm for acute urinary retention

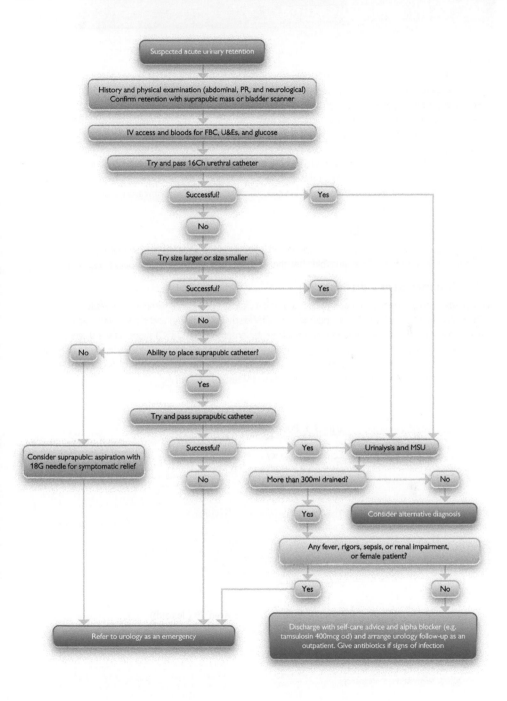

Suspected acute urinary retention

History and physical examination (abdominal, PR, and neurological)
Confirm retention with suprapubic mass or bladder scanner

IV access and bloods for FBC, U&Es, and glucose

Try and pass 16Ch urethral catheter

Successful? → Yes

No

Try size larger or size smaller

Successful? → Yes

No

No ← Ability to place suprapubic catheter?

Yes

Try and pass suprapubic catheter

Successful? → Yes → Urinalysis and MSU

Consider suprapubic: aspiration with 18G needle for symptomatic relief

No

More than 300ml drained? → No

Yes

Consider alternative diagnosis

Any fever, rigors, sepsis, or renal impairment, or female patient?

Yes

No

Refer to urology as an emergency

Discharge with self-care advice and alpha blocker (e.g. tamsulosin 400mcg od) and arrange urology follow-up as an outpatient. Give antibiotics if signs of infection

10. Per-vaginal bleeding

Introduction

- If the patient has collapsed, is in haemorrhagic shock, has heavy bleeding, or has severe abdominal pain, move to the resuscitation room and instigate resuscitation measures, as shown on the algorithm. Call for help early, e.g. senior obstetric, gynaecology, and anaesthetic teams
- Perform a urine or serum β-HCG to determine pregnancy status (consider catheter if the patient is unwell and urgent determination of pregnancy state is needed). If in doubt, treat the patient as if she *is* pregnant
- A PV examination may be lifesaving in the event of an open os during a miscarriage—ensure IV access and fluid resuscitation is ongoing. The aim is to remove products from the os to enable it to close to prevent further bleeding. If this fails, refer immediately for an examination under anaesthetic. During heavy PV loss due to a miscarriage, vagal stimulation may result in bradycardia as opposed to tachycardia. Consider the use of atropine in these patients

Anti-D immunoglobulin use

Anti-D Ig is given to women who are D-negative and who have been exposed to a 'sensitizing event' (Box 9.1). It should be administered as soon as possible after the sensitizing event and within 72 hours (Table 9.4).

Pelvic inflammatory disease

A full sexual history is needed in patients with a possible diagnosis of pelvic inflammatory disease (PID).

The collection of symptoms (fever, abdominal pain, PV discharge/bleeding) and signs (lower abdominal tenderness (usually bilateral), adnexal tenderness, cervical excitation, and fever >38°C) supports this diagnosis.

All patients should be discussed with the gynaecology team and have swabs taken for gonorrhoea and chlamydia. Inpatient vs outpatient treatment depends on many factors (see British Association for Sexual Health and HIV (BASHH) guidelines). All patients should be offered an HIV test.

Follow local hospital guidelines about antibiotic regimen.

Box 9.1 Potentially sensitising events

Ectopic pregnancy
Intrauterine death and stillbirth
Abdominal trauma
Miscarriage
Therapeutic termination of pregnancy
Delivery
Molar pregnancy
PV bleeding in pregnancy
Amniocentesis, cordocentesis

Table 9.4 Anti-D Ig use in pregnant women (should be given IM (deltoid))

<12 weeks (250 IU minimum)	12–20 weeks (250 IU minimum)	12–20 weeks (250 IU minimum)
Ectopic pregnancy	Any sensitising event	Any sensitising event
Molar pregnancy		
Therapeutic termination of pregnancy		

Further reading

Royal College of Obstetricians and Gynaecologists, Pelvic Inflammatory Disease (Green-top Guideline No. 32)
British Association for Sexual Health and HIV (BASHH) guidelines
UK National Guideline for the Management of Pelvic Inflammatory Disease. 2011

Algorithm for per-vaginal bleeding

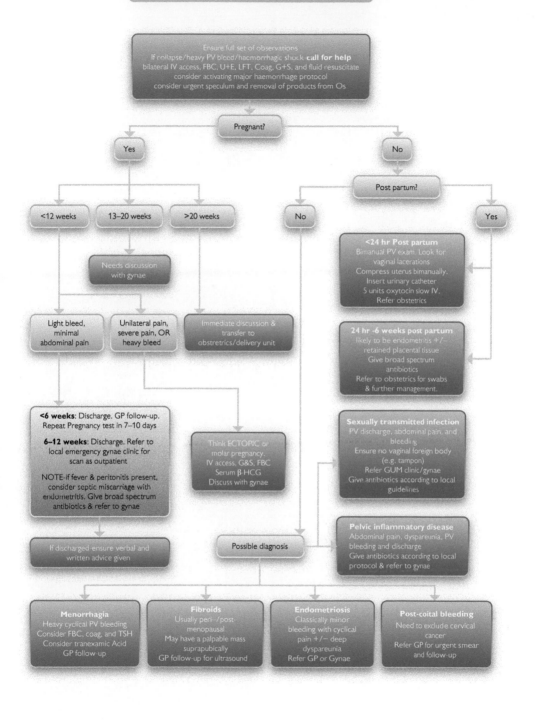

Ensure full set of observations
If collapse/heavy PV bleed/haemorrhagic shock **call for help**
bilateral IV access, FBC, U+E, LFT, Coag, G+S, and fluid resuscitate
consider activating major haemorrhage protocol
consider urgent speculum and removal of products from Os

Pregnant?

Yes

No

Post partum?

<12 weeks   **13–20 weeks**   **>20 weeks**   **No**   **Yes**

Needs discussion with gynae

<24 hr Post partum
Bimanual PV exam. Look for vaginal lacerations
Compress uterus bimanually.
Insert urinary catheter
5 units oxytocin slow IV.
Refer obstetrics

Light bleed, minimal abdominal pain

Unilateral pain, severe pain, OR heavy bleed

Immediate discussion & transfer to obstretrics/delivery unit

24 hr -6 weeks post partum
likely to be endometritis +/- retained placental tissue
Give broad spectrum antibiotics
Refer to obstetrics for swabs & further management.

<6 weeks: Discharge. GP follow-up. Repeat Pregnancy test in 7–10 days

6–12 weeks: Discharge. Refer to local emergency gynae clinic for scan as outpatient

NOTE-if fever & peritonitis present, consider septic miscarriage with endometritis. Give broad spectrum antibiotics & refer to gynae

Think ECTOPIC or molar pregnancy.
IV access, G&S, FBC
Serum β-HCG
Discuss with gynae

Sexually transmitted infection
PV discharge, abdominal pain, and bleeding
Ensure no vaginal foreign body (e.g. tampon)
Refer GUM clinic/gynae
Give antibiotics according to local guidelines

If discharged ensure verbal and written advice given

Possible diagnosis

Pelvic inflammatory disease
Abdominal pain, dyspareunia, PV bleeding and discharge
Give antibiotics according to local protocol & refer to gynae

Menorrhagia
Heavy cyclical PV bleeding
Consider FBC, coag, and TSH
Consider tranexamic Acid
GP follow-up

Fibroids
Usually peri-/post-menopausal
May have a palpable mass suprapubically
GP follow-up for ultrasound

Endometriosis
Classically minor bleeding with cyclical pain +/- deep dyspareunia
Refer GP or Gynae

Post-coital bleeding
Need to exclude cervical cancer
Refer GP for urgent smear and follow-up

SECTION 10

Miscellaneous

1. Suicidal ideation

Introduction

Suicidal ideation and behaviour are among the most common psychiatric emergencies, and an estimated one million people die by suicide worldwide each year. Assessment of the patient exhibiting suicidal ideation is vital to try to prevent the patient going on to attempting self-harm or suicide.

Assessment of suicide risk

It can be challenging for clinicians in the Emergency Department to assess suicide risk in patients. The Modified SAD PERSONS Scale attempts to assist non-psychiatrists in assessing this risk by arranging a number of risk factors into a mnemonic that can be used to assess potentially suicidal patients (Table 10.1).

This score is then mapped onto a risk assessment scale as follows:

- 0–5: May be safe to discharge (depending upon circumstances)
- 6–8: Probably requires psychiatric consultation
- >8: Probably requires hospital admission

The Scale is helpful, but evidence suggests it is not reliable in isolation in assessing this group of patients. Other risk factors should also be taken into account.

Other risk factors

- Psychiatric disorders/diagnosis and physical health
- Hopelessness
- Occupation (e.g. military service)
- Family history

Who to refer

Patients scoring highly on the Modified SAD PERSONS Scale or with other worrying risk factors should be referred to mental health services. A low threshold should be maintained for discussion with mental health services for all suicidal patients as this enables information sharing and helps to ensure appropriate review and/or follow-up with mental health services.

Table 10.1 The Modified SAD PERSONS Scale

	Meaning	Score
S	Male sex	1
A	Age 15–25 or 59 + years	1
D	Depression or hopelessness	2
P	Previous suicidal attempts or psychiatric care	1
E	Excessive ethanol or drug use	1
R	Rational thinking loss (psychotic or organic illness)	2
S	Single, widowed, or divorced	1
O	Organised or serious attempt	2
N	No social support	1
S	Stated future intent (determined to repeat or ambivalent)	2

Further reading

Jennifer Schreiber, Larry Culpepper. UptoDate: Suicidal Ideation and Behavior in Adults.

Wyatt JP, Illingworth RN, Graham CA, Hogg K, Robertson C, Clancy M. Oxford Handbook of Emergency Medicine, 4th edn. Oxford: Oxford University Press, 2012.

Algorithm for suicidal ideation

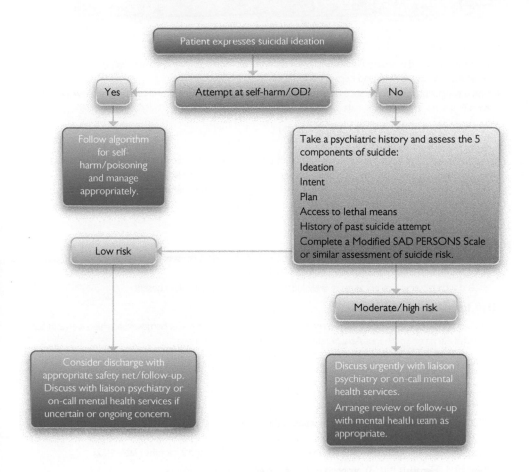

Patient expresses suicidal ideation

Attempt at self-harm/OD?

Yes

No

Follow algorithm for self-harm/poisoning and manage appropriately.

Take a psychiatric history and assess the 5 components of suicide:
Ideation
Intent
Plan
Access to lethal means
History of past suicide attempt
Complete a Modified SAD PERSONS Scale or similar assessment of suicide risk.

Low risk

Moderate/high risk

Consider discharge with appropriate safety net/follow-up. Discuss with liaison psychiatry or on-call mental health services if uncertain or ongoing concern.

Discuss urgently with liaison psychiatry or on-call mental health services.
Arrange review or follow-up with mental health team as appropriate.

2. Needlestick injury

Introduction

- Exposure to blood or bodily fluid may result in transmission of blood-borne viruses (BBVs)
  - These may include HIV and hepatitis B and C virus
- Risk is proportional to prevalence of the infection in the population served, and to a healthcare worker from an infective patient is approximately

Transmission (significant exposures)

- Injury from hollow needles
- Contamination of mucous membranes, eyes, mouth, or broken skin with infected blood or other infectious material
  - Risk is much lower after mucocutaneous exposure (<1 in 2000 for HIV)
  - High-risk body fluids include blood, CSF, amniotic fluid, breast milk, peritoneal, pleural, pericardial, or synovial fluid, vaginal secretions, semen, and tissue fluid exudate
- Bites that break the skin of the person bitten

Testing

- Source patient's consent to testing must always be obtained (cannot consent if unconscious)
  - By someone other than that who sustained the injury
  - A donor refusing consent is more likely HBsAg positive than those who consent

Risk factors

- IV drug abuse, blood transfusions (earlier than 1992), chronic liver disease, homosexual males, native of Sub-Saharan Africa or South East Asia, prostitute, multiple tattoos or piercings
- 'Window period' of 6–10 weeks from infection to detection of measurable antibodies

Treatment

- Post-exposure prophylaxis (PEP) reduces the risk of infection following an exposure
  - Rarely indicated following exposure to unknown source
  - Ideally commenced within 1 hour, certainly within 72 hours, and continued for 28 days
  - Standard regimen of 1 Truvada® bd + 2 Kaletra® bd
- Accelerated course of hepatitis B vaccine consists of doses at 0, 1, and 2 months (Table 10.2).

Table 10.2 Hepatitis B (HB) prophylaxis for reported exposure incidents

HB virus status of exposed person	Significant exposure				Non-significant exposure	
	HBsAg +ve source	Unknown source	HBsAg –ve source	Continued risk	No further risk
≤1 dose HB vaccine pre-exposure	Accelerated course of HB vaccine + HBIg	Accelerated course of HB vaccine	Initiate course of HB vaccine	Initiate course of HB vaccine	No HB virus prophylaxis. Reassure
≥2 doses HB vaccine pre-exposure (anti-HBs not known)	One dose of vaccine followed by 2nd dose 1 month later	One dose of HB vaccine	Finish course of HB vaccine	Finish course of HB vaccine	No HB virus prophylaxis. Reassure
Known responder (anti-HBs ≥10 million units/mL)	Booster dose of HB vaccine	Consider booster dose of HB vaccine	Consider booster dose of HB vaccine	Consider booster dose of HB vaccine	No HB virus prophylaxis. Reassure
Known non-responder (anti-HBs <10 million units/mL)	HBIg + one dose of vaccine followed by 2nd dose at 1 month	HBIg + one dose of vaccine followed by 2nd dose at 1 month	No HBIg. Consider booster dose of HB vaccine	No HBIg. Consider booster dose of HB vaccine	No HB virus prophylaxis. Reassure

Reporting of Injuries, Diseases and Dangerous Occurrences Regulations (RIDDOR) mandates reporting of significant exposure in the workplace.

Source: Data from Immunisation against infectious disease: the green book. Department of Health, September 2013. https://www.gov.uk/government/organisations/public-health-england/series/immunisation-against-infectious-disease-the-green-book (accessed October 2013).

Further reading

Department of Health. Immunisation against infectious disease: the green book. https://www.gov.uk/government/organisations/public-health-england/series/immunisation-against-infectious-disease-the-green-book, 2013.

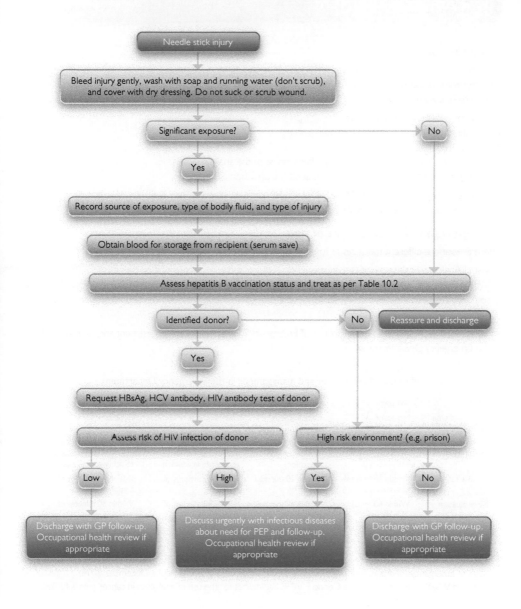

Algorithm for needlestick injuries

Needle stick injury

Bleed injury gently, wash with soap and running water (don't scrub), and cover with dry dressing. Do not suck or scrub wound.

Significant exposure? → No

Yes

Record source of exposure, type of bodily fluid, and type of injury

Obtain blood for storage from recipient (serum save)

Assess hepatitis B vaccination status and treat as per Table 10.2

Identified donor? → No → Reassure and discharge

Yes

Request HBsAg, HCV antibody, HIV antibody test of donor

Assess risk of HIV infection of donor

High risk environment? (e.g. prison)

Low

High

Yes

No

Discharge with GP follow-up. Occupational health review if appropriate

Discuss urgently with infectious diseases about need for PEP and follow-up. Occupational health review if appropriate

Discharge with GP follow-up. Occupational health review if appropriate

3. Pain management

Introduction

Recognising and alleviating pain is vital in order to help relieve distress, aid patients in giving useful details of history, and help with cooperation with further investigations and treatment.

As clinicians we need to:

- Recognize that patients are in pain
- Be able to quantify and assess how much pain they are in
- Relieve the pain
- Reassess the pain in order to assess the effectiveness of the analgesia given
- Ensure that we have processes in place to audit the provision of analgesia

The Royal College of Emergency Medicine states that patients in severe pain should receive analgesia within 20 minutes and be reassessed within 30 minutes of that analgesia being given.

Recognition and assessment of pain

There are various different mechanisms to quantify the level of pain a patient is in, including:

- Visual Analogue Scale: scale of 0–10. Severe pain is diagnosed with a score of 7 or more
- Wong–Baker FACES® Pain Rating Scale. This is a picture card of various faces that look happy (pain free), not so happy (moderate pain), or very tearful (severe pain). This is useful for children and those with language barriers

Table 10.3 is a guide from the Royal College of Emergency Medicine regarding assessment and treatment of pain in the Emergency Department.

Table 10.3 Guide on pain assessment and management in the Emergency Department

	No pain	Mild pain	Moderate pain	Severe pain
Route and type of analgesia	No action	Oral analgesia	Oral analgesia	IV opiates
Suggested analgesia	None	Oral paracetamol or NSAID (e.g. ibuprofen)	Paracetamol and NSAID, and consider codeine phosphate in addition	IV morphine, start at 2.5 mg. Titrate as needed to achieve analgesia
Initial assessment	Within 20 minutes of arrival	Within 20 minutes of arrival	Within 20 minutes of arrival	Within 20 minutes of arrival
Re-evaluation	Within 60 minutes of initial assessment	Within 60 minutes of analgesia	Within 60 minutes of analgesia	Within 30 minutes of analgesia

Further reading

College of Emergency Medicine. Best practice guidelines. Management of pain in adults. December 2014.
Ventafridda V, Saita L, Ripamonti C, De Conno F. WHO guidelines for the use of analgesics in cancer pain. *Int J Tissue React.* 1985;7(1):93–96.
World Health Organisation Analgesia Ladder.

Algorithm for pain management

ACUTE PAIN. ANALGESIA OPTIONS

Intranasal
E.g. diamorphine
Good for patients with
difficult IV access or
children

Distraction
E.g. play therapy
Good for children or
adults (relatives can
play a large role)

Definitive treatment
E.g. trephining a
subungual
haematoma or
fixing a fracture

Ice/heat packs
Good for sprains
and soft tissue
injuries

Topical
E.g. dressing or local
anaesthetic patches/creams
Good for burns or children

Empathic communication and explanation
Good for everyone-
explain why the pain is
happening and your
plan to treat it

Immobilization
E.g. Back slab/plaster of
Paris, sling, bandage
Good for fractures

Acute Pain

Procedural
E.g. NG tube
Good for pain from
bowel obstruction
E.g. catheter
Good for urinary
retention

Nerve block
E.g. femoral nerve block-
useful in femoral fractures
E.g. digital nerve block-
useful in finger injuries

Intravenous medications
E.g. morphine/diamorphine
Good for severe pain

Oral medication
Good for mild to
moderate pain
E.g. paracetamol,
ibuprofen,
codeine phosphate,
nefopam

Intramuscular medication
Rarely used acutely; (one
exception is buscopan
(hyoscine butylbromide)-
Useful in spasmodic
abdominal pain
Do NOT use IM morphine

Subcutaneous medications
Occasionally used
E.g. sumatriptan-good for
migraines
E.g. morphine in a syringe
driver in palliative care

INDEX

For the benefit of digital users, indexed terms that span two pages (e.g., 52–53) may, on occasion, appear on only one of those pages.

Tables, figures, and boxes are indicated by *t*, *f*, and *b* following the page number